11418

D0360028

Library
Oakland S.U.M.

Covering Home

Covering Home

Ruth Ryan

WORD PUBLISHING

Dallas   London   Vancouver   Melbourne

PUBLISHED BY WORD PUBLISHING,
DALLAS, TEXAS

Covering Home
Copyright © 1995 by Ruth Ryan. All rights reserved.
No portion of this book may be reproduced, stored in a retrieval system,
or transmitted in any form or by any means—electronic, mechanical, photocopy,
recording, or any other—except for brief quotations in printed reviews,
without the prior permission of the publisher.

Jill Smith Lempke's poem, "Being a Baseball Wife," is used by permission of
The Waiting Room, a publication for Women in Professional Baseball, edited and published
by Maryanne Ellison Simmons, 1982–1984.

Book Design by Mark McGarry
Title and Part Title illustration by Sharon Allen
Set in Bernhard Modern

LIBRARY OF CONGRESS CATALOGING-IN-PUBLICATION DATA

Ryan, Ruth, 1949–
Covering home : my life with Nolan Ryan / Ruth Ryan.
p.   cm.
ISBN 0–8499–1098–6
1. Ryan, Nolan, 1947–   .
2. Baseball players—United States—Biography. I. Title.
GV865.R9R93   1995
796.357'092 — dc20
[B] 94–44258 CIP

PRINTED IN THE UNITED STATES OF AMERICA

5 6 7 8 0 1 2 3 9   RRD   9 8 7 6 5 4 3 2 1

This book is dedicated to my three wonderful, loving, and understanding children—Robert Reid, Nolan Reese, and Wendy Lynn Ryan—and to the man whose life and love I have shared for most of my life, Lynn Nolan Ryan Jr.

Special appreciation goes to my mother and father, Larry and Ingrid Holdorff; my sister, Lynn Shigekawa; and my brothers, Bruce, Larry, and Steve Holdorff, for an idyllic childhood full of loving memories.

Also, a special "thanks for the memories" goes to all the baseball wives whose lives have crossed my path and with whom I will always share a special bond of friendship. This poem, written by Jill Smith Lempke (sister of former baseball wife Jody McClure) and published in 1982 in *The Waiting Room*, a magazine for baseball wives, is dedicated to them:

> Moving, travel, money and fame,
> Reaching for stardom, an important name,
> Giving love and security, in this little boy's game,
> All part of being a baseball wife.
>
> Pain and sorrow,
> Misunderstood enchantments,
> Assuming, concluding as loneliness advances,
> But oh, the loving second chances,
> In being a baseball wife.
>
> Everything I wanted to be,
> Anything that's left of me,
> Hopes and dreams, the reality,
> All goes to being a baseball wife.
>
> Love and laughter,
> Children's faces,
> Everything that God embraces,
> Lets me know I'm so much more,
> Than just a baseball wife.

Contents

Contents

Foreword

. . . .

The statisticians can tell you how many games I've pitched, how many batters I've faced, how many strikeouts, shutouts, no-hitters, and maybe even how many pitches I've thrown. All I know is that I've spent almost every year of my life on the mound. I started playing baseball as a kid, and aside from a little ranching and banking, that's about all I've done as an adult for the last twenty-seven years.

Nowadays I go out to the stands and watch my boys pitch and my daughter play volleyball. And sitting next to me, making as much noise as I do about some ref's call, is the woman who's been there for me for all the time I can remember, from Alvin to New York to Anaheim to Houston to Arlington and back. But even now, after all these years, when I look at Ruth I see the girl who used to play football or baseball with us boys in Alvin.

During my last spring training, I pitched to Ruth a few times, and she got a hit off me, flying down the baseline to first, grinning at me the whole distance. As always, she struck me as the prettiest girl I'd ever seen.

Ruth is my best friend as well as my wife. She knows me better than anyone. If I confide my thoughts and feelings to anyone, it's to her. Our marriage has lasted this long because we made a commitment to each other that we both took seriously. We didn't know exactly what we were getting into when we got married, but we've learned over time what it's like to be husband and wife. That's not an easy job for any two people, but it's especially hard when one of them is a ballplayer. We've worked hard at our marriage, and I've learned to be sensitive to Ruth's needs as much as she has learned how to live with me and my crazy schedule.

Ruth has supported me during all the games over all those years. Although she couldn't do anything on the field to help me when I'd get into a tight spot, she was my best cheerleader and more.

Foreword

For almost a dozen years, Harry Spilman, one of my closest friends and neighbors, was my catcher during the off-season. There's a backstop on our property, and I'd throw a certain number of pitches to Harry as part of my daily workout when I was getting ready for spring training. But Harry moved just as I was going into my last season, so Ruth put on the catcher's mask and helped me get ready for my final season in the majors. And I got to thinking that that was what our marriage has been like for these many years. Ruth has always been there for me. But not just for me; she's also been there for our kids—Reid, Reese, and Wendy. Ruth's been behind each of us, quietly doing what a wife and mother has traditionally done for her husband and family. And as many times as we talked about how we couldn't do what we did and accomplish what we did without Ruth being there for each one of us, it's not enough to say that I love her, that we all love her. She's the most special person I know. And she put up with a lot to help me get through a career in major-league baseball.

They call Yankee Stadium "the house that Ruth built," referring to the legendary Babe Ruth. Well, it's no small comparison to say that the Ryan household is the house that Ruth built and nurtured and loved into what it is now. She did the same thing for me. Every now and then I think of how I felt when I was on the mound on a humid night in some faceless stadium looking at a hitter who thought he might be due for a hit off me. My arm might not have felt its strongest. But I knew that Ruth was there for me, watching one way or another and pulling for me. I knew that she was doing all she could to help me get that next batter out, that last inning over. And I knew I wasn't going to let down, that somehow I'd get out of that spot.

Well, I've pitched to that last hitter, and I've seen my last inning, and Ruth was there for me. And afterward we came home to Alvin. Since then we have begun to do a little more as a family without the glare of the klieg lights, away from the big-league ballparks. What adjustments I've had to make to life after baseball have been minimal because Ruth has always been there for me, always backing me up, always covering home.

Nolan Ryan

Acknowledgments

. . . .

Special thanks to Mickey Herskowitz for his invaluable assistance with this project. His gathering of sports statistics and other information was a great help to me, and I am grateful to him for his ideas as well as his work.

My appreciation also goes to Sue Ann Jones whose keen judgment and precise editorial skills helped me shape my story.

Prologue: The Last Pitch

Seattle, September 22, 1993.

For years I had known this game—the last game—could come at any time, with any pitch. But I had prayed it wouldn't happen this way . . .

At the beginning of 1993 we had hoped that Nolan's pitching arm—the arm that had thrown more no-hitters, more strikeouts, and set more records overall than any other pitcher's arm—would hold together just one more season with the Texas Rangers. He had already announced that 1993 would be his last year. After twenty-seven seasons, he was abdicating the mound to the younger players.

Only a few people knew about the time bomb ticking away in Nolan's body. He was trying to pitch with numerous problems—a partial tear in the rotator cuff in his shoulder, a partial tear in his elbow, a cartilage problem in his knee, and a bulging disc in his back. But the most worrisome problem was the elbow. A specialist in California had done an MRI on Nolan's arm in 1991. Afterward the doctor had pointed to the film and shown us the tiny tear in the ligament.

"It could be okay for a while," the doctor said. And then he paused before continuing. "Or it could go on the next pitch."

Prologue

We had kept the secret to ourselves for those following years, telling only a handful of people about these problems. Living and working through pain was just part of being a pitcher in the major leagues, but gradually it was becoming an insurmountable problem, and we both knew Nolan was reaching his limit. Since then I had probably watched him launch a thousand fastballs toward home plate. And each time he threw the ball, I watched his face.

I was pretty sure I would know when the last pitch came. I felt certain I would be able to see it on his face. Many times I sat in the stands, worrying about his physical problems, watching and wondering, *Will this be it? Will he literally throw his arm out? Will this be the last game?* Whenever I saw a flash of pain cross Nolan's face as he hurled that baseball toward home, I would hold my breath and pray.

But pain is any pitcher's constant companion, and Nolan had kept going strong. I had seen it numerous times before—Nolan had pitched with a sore arm, a broken foot, a bad back, or other injuries. He did it again through the 1991 season, pitching his seventh career no-hitter in May against the Toronto Bluejays. In 1992 he struck out 157 more batters; by the end of the '92 season he had a career strikeout record of 5,668.

Then came 1993, the last season. We had hoped it would be a happy ending to a long and rewarding career, but it turned out to be a real struggle. His knee kept swelling and hurting so badly that he finally consented to have surgery in April. Later he tore a muscle away from his hip bone as a result of his rushing to come back and pitch again too soon. The pain caused him to favor his knee—and throw out his hip. A gashed foot had sidelined him for most of May and June.

Then things had seemed to turn around for a while. In Cleveland he won what turned out to be his 324th (and last) big-league game, and the Cleveland crowd on that August 15 afternoon gave him two standing ovations. I had not been able to attend all his road games, but I was determined to try to go to as many as possible during that last year, and I was at the Cleveland game. When people around me found out I was Nolan's wife, a steady stream of fans stopped by my seat to tell me how much they loved Nolan. I will never forget the feeling of adoration and respect those Cleveland fans showed him that day.

Best of all, Nolan pitched his best game since April.

But Nolan's body was definitely telling him it was nearly time to quit, and although we both knew this, we also wanted him to be able to finish the season and uphold his contract. His fierce determination had carried him through similar challenges before. Now, we thought, that same determination would get him through just a few more games, and then he could let go.

But in August a ribcage problem cropped up, and he was on the disabled list for the third time that season. When he returned to play on Nolan Ryan Day at Arlington Stadium on September 12, the old worries returned too—for me, at least. But Nolan wasn't one to dwell on the negative. He focused on one game at a time, one pitch at a time. And he gave it all he had. The Rangers wanted him to pitch six innings that day, and he almost made it. In the sixth inning, with two outs and two men on base (on walks), the score was tied at 1-1.

The next two hitters drove in three runs.

Nolan left the game.

The Rangers lost to Minnesota 4-2.

The next games were road trips.

In Anaheim, the Angels fans were wonderful, standing and cheering for Nolan as he took the field. Although the game was a no-decision (neither pitcher was declared the winner), I remember feeling a bit of relief, thinking, *It's going to be okay. He's going to make it through the season.*

But after that game Nolan told me, "You know, my elbow feels like it's ready to go."

I wanted to ask a thousand questions, to sit down and talk it out; I've always been one who wanted to know everything that's going on. But in twenty-six years of marriage I'd learned that wasn't what Nolan wanted. He is good at hiding his feelings, and he doesn't like to be questioned about what's going on inside him. It's frustrating for me. Sometimes I want to say, "I'm not a reporter. I'm not being nosy. I love you and care about you, and I want to know what you're thinking and feeling."

But I couldn't. All I could do was wait and listen when he was ready to talk about it. All he said that day was, "If I can just get through a few more games, then I can rest my arm and maybe it'll be okay."

With Nolan's words bouncing around my head, I flew to Seattle for the Rangers' game against the Mariners. Only eleven days remained in the 1993 season.

The family of one of our son's friends joined me there. I hadn't met Rodger and Marsha Merrick and their daughter, Kelli, but we were very fond of their son, Brett, and they were longtime Mariners season ticket holders and baseball enthusiasts, so I looked forward to watching the game with them. They sat with me in the wives section of the Kingdome.

I was apprehensive as the game started, even though it began with an outpouring of warmth and appreciation. As Nolan ran out to the mound for the start of play, the crowd of forty thousand fans rose to their feet and cheered for him. He was the opponent, yes. But he was also a veteran, hardworking athlete, and they were letting him know they admired and respected him.

Marsha Merrick said later, "Those people weren't there to see the Rangers. They probably weren't even there to see the Mariners. They had come to see Nolan Ryan. They knew it was his last season, and they wanted one more chance to see him play."

But as soon as the game began, I saw signs of stress on Nolan's face and knew things were bad. The arm was bothering him. Each time he released the ball, a flash of pain made him wince.

Maybe someone else would have eased up and tried to save his arm. But that wasn't Nolan. In my mind I was saying, *Come out of the game, Nolan. Don't push it. At least hold back a little.* But I knew that wasn't the way Nolan Ryan worked. He would go all out, giving it everything he had.

Right up to the end.

From the beginning, Nolan's pitches were wild that night. It was another sign that he was hurting. I knew when he got his pitches up and wild he was either tired or in pain. But it was only the first inning; he wasn't tired.

He loaded the bases. Then Dann Howitt hit an opposite-field home run, driving in four runs.

The Last Pitch

I'm sure the Mariners crowd must have cheered for the grand slam, but strangely enough I remember the stadium as being very quiet. For a few seconds it was as though we were all holding our breath, our eyes on Nolan, wondering what was going to happen. I said to Marsha and Rodger, "I know his arm is hurting." Then I whispered, more to myself than to them, "This may be it."

Dave Magadan, the seventh hitter in the Mariners' lineup, stepped up to the plate. Grimacing with each throw, Nolan racked up a 2-0 count. Then he threw one more. A fastball.

The last pitch.

I saw it happen. I knew the instant it occurred. A split-second stab of anguish distorted his face as his elbow popped, then Nolan's right arm dropped, limp, to his side. Grimacing with pain, he motioned awkwardly to the trainer, Danny Wheat, lightly brushing his left hand across his chest while his right arm flopped helplessly against his belt. Danny and Kevin Kennedy, the team manager, popped out of the dugout and trotted toward the mound, but Nolan was already on his way in.

The huge stadium was silent. You could almost hear the men's footsteps as their cleats punctured the turf on their way back to the dugout.

Everyone knew it was the end.

As Nolan neared the dugout, the silence changed to polite applause. Then, around the stands, the fans rose out of their seats and the polite applause turned into a thundering ovation.

The audience cheered and whistled and whooped and wouldn't stop. As Nolan ducked into the dugout, he turned back for a second, his face grim. He lifted his left arm to take off his cap and wave it at the wildly cheering fans. Marsha thought he seemed to glance back toward our seats in the wives' section and jerk his chin up with a tight little smile that said, "I'll be all right." But I couldn't see through the tears. I just remember seeing his back as he disappeared into the locker room.

The crowd continued to stand and applaud, hoping he would come back out and wave to them one more time, but he didn't.

One of the Rangers' pitchers, Kevin Brown, later described what it was like in the dugout. "Everybody just got real quiet," he said. "It was like no one really wanted to think about it."

Prologue

I sat in my seat and cried as Marsha gently eased her arm around me. Watching Nolan take that last, sad walk from the mound to the dugout broke my heart. I wanted to run down to the field and grab him and say, "It's not fair! It shouldn't end like this! You've worked so long and so hard, and you've given so much of yourself. You deserve to go out in a blaze of glory, not walking off the field with your arm hanging like a wet rag at your side. It's just not fair!"

But a baseball wife, especially a baseball wife of twenty-six years, would never make such a scene. I stayed in my seat and waited. In a few minutes, Zack Minasian, the Rangers equipment manager, appeared in the aisle by our seats and beckoned toward me. He was dressed in street clothes, so most people didn't notice.

"He's gonna be okay," Zack said, trying to muster a little smile. "He wanted me to come and tell you that."

"How bad is it?" I asked.

"We don't know yet; they're doing the x-rays now. But . . ." He grimaced and put a hand on my shoulder.

"Okay," I said, stonefaced, then returned to my seat as Zack trotted back up the steps.

A few minutes later he was back in the aisle, beckoning to me again.

"He's okay," he repeated. "He said to tell you he's doing fine. But the arm's gone. It's over, Ruth."

I returned to my seat to wait out the rest of the game. It seemed to last for eons instead of hours. During the final inning Rodger and Marsha walked with me down to the pressroom. I knew there would be a press conference, and I wanted to be there even though it would be painful to watch.

When the reporters' questions came, Nolan took them all in his usual good-natured style, answering with his own special blend of frank honesty plus a smile: "I guess if I was going to injure myself and finish my career, that was the way to do it—throwing my bread-and-butter pitch, the fastball that was the basis for everything I accomplished."

He had faced seven Mariners and hadn't retired any of them. It was only the third time that had happened in his entire career.

The Last Pitch

Listening to it all, I stood at the back of the room, quietly wiping away tears. I was grateful that none of the photographers took my picture as I stood there in misery, watching my husband give up the career he loved. Someone told me later it was a sign of the reporters' and photographers' respect for Nolan and me. "They like you, Ruth," she said. "They knew you were hurting, and they left you alone."

Before the game began, the plan had been that the Merricks would take me back to my hotel and Nolan would go on the team's bus to the airport. Then, the next day, I would go home to Texas and Nolan would continue on with the team. But after the press conference, Nolan took my arm and said, "Let's go."

We hailed a cab and rode in silence, anxious to be alone and out of the spotlight. Later we went to eat and were lucky to find a restaurant where the staff, who had heard what had happened, gave us a quiet, out-of-the-way table where we could be alone.

Sitting there with Nolan, it was hard not to get teary-eyed as we tried to put the whole thing in perspective and talk about what would happen next.

Then the conversation turned to nostalgia. We talked about what a good life baseball had given us, what a ride it had been. It hadn't always been easy; but overall, it had always been good . . .

As the final season had begun, I had considered the idea of writing a book, but I was determined that if I did write one, it would be about more than the final season. I couldn't even imagine then that 1993 would turn out to be only a *fraction* of a season.

In 1993 Nolan would spend 126 days on the disabled list with four major injuries, including that career-ending snap of his elbow in Seattle. That was the last way Nolan wanted to leave baseball, with his arm failing him, but that is the reality of the sport.

Baseball has its peaks and valleys, just like real life. But for us, this roller-coaster ride had just come to a screeching halt, and we were heading home to Texas, where it had all started on that Little League field in Alvin . . .

Part One

. . . .

Childhood Sweethearts

1

Little League

$\mathcal{O}$n most early-summer afternoons in 1959, you could find me at Shroeder Field, the baseball field in Alvin, peering longingly through the chain-link fence. Sprawled in the grass, squinting against the harsh sun, and wiping the sweat off my ten-year-old freckled face, I came often to watch the Little League team—ironically named the Rangers—compete against various other teams.

It wasn't that I enjoyed *watching* baseball. And I certainly wasn't watching any of the boys with romantic intentions—not even the skinny Ryan kid who alternated between pitching and playing shortstop. (He told a newspaper reporter many years later that I caught his eye that summer as I watched through the fence, but to me, he was just another player on the team.)

No, I wasn't there because I loved to watch. I was watching because I loved to *play.*

I wanted to be out there with the team, the same guys I'd played baseball with as long as I could remember on the vacant lot next to my house. Every spring the kids would be out there with lawn mowers, clearing the baseline and repairing the old backstop. There wasn't a lot to do in Alvin, a sleepy little South Texas town of about seven thousand people. Baseball was our primary means of entertaining ourselves during the long, hot summers. It didn't matter that the temperature and the humidity were often in the high nineties on most summer afternoons. We loved the game, and we played whenever we could.

But when the boys got old enough to play Little League, things changed. They moved over to Shroeder Field, a *real* baseball diamond with a pitching rubber, batter's boxes, and bleachers for the fans. It even had lights.

With all my heart I wanted to be out there with the boys, wearing one of those wonderful, baggy-pants uniforms and tipping the brim on one of those coveted caps. Instead of tripping over homemade bases made out of bits of trash in the empty lot across the street, I wanted to be out there on the turf, digging my toes in beside a real home plate and scuffing the chalk-dust baseline as I trotted to my position as shortstop. That would really be the best, I thought, imagining myself on the field, yelling that cool, Little League chatter as I slammed my fist into my glove, waiting for the next play.

The team was very competitive. All the boys dreamed of making the All-Star team or even of going to the Little League World Series, which was held back then in Williamsport, Pennsylvania.

It's not fair! I thought, hating the rule that prohibited girls from playing on Little League teams. As an athletic fourth-grader who could outhit, outcatch, and outthrow some of the boys, this seemed like a terrible injustice. It might have even been enough to make me cry, except that, of course, a true tomboy, as I was, would *never* do that! And I wasn't one to do a lot of complaining and pouting. My parents, who have always been very calm and poised, taught us kids that losing your temper is a sign of stupidity. By their example, they trained us to keep our emotions hidden from public display. Of the five of us kids, that training surely has helped me the most during my three decades of life in the public eye.

Luckily, baseball wasn't the only sport in Alvin. As summer turned to fall, the vacant lot near our house was transformed from a baseball diamond to a football field, and I was able to rejoin the boys in after-school matchups. I delighted in these exuberant, rough-and-tumble games when I would snare a high, spinning pass from the quarterback, lock the ball between my arm and ribcage, and weave and dodge my way to the goal, a trail of defenders in my wake. Oh, those victories felt good!

I was also pretty good at punting. In fact, by the time I was in sixth grade, someone kidded my dad, Larry Holdorff, that I could kick the football farther than the boys. That's when he went out and bought my first tennis racket.

"We didn't think football was very feminine," he would say with a sheepish smile.

And tennis was okay with me. I was ready for some one-on-one competition.

When my older sister, Lynn (now Lynn Shigekawa), was a sixth-grader in Alvin Elementary School, she was in the same class as Nolan Ryan. She and I were supposed to walk home together every day, so I often waited outside her classroom because my class was usually dismissed before hers. Nolan and Lynn were friends that year—and I was just the little sister.

I really noticed Nolan for the first time a few years later, when I was in seventh grade. That was the year I started playing tennis in earnest. Alvin had a high school tennis team and one coach, Aubrey Horner, who coached everything. I would often go to the school to hit balls against the backboard after school, and he offered to work with me after he finished with the high school team's practice sessions each day. My parents didn't have money for private lessons, so it was really a help to me to be able to hit balls with him every day. He was a good, fundamental coach, and I'm very fortunate he was willing to take the time to work with me. He ended up letting me tag along to tournaments with the high school players, and eventually I joined the team. My partner, Rachel Adams, and I even won the 1965 AAA girls doubles state championship.

It was on one of those afternoons when I was a seventh-grader, hitting tennis balls against the backboard while I waited for the coach

Childhood Sweethearts

to finish up with the high school students, that two boys rode by on a motorscooter.

The scooter slowed down a little bit as it rolled past the tennis courts, and the driver honked and waved to me. I heard the boy in back, the skinny Ryan kid, yell to the driver, "Who's that?"

"That's Lynn Holdorff's little sister," he answered.

My racket slung against my shoulder, I smiled and waved back.

It's funny how such an insignificant moment stands out in my memories. Nolan and I grew up in the same town, and our paths had undoubtedly crossed hundreds of times before that school-day afternoon in 1961. But that was the beginning.

A year later, when I was just thirteen, we had our first date.

2

Home Team

*N*olan's first car was a 1952 Chevy, fire-engine red and polished to a shine as bright as Christmas. In my mind I can still see that car waiting in front of our house the night Nolan picked me up for our first date.

I was thirteen, an eighth-grader, and so nervous I could hardly get into the dress Lynn was letting me borrow. At fifteen, Nolan had already had his driver's license—and his own car—for more than a year. (At that time Texas allowed residents to get a license at age fourteen.) He admits now that he was nervous, too, especially since good manners required him to come in and chat with my parents while I nervously finished getting dressed. But to me, Nolan, the sophisticated sophomore, seemed cool and confident that night.

My mother hadn't wanted me to start dating, and she had made it clear that we could go this once by ourselves, but after this we would have to double-date for a while. My parents were willing to let me go because, after all, this was 1962 in Alvin, Texas, and they knew Nolan and his family. In fact, my father first "met" Nolan under a bed when Nolan was just a toddler. Dad tells the story of when he was working as an appliance repairman and was called to the Ryans' home to repair their refrigerator. When it was time to leave, he discovered a couple of his tools were missing. He eventually found them, along with two-year-old Nolan, under the bed. He had to crawl under there with Nolan to get his tools back.

My mom was (and still is) a kind and loving woman who was very protective of her five children. She wouldn't allow us to go to a movie unless she had read about it first in *Parents* magazine and made sure it was okay. There was only one theater and one drive-in in Alvin back then, and each had only one screen. So Nolan and I were lucky that *Rome Adventure,* starring Suzanne Pleshette and Troy Donahue, was one of the two movies playing in town that night; it had received Mom's seal of approval.

Walking together down the sidewalk toward that bright red car, my heart was doing flip-flops. I was thrilled at being on my first date, delighted to be with Nolan—and full of so much nervous energy I probably could have set some sort of speed record running all the way to the movie theater instead of riding.

Nolan opened the door for me, and I scooted over to sit in the middle beside him. That was before seatbelts, of course, or my mother would have insisted that I be securely belted in—just as I insist with my kids today.

Ironically, I can't remember a lot of other details about that night. I know Nolan slid a dollar through the slot in the box-office window to pay for our two tickets—and got fifty cents back in change. He probably bought me a Coke, and we may have shared some popcorn. After the movie, we went to Dairyland, Alvin's only fast-food place back then. I don't remember what we talked about that night, but I remember that we *did* talk. Most of all, I remember having a real good time. I was on cloud nine.

The date ended at my front door right on time; I don't remember what my curfew was, but it was probably pretty early. Nolan didn't kiss me good-night. We both knew that wasn't a proper thing to do on a first date.

After that, our lives gradually became more and more intertwined. It seemed like such a natural thing, not just because we enjoyed being together, but also because we enjoyed the same things—namely, sports—and we came from similar backgrounds: large families reared on strong Christian values.

Nolan was the youngest of six children, and I was the second of five kids. We were both reared in small homes with one bathroom—and didn't think anything of it. Everyone we knew lived in that kind of house.

Our fathers worked hard to support their families, and our mothers devoted themselves to guiding us through the ins and outs of childhood, the turmoil of adolescence, and the beginning of adulthood. When I read about all the issues facing many of today's children: divorce, a parade of stepparents, molestation, and other trauma, I marvel at how lucky Nolan and I were to grow up in such loving, nurturing families. That legacy has continued into our adult lives.

The Ryans came from Ireland to Texas more than a hundred years ago, so they have some Texas seniority over the Holdorffs, who didn't arrive in Alvin until 1948. Maybe that's why my native New Yorker parents' culinary traditions haven't been completely converted to the ways of the Southwest. My mother often invited Nolan to join us for meals when he and I were dating, but he was always wary of the boiled meat and vegetables or other New York recipes he would find on our dinner table. Mom would sometimes tease Nolan by mimicking his Texas drawl and asking, "Don't y'all ever have any American food?"

Sadly, Nolan's dad, who had such a significant influence on Nolan, died in 1970, and his mother passed away in January 1990. Their deaths leave a void in our lives, and there's probably not a day that goes by that we don't think of them or feel their influence in our lives. I'm just grateful that our kids got to know Nolan's mother, Martha Ryan. They loved her so much. If one of them got sick at school they would call me and say, "Mom, take me to Grandmother's house." They knew she would baby them and fuss over them, and soon they would forget about feeling sick. She was an anchor, a pillar of our family who gave us deep roots and strong love.

Thankfully, I'm still able to enjoy seeing or talking with my parents every day I'm home in Alvin. They are a wonderful blessing to me, and

Childhood Sweethearts

I cherish them for all they are to me and my family. My father and mother would do anything in the world for us, and I am thankful my children have been able to live close to them, as I never really knew either one of my grandfathers. Even now, my dad enjoys driving to Fort Worth, where our sons, Reid and Reese, go to college. He brings along his special cooking pots and stays a couple of days to visit and cook for the boys and their friends.

Our parents taught us strong values, not only with words, but by the way they lived their lives. Nolan's dad held two jobs for as long as Nolan can remember. He worked for American Oil Company during the day. Then at night—in the middle of the night, actually—he delivered the *Houston Post* to fifteen hundred homes over a fifty-five-mile route. As soon as Nolan was old enough to help, he got up with his dad at 1 A.M. to roll the papers and toss them from the car window. When Nolan got his driver's license at age fourteen, he split the motor route with his dad. About 5 A.M. they would drop back into bed for a couple more hours of sleep before his dad went to work and Nolan went to school.

Nolan's parents trained him to follow the Golden Rule: to always treat other people the way he wanted to be treated—"with honesty and integrity," he says. If a customer called to say he or she didn't get a paper that morning, the Ryans didn't argue or complain. They got in the car and got that paper to the customer as quickly as possible. In that way and a dozen others, Nolan's dad taught him the importance of being dependable and having a good reputation.

Continuing his father's example of hard work, Nolan held various summer jobs throughout his high school years, and none of them was easy. One summer he worked for a lumber company, unloading boxcars all day long. Another summer he worked for an appliance company.

My father has also worked hard all his life; he is the son of a ship's captain who had immigrated to New York from Norway. My seagoing grandfather married a young woman who also had immigrated from Norway, but soon after my father was born, they separated. My father spent most of his growing-up years living with his paternal grandmother in Poughkeepsie, New York, until he was thirteen. He came home from running an errand for her and found his beloved grandmother lying dead on the floor. After that he alternated between living with his dad in Poughkeepsie and his mother on Staten Island.

Despite these hardships—his parents' separation, his dad's long absences, and his grandmother's death—my dad speaks fondly of his childhood. (It's that old Holdorff philosophy that demands optimism and good humor, even in the face of tragedy.) He remembers as a boy coming along on my grandfather's ship occasionally, riding from Poughkeepsie down the Hudson River to New York, then ending up in the Camden, New Jersey, shipyards, where he would meet a family friend, a stevedore, who would take him home to stay with his family until my grandfather's ship returned.

Dad reached adulthood in the late 1930s, just in time for World War II. He and his father both went to war—Dad in the army and my grandfather in the navy. My dad's future was shaped by a chance encounter with his father in 1946 when they both ended up on a brief furlough together somewhere in the Pacific. They were together for only a few hours, but what they discussed there affected my dad's life forever.

As dad tells it, his father asked him, "What are you going to do after the war?"

Dad had been working with refrigeration units during the war, and he told his father he was considering going into the relatively new field of air conditioning.

"Well," my grandfather replied, "if you're going into air conditioning, you ought to go to Texas. It's hot down there, and air conditioning is going to be big."

My grandfather had docked in Houston and Galveston when he was the captain of a commercial ship, and he had the insight to realize Texas was a place where air conditioning was soon going to be in great demand.

So when Dad got home from the war, he followed my grandfather's advice and enrolled in a correspondence course to train as an air-conditioning technician; the next year he went to technical school full time. He and my mother lived on Staten Island then; my mother, a native New Yorker reared by Swedish-immigrant parents, worked in Manhattan. When Dad finished school in 1948, he bundled my mother and my older sister, Lynn, then a toddler, into their 1937 Lafayette and headed for the Lone Star State.

The car broke down in Chattanooga, but somehow Mom and Dad made it to Texas and eventually settled into a renovated army-barracks home three miles outside of Alvin. I was born a few months later, in 1949, in Saint Mary's Hospital in nearby Galveston.

It must have been a real challenge for my mother, the lifelong city girl, to keep up her strength and her sanity when she found herself trying to be a mother and wife in what probably seemed like the outskirts of no man's land. She didn't know how to drive, so when my dad went off to work each morning, she was alone in the hinterlands with Lynn and me. It must have been both frustrating and frightening for her, but I've never heard her complain about it. She and my dad have always tried to make the best of any situation, then and now.

My grandfather helped make the place a little more bearable when he came for a visit. He rigged up a little swimming pool by hanging canvas from a wooden frame—maybe it was something old-time sailors built to collect rainwater. To be honest, I don't remember the army-barracks home and the makeshift pool, but when I look at the old photographs, I always notice that Lynn and I, wearing swimsuits Mom had sewn for us and splashing in that makeshift swimming pool, are smiling the smiles of happy, secure children who know they are loved.

My dad did try to teach my mother to drive so she wouldn't be stuck in our rural home all day, but the old Lafayette's four-on-the-floor stick shift was just too much for her.

The second year my family was in Alvin, my mother flew back to New York to visit her mother, and she took Lynn and me with her. When I think of her making that trip, I remember what a struggle it was for me as a young mother many years later when I had to travel alone with any of our children as infants. Yet in the photograph taken as we were leaving on that trip, my mother is smiling her brightest, most confident smile, and Lynn and I are wearing adorable little coats with matching hats—all made by Mom.

She was such a talented seamstress she probably could have been a successful designer if our parents had stayed in New York. She never needed to buy a pattern. She would sketch out a design (or just envision it in her head), then make her own pattern, cut the fabric, and head for her old Singer sewing machine. Our family albums are filled with pictures of the wonderful clothes she made for us—everything from cowgirl outfits, dance costumes, prom gowns, and bridesmaid dresses to maternity tennis sets for me to wear after I was married.

Whenever there was an important occasion in the lives of us kids, we were usually wearing carefully tailored clothes that had been lovingly made for us by Mom. They weren't fancy, but they were stylish and always very well made. To this day when I buy something new, I turn it inside out and check the seams and hems and pull on it to see if it puckers or gives. That's my mom's legacy coming out in me. The amazing thing is that Mom sewed all these clothes for us, but I can't really remember seeing her at that sewing machine—the beautiful clothes just seemed to appear magically. Once I asked her, "Mom, when did you make all those things for us?"

She said, "Oh, usually between 10 P.M. and 3 A.M."

Such stories remind me of the sacrifices she and my dad made for us kids. Yet my mother never, ever played the role of martyr. She and Dad have always made us feel so special, so wanted. My mother never let a birthday or a holiday slip by with just a song and a present. No, not at the Holdorffs' house! We always had exuberant celebrations with decorations and games and special food and lots of fun and laughter.

When my mom and dad first hit town back in 1948, my dad had applied for a job at the appliance store in Alvin. The owner told Dad he didn't have any openings there; but he owned the Chevy agency, and he told Dad he could work there until he had an opening in the appliance store.

It was at the Chevy agency that the answer to my mother's driving problem was solved a few years later when Dad bought her a 1953

Childhood Sweethearts

Chevy. It was the first Chevy model to have Powerglide automatic transmission. Mom mastered driving in a snap once she didn't have to struggle with the Lafayette's stubborn shifter and stiff clutch. Finally, Mom was mobile!

Ironically, it was just about that time that we moved into town to live in an Alvin duplex my grandfather had built as an investment—and as a home for us. I remember hanging from limbs—upside down, of course—on the big live oak trees in the yard and shopping at the Walgreen's not too far away. One of my favorite playmates was George Pugh, whose family lived on the other side of the duplex. Today George and his wife, Karen, are still two of our favorite Alvin friends.

Later, our family moved to a house across from the Alvin school that had served as the parsonage for the First Methodist Church, which the Ryans attended. By this time the family included my three brothers, Bruce, Larry, and Steve, as well as Lynn and me. So it was a good thing this house had three bedrooms and, even better, *two* bathrooms. What luxury!

In my memory, my childhood years form a mellow hodgepodge of love, joy, and the thrill of conquering new challenges. I was definitely a tomboy, but somehow my mother persuaded me to take ballet lessons, and I've always been grateful for that. The teacher was a woman from Russia who had moved to the area for some reason, and she was a very strict, very disciplined instructor. She taught lessons once a week in the American Legion Hall, and her mother would come along to play the piano for us while we danced. My mother sewed all my costumes for the recitals, of course—elaborate sequined-and-feathered outfits that seem just as enchanting today in the old photographs as they did so many years ago.

After the Russian teacher moved away, Mom drove me to Angelton, a town about twenty miles away, so I could continue dance lessons with Ruth and Sara Munson, two sisters from West Columbia. One of them later became a talented artist who painted a portrait of Nolan that now hangs in our home; her sister studied drama and now is an English professor in Tampa, Florida.

I took ballet lessons through my junior high and high school years, and I think that highly disciplined training helped me a lot in later life—not just in coordination and agility, but in disciplining myself and in appreciating the value of exercise and fitness. My mother tells the story of the time I nearly cut off my toe in the spokes of a bicycle the day before one of my big recitals. The doctor told us I should stay off that foot until the cut healed, but I wouldn't hear of it. I swapped my toe-shoes for flats and danced my heart out in the program the next evening.

I'm sure my brothers and Lynn and I must have gotten into mischief from time to time as we grew up, but I can't really remember any serious incidents. My parents didn't spank us, but when we misbehaved Dad would sit us down and deliver a lecture that we considered worse punishment than any spanking could ever have been. The lectures weren't angry tirades that made the rafters rattle; our parents rarely raised their voices. They gave us boundaries and expected us to abide by them. And most of the time, we did.

They also taught us to stand up for what is right. But again, those lessons didn't come from dinner-table lectures; they were taught by example. When my dad helped integrate Alvin's Little League, I certainly understood the injustice he was correcting. After all, if it was hard for a girl to watch longingly through that fence, wanting to join the team on Shroeder Field, how much harder it must have been for a little boy who was kept from playing simply because his skin was a little darker than the other boys'!

Dad also caused a stir when he invited some African-American friends to our church. There were church members who got mad at him for that. But he was doing what he knew was right: welcoming God's people, regardless of their skin color, to God's house.

The same thing happened to me—on a much smaller scale—when some of the kids jeered and argued with me after I made a speech in speech class that described Dr. Martin Luther King as a great leader. The way I saw it, he and my dad were working for the same cause. The only difference was their perspective: Dr. King was working to give all Americans equal rights. Dad was just focusing on his little corner of Alvin.

Childhood Sweethearts

If there is one difference in my upbringing and Nolan's, it's that he had to work a lot harder than I did as we were growing up. Whether he was helping his dad with the newspaper route or working at summer jobs or just handling chores and responsibilities around the house, Nolan was always working. As a result, he has a great appreciation for honest labor and the feeling of accomplishment and fulfilled responsibilities.

In contrast, my parents didn't push us to work and do chores around the house; instead, they urged us to focus on our schoolwork and our sports endeavors. The truth is, I had never run a washing machine until I was married, and my sister and I almost never even helped with the dishes—at least not willingly! Doing dishes was our punishment if we didn't get our homework done—so we almost always did our homework first thing when we got home.

In fact, I didn't have a clue about how to cook when I got married. A few years ago my brother Larry told a newspaper reporter about the time I was trying to heat up some store-bought dinner rolls and put them, wrapper and all, into the hot oven.

"She didn't even know you were supposed to take the plastic off," he said.

It's true. I wasn't much of a cook—and it's still not one of my favorite activities. There were (and are) so many other things I found more appealing—and my parents encouraged me to be out of the house, enjoying life and pushing myself to excel in other areas.

Because of this focus on academics and sports, I made straight A's all through high school, and my tennis game improved so that I was often competing in tournaments all over South Texas—and winning quite a few of them.

A very familiar scene in my mind is my dad, sitting in his lawn chair, watching from the sidelines as I competed in tennis matches around the area. Somehow he was always there. It was rare for dads to attend weekday matches, but somehow Dad made it seem natural for a man with a full-time job to show up in Houston or Galveston or some other city to watch as the first set began. He would make light of it, saying, "Oh, I had a service call to make in Houston, so I just scheduled it on the day when you were playing here." But now that I'm a mother trying to keep up with the sports schedules of just three children (and remember, he had five), I can appreciate what he must have gone through to arrange his schedule so he could be there at courtside in his lawn chair wherever I was playing.

He would bring along a cooler with some cold soft drinks for all of us, and he would cheer for us when we won and hug us when we lost. Sometimes when things went wrong on the court, I'd lose my temper and stomp around the sidelines or make a face. Then I'd see Daddy sitting over there, giving me the look that said, *Keep your cool, keep control of your temper, and keep your chin up,* and I'd take a deep breath and get back into the game.

One of the biggest problems I had as a child was sitting still. I was the kind of kid who always had to be doing something—and it had to be something *active.* I only endured a couple of years of piano lessons, for example, and even though my mom was an expert seamstress, I only learned the basics of sewing. One summer my sister and I went all over the neighborhood organizing a little library, collecting books from some of the families and devising a lending system for the neighborhood kids. Another summer we spent our time putting on "shows" in our garage or hosting "Miss America" pageants. Sometimes our parents would take us to the beach. All in all, it was a busy, idyllic childhood.

But too soon my childhood days were behind me. While I was still a teenager, I stepped into a marriage that would lead me out of my sheltered, cozy life in Alvin and into the fringe of the spotlight.

3

Young Love

*S*tudents in all four grades of Alvin High School were invited to the spring prom when I was a student there, but I only went to one— and it was a disappointing experience.

When I was a freshman and Nolan was a junior, he asked me to go to the prom, but I think he did it just because he knew I was hoping he would ask me. His heart just wasn't in it.

We got all dressed up the way you were supposed to. Nolan wore a dark suit and bought a corsage to pin on the prom dress my mom had made for me. It was a simple sleeveless sheath of yellow *peau de soie* with ruffles around the neck. Decked out in all our spring finery, we climbed into the '52 Chevy and headed out for the big night.

I liked to dance, and I was looking forward to spending the night out on the floor, being held in Nolan's arms for those dreamy slow dances or smiling and laughing together as we twisted and turned to the latest rock-'n'-roll tune.

But that's not what happened. Yes, I liked to dance—but Nolan definitely didn't. We only danced to one song the whole evening. The rest of the time we stood against the wall, watching the others, or hovered around the refreshments table, sampling the punch and cookies.

Childhood Sweethearts

It might have been a disastrous evening—except that I was so delighted to be with Nolan that nothing else really mattered. I was happy when we were together, regardless of what we were doing.

And I was involved in plenty of other interests to fill my time when we weren't together. I was working hard at my tennis game, I went to Girls State my junior year, I was still making straight A's, and I was a cheerleader my first three years of high school.

Alvin High School's cheerleaders cheered for both football and basketball—and any other event where spirited yelling and colorful pompoms were allowed. Our uniforms were orange V-neck pullover sweaters worn with pleated white wool skirts that had to touch our kneecaps. I suppose they would look positively Victorian compared with the revealing uniforms many modern cheerleaders wear.

My first two years of high school were my favorites because Nolan was there and he played basketball, so I put my heart into cheering for him. During his senior year, 1965, he won the school's Outstanding Athlete Award for being the best all-around athlete; that was the same year Rachel Adams and I won the state tennis championship. I also spent a lot of time watching Nolan play baseball on the high school diamond, the same field where I would watch our two sons play several years later. That year Nolan pitched his team to the state tournament and was named to the All-State team.

Thinking back on it, I see myself standing at the gate after those high school games, and I wonder just how much of my life I've spent during the last thirty-plus years waiting for Nolan outside of baseball parks. That comes to mind when I'm supposed to pick up Nolan at the airport and I'm a few minutes late. When he fusses about my being late sometimes, I can't help but remind him of the years I've spent waiting for him under the bleachers. Of course, he quickly points out that I could stand there in peace without being mobbed by autograph-seekers; I suppose that does make a difference!

When Nolan was a senior and I was a sophomore, we were elected "Most Beautiful Girl" and "Most Handsome Boy" in Alvin High. Today our kids get a kick out of teasing us about that claim to fame, mimicking the way those titles would be ridiculed by modern teenagers. But those were different times, and to us the titles were a special honor.

When Nolan and I were together, I was the happiest girl on earth— and he says he felt the same way. We both liked animals as well as sports, and sometimes we would share bits and pieces of our dreams. Nolan thought he might like to be a veterinarian, and I had visions of being a teacher—a coach, of course.

We felt comfortable together, and we saw each other every day at school. (Nolan would walk me to all my classes, then hurry to get to his own before the bell rang.) When we weren't playing tennis or baseball, or whenever Nolan wasn't working, we were almost always together.

That explains why one of the most miserable days of my life was the day during the summer before my junior year when Nolan left for the minor leagues.

He was anxious to get away from Alvin, just like kids have always been anxious to get away from their small-hometown roots. He wanted to be on his own and explore any opportunities the future held for him. The first opportunity developed as major-league scouts started showing up at Alvin baseball games.

One of them, Red Murff, a scout for the New York Mets, was there in March 1963 to watch Nolan pitch in a high school tournament. "I'm a hunter, and I know something about ballistics," he said later. "When I filled out my report for the Mets I said that Ryan was in the hundred-mile-per-hour range, that his ball stayed level in flight, rose as it got to the plate, and then exploded."

By his senior year, others were starting to notice Nolan's fastball, but Nolan himself seemed to be one of the last to recognize his potential. His self-confidence wasn't helped much when he was the 295th selection that spring in the major-league draft. Instead of being ecstatic that he'd been drafted, he seemed to focus on the fact that the major leaguers considered 294 other players better than he was. He wasn't even sure he *wanted* to play major-league ball. He had envisioned going to college and maybe playing basketball, but there were not too many colleges interested in a six-foot-two post man who weighed 140 pounds.

Childhood Sweethearts

After haggling back and forth with the Mets for a couple of weeks, Nolan still couldn't decide whether to play baseball or enroll in college. On June 28, 1965, the contract was lying on the Ryans' kitchen table. Nolan looked at the contract again—five hundred dollars a month plus a twenty-thousand-dollar signing bonus—then he looked into his father's eyes and thought of how he had worked at two jobs to raise six children. He thought about how long it would take his father to earn twenty thousand dollars. He picked up the pen and signed. He used the bonus money to pay off his parents' mortgage, and he bought himself a car. He said he figured he could use the rest of the money to go to Texas A&M and get his veterinarian's degree when the baseball thing was over.

About a week later, eighteen-year-old Nolan made his first trip by airplane and joined the Mets' Appalachian League team in Marion, Virginia. The Appalachian League, the bottom rung of the farm system, was comprised of teams of rookies.

On the day he left, my world came to a screeching halt. I went with his parents to Hobby Airport in Houston to see him off, and I will never forget that lonely feeling as I watched that plane fly away. When I got back home, I stormed into the house, dramatically slamming doors and crying as though my life had ended.

As I've said, the Holdorffs have never been ones to carry on in public—or even in front of family, for that matter. So my parents knew right away this uncharacteristic tantrum was heartfelt and devastating. I wasn't just putting on a show; I actually thought I would die of grief.

"Don't worry, Honey. It'll be okay. We'll work it out," Dad cooed to me, wrapping me in his arms and trying to soothe my shaking shoulders.

"How can you work anything out?" I sobbed, pushing back from him and glaring into his eyes that reflected my pain. "I'll never see him again!"

As I turned and ran up the stairs, Daddy called after me, "Maybe we can go see him."

I answered sarcastically, "Yeah, right!" and ran into the room I shared with Lynn, sprawling on my bed and crying as I'd never cried before. *Surely,* I thought, *no one in the whole wide world is as miserable as I am right now.*

Young Love

What followed was the longest, saddest, most wretched summer of my life. My only consolation was that Nolan, who regularly sent me little notes from Virginia, assured me that he was just as miserable as I was. I wrote him at least once a week, and he answered faithfully, describing how he had had to wait until someone was cut from the team before they had a uniform for him. Unfortunately, the first player to be cut was a guy who was so little his uniform pants had been shortened several inches. At six-foot-two, Nolan must have looked like he was wearing Bermuda shorts when he pulled on those trousers!

We both believe the only thing that saved either of us from becoming mentally unstable that summer due to a horrible case of lovesickness was the fact that my dear dad did, indeed, take me to see Nolan. He took off work and drove me all the way to Virginia in the old family station wagon so I could see this boyfriend I missed so much.

Except for a couple of trips to New York when I was little, I had never been outside of Texas—and rarely ventured out of the area around Alvin—so it was quite an adventure for me to ride all the way to Virginia. Dad took George Pugh, our neighbor and lifelong pal, as well as my three brothers and me, and we ended up in those beautiful Blue Ridge Mountains where it was cool and peaceful and . . . at least to me, very romantic. We stayed in an old hotel and watched Nolan's games whenever his team played or practiced that week.

Right away I noticed that Nolan was a little more demonstrative of his affection. Back in Alvin, he had never been one to hold hands or put his arm around me in front of other people, but here—perhaps because he was so glad to see me—he was willing to be a bit more outgoing, a little less shy of showing me how much he cared for me.

I remember those games in Marion as being a lot different from what I had expected of something connected with major-league baseball. Nolan pitched every fourth night, and the team had road trips every week or so. The small but enthusiastic crowds would pack themselves into the rickety old stands, hooting and hollering so boisterously you could hardly hear the announcer.

Childhood Sweethearts

I also remember one special group in the audience. There was a mental hospital up the hill from the ballpark—Nolan and the team members called it an asylum—and many of the mentally disabled patients there would be brought to the park for the games. Some of them would get so excited about every play, you couldn't help but catch their enthusiasm. They didn't care who was winning; they probably had no idea who was even playing. They just loved to be out in the fresh air, and they made the rest of us appreciate our good health and our many blessings. Their mental capacity might have been lacking, but their spirits were high.

Another thing I remember is the 1965 Impala Nolan bought that summer—his first *new* car. It was maroon with a red interior, and riding in it beside him was a real thrill for me.

But too soon the visit was over, and Nolan and I were saying good-bye again. I was silent most of the way home. It's a miracle my dad and brothers didn't kick me out of the car somewhere in Kentucky; I'm sure they got pretty tired of my bad mood. But they didn't, of course. They comforted and consoled and teased and tormented me until, for a few moments here and there, I could think about something besides Nolan. Still, it was a long, lonely summer back in Alvin. I didn't see Nolan again until he came home that fall at the end of the season.

When school started in August I was grateful that I had enough activities to keep me busy so I didn't miss Nolan quite so much. But before my junior year, a new school policy went into effect that prohibited girls from being cheerleaders more than two years. I had already been on the squad for two years, so I was automatically eliminated—and I was crushed by the new rule.

But there were plenty of other activities during those last two years of school to help distract me. I was active in several school functions, and I worked hard at tennis. I was lucky to have a lot of friends, and I enjoyed being with them. I realize now, however, that I missed out on a lot of things because I was so devoted to Nolan—and to tennis. For example, the seniors always had a "Kid Day," when everyone dressed up like little kids. It was just a fun thing to do, and every-one enjoyed it; but I was out of town for a tennis match, so I didn't participate. I didn't go to any more proms or dances, either, because Nolan wasn't there to go with me—and even if he had been, we might have agreed not to go, considering how disappointing that first prom had been.

I didn't date any other guys except one time. During my junior year I was voted to be the high school's Halloween coronation queen, a big occasion in the fall. I asked my friend George Pugh to be my "king" and escort. I had a few other casual dates to the beach or a movie with a friend, but no other serious boyfriends. There was really only one guy I wanted to be with.

The summer between my junior and senior years of high school, I was selected to go to Girls State in Austin, our state capital. Girls from all over Texas would go there for ten days to learn all about state government. Each girl would run for a city, county, or state office, and we were divided into two parties. Even though I did not have that much interest in government, I did learn a lot. Our keynote speaker for the week was a former Miss America, Marilyn Van Derbur. I can distinctly remember her talk—the main idea being to set high goals for ourselves, to follow our dreams, to become career women. She told us that if we were considering marriage, we should put that idea on hold and go to college. I suppose I felt that she was talking to me, but at the same time I was missing Nolan, and I felt like I could go to college and still be with him.

I remembered all this last year when I read an extremely sad arti-cle about Miss Van Derbur in *People* magazine. In the article she told of being sexually abused by her father when she was a child, and she said she wanted to help other victims of abuse by coming out with her story. I thought of how she must have pushed all those feelings inside as she presented such a positive, enthusiastic image to us girls who attended that Girls State gathering. It also must have been very dif-ficult for her to eventually have the fortitude to use her fame to speak out about something so emotionally painful.

Childhood Sweethearts

I think about that experience at Girls State, and I remember enjoying all the activities but also thinking constantly about Nolan. That's what comes to mind when someone asks me how I knew I was in love. All I can say is that the only thing we thought about—except maybe during a ball game or before a big test or at something like Girls State—was being together. We didn't really think beyond that. As Nolan says, "The only real ambition I had was to see my girlfriend."

So the next step seemed perfectly natural.

Part Two

Married to Baseball

4

A Bad Year—and the Wedding

$\mathcal{N}$olan never did propose in the formal sense, but he gave me an engagement ring in September 1966, just after school started in my senior year.

He had moved up to Class A ball that year and had spent most of the summer playing on the Mets' farm team in Greenville, South Carolina. Nolan's parents and youngest sister, taking their turn at trying to keep young hearts from breaking, had driven me up there during the summer so we could be together for a few days. It was during our visit that Nolan told me, "I really want to get married. How soon do you think we could?"

I believe that the loneliness of the baseball life and our missing each other so much had a lot to do with that decision. The only thing that stood in our way was my senior year in high school, and I had promised my parents I would wait until after graduation. I was only eighteen, and Nolan was twenty. Neither of us had any idea what we were getting into—only that we were in love and missed being together.

On one of those afternoons in Greenville, when we had a few hours to ourselves, we went into Kingoff Jewelers and picked out engagement and wedding rings. Nolan left a down payment of two hundred dollars on the set (which I think cost a total of about six hundred dollars—more than a month's salary for him then) and paid the rest off a little bit each month during that summer. When he came to Houston in September, he gave me the diamond.

It was obvious to everyone that Nolan's star was rising. The game his parents and I got to see was a seven-inning contest in which nineteen of the twenty-one outs came on Nolan's strikeouts. He was becoming known as a dangerous pitcher—in more ways than one. In Greenville, one of his pitches broke the arm of a woman who was leaning against the screen behind home plate.

By the end of his Class A play, he had been named the winning pitcher in seventeen games with only two losses, and he had thrown five shutouts and accumulated 272 strikeouts in 183 innings.

Near the end of the summer he moved up to play three games of AA ball with the Mets' team in Williamsport, Pennsylvania. Then, at the end of the season, when the major-league teams could traditionally expand their roster to forty players, Nolan was called up to play with the Mets in New York. He did so on the condition that he could stay in Alvin and start college after the Mets came to Houston to play the Astros in late September.

He pitched in a couple of games and recalls now that he learned very quickly that pitching in the majors, against the best hitters in the world, was no picnic.

I had followed his progress that summer with mixed feelings; I was certainly happy for Nolan, but all the good numbers and stats didn't make up for the terrible loneliness I felt when he was so far away. The truth was, I didn't care about any of that stuff; I just wanted him to come home.

Sometimes I think that our lives would have turned out completely different if he had not gone away to play ball. Absence certainly did seem to make our hearts grow fonder of each other. Would we have felt the same way and still married at such an early age had he remained in Alvin? I don't know . . . I really don't know.

A Bad Year—and the Wedding

Throughout that year, I rushed to beat everyone else to the telephone when it rang, hoping it was Nolan. We only had one phone in the house—in the center hallway downstairs—and my only hope for privacy was to take the phone with me into the hall closet, where I'd sit in the dark, talking to my boyfriend a thousand miles away. My kid brothers' favorite trick, when they saw the phone cord trailing out from under the door, was to lock me in the closet.

I was only seventeen years old, but I knew Nolan was the man I wanted to spend my life with. So when he asked, I didn't hesitate.

I said yes.

The wedding was scheduled for the following June, about a month after school ended. Looking back, I can't help but compare myself then with our daughter, Wendy, who's now the same age I was when I married Nolan. I think, *She's so young. She couldn't possibly know if she's in love.* Maybe I didn't know either. Maybe Nolan and I were just lucky. Maybe I would have been smarter to have waited awhile before I got married, to have dated other guys and gone to those proms and dances and finished college. Maybe. Sometimes I do have a few regrets, and I've admitted that it might have been a mistake to get married so young. But I've never thought I made a mistake in who I married.

Never.

I can't say our marriage got off to the best start, however. In fact, Nolan says except for getting married, 1967 was the worst year of his life.

The Vietnam War was gearing up, and Nolan had gotten a draft notice in 1966. By then, sportswriters had discovered him, and he had received a lot of attention. So that he could keep playing baseball, the Mets were determined to get him into an army reserve unit, which required a six-month tour of active duty, then six years of weekend sessions every month and two weeks of training camp in the summers. They finally found a reserve unit for him, and he made the six-year commitment, beginning with basic training in Fort Leonard Wood, Missouri.

It was a difficult time for everyone. So many people were either being drafted or were enlisting. Nolan's brother, Robert, was in the air force and served in Cambodia during the war. I remember watching the television news and thinking about friends and relatives who were involved in the war. It did not really hit home, though, until the day we found out that Billy Dixon, my next-door neighbor and one of Nolan's classmates, who had enlisted in the marines with some Alvin friends, had been killed in Vietnam. I have always been thankful that Nolan and my own brothers did not have to go to Southeast Asia.

While I finished my senior year in high school, Nolan completed his six months in basic training, then returned to play with the Mets' minor-league team in Jacksonville, Florida. He was striking out a lot of batters, and the Mets' minor-league team was starting to use his name in advertisements and promotions.

They made a big deal out of the fact that he would be pitching in one of the games, and one day a big crowd had arrived at the stadium to see this new phenomenon. But while Nolan was warming up before the game, something in his arm popped. He had no idea what was wrong, but he knew he couldn't play. He couldn't throw the ball ten feet. He went to the general manager and said simply, "I can't pitch."

The general manager was irate. "What do you mean you can't pitch?" he roared. "We've got a sellout crowd here, and they've come to see you pitch! What do you expect me to do?"

Nolan just stood there, holding his arm and saying he was sorry but he was injured and he simply couldn't pitch.

"Well, I'll tell you what *you're* going to do," the general manager yelled. "You walk out there on the mound, get a microphone, and tell these people you can't pitch!"

It was as if the general manager had no idea what to do with all the spectators. Nolan told him he wouldn't do that and suggested the team owner give the people their money back if they didn't want to stay to see the game. I think they offered the refund, but they weren't happy about it.

The Mets wanted the team doctor in New York to look at Nolan's arm, and when Nolan went to see him, the doctor wanted to operate right then. But Nolan said no.

A Bad Year—and the Wedding

When I think of this story, I can't help admiring Nolan for having a sixth sense about what was right for him. He was so young—not quite twenty years old—but he knew himself, and he knew this didn't feel right. He told the Mets he would quit before he let anyone cut up his pitching arm.

If it had been me I would have thought, *This guy is an expert; he knows what he's doing. I may have second thoughts, but he's probably right.* But Nolan didn't believe surgery was the right thing to do, and he refused to have it.

He was still on the disabled list—and worried about his future—when our wedding date rolled around. Nolan had to come home for one of his army-reserve weekends, and he asked the team for an extra day off so he could get married. The Mets agreed but insisted that he be ready to rejoin the team the next day, Tuesday, June 27. The wedding was scheduled for Monday evening, June 26, 1967.

Nowadays when I hear brides talking about all the preparations that go into a big church wedding, I realize just how hard my mother worked to make mine a dream come true. I did hardly anything; she pulled the whole thing together maintaining her usual optimistic smile and calm demeanor. I don't really remember doing anything but choosing my wedding dress and going to the jewelry store to "pick out my patterns." Mom even had to go with me to do that; when she told me it was something I should do, I asked, "What patterns?" I had no idea what she meant.

I wore an A-line gown of white silk organza with *point-device* lace, purchased on sale for seventy-five dollars at Foley's in Houston. The bridesmaids' yellow dresses for my sister, Nolan's sister Jean, and my two friends came from Foley's too. My mother made the dresses for my two nieces who were the flower girls. Mom also made all the arrangements for the flowers, the reception, and the photographer. And through it all, she kept up her good humor and her wonderful sense of peace and tranquility. My daughter will be lucky if I can be half as calm on her big day.

My family attended the Presbyterian Church, but we decided to have the wedding at the Methodist Church, which the Ryans attended, because it was bigger. We needed the space for the three hundred guests we had invited.

I got dressed in the church nursery, and when Daddy tapped on the door to say it was time to go, he was wearing the biggest, proudest smile in the universe. As we started down the aisle, I sensed that the church was bulging with dozens of smiling friends and family members, but I only remember seeing one person in focus: the tall, dark-haired, athletic-looking guy waiting down by the altar. I'd always thought Nolan looked very appealing wearing blue jeans or a baseball uniform, but seeing him standing there in that white tuxedo dinner jacket, I believed with all my heart that I was marrying my own Prince Charming and embarking on a dream come true.

The ceremony proceeded without a hitch, then we all moved over to the parish hall for the reception featuring punch and wedding cake. It was then that the irony of the day hit me. It was the happiest day of my life, true, but it was a day tinged with sadness. That morning, Nolan's dad had become very ill. He had asked the doctors to give him something that would allow him to attend the wedding, but they said it was out of the question. He was admitted to the hospital a couple of hours before the ceremony began.

The problem was cancer, the price of a lifetime of heavy smoking.

Trying not to spoil my big day, no one told me about Nolan's dad, and I was so concerned with all my prewedding jitters that I didn't even notice he was not there when the wedding began. Now I realized that Nolan must have borne a heavy burden throughout the day, feeling torn up about his dad and just as nervous as I was about the wedding. He also knew that we had airline reservations early the next morning to rejoin the team in Florida. It must have been a very stressful day for him, but as usual he didn't show his feelings. He was patient while the photographs were taken and the wedding cake was cut, then he joined me in mingling through the reception, greeting all the guests and thanking them for coming.

One of those guests was Red Murff, the Mets scout who had first discovered Nolan. When I had shown him my engagement ring a few months earlier, he had said, "It's not easy being a baseball wife. You know, you're going to have to share him with the world."

I wasn't sure what he meant, but I thought to myself, *I'm not sharing him with anybody!*

Now, as Nolan's edginess increased and he became anxious to leave, I realized I *would* have to share him, beginning with his close-knit family here in Alvin. "I'd like to check on Dad," he said.

We changed clothes and made our exit, squinting against the storm of rice that fell on us as we ran to the maroon Impala. Then we went home to get our luggage.

Our next stop was the hospital.

5

Stranded on First

$\mathcal{O}$ur visit to see Nolan's dad in the hospital was short and poignant. He was groggy from all the medication, and breathing was a chore for him. He nodded and blinked at us, and as Nolan squeezed his hand to say good-bye I thought I saw him smile.

It was hard for Nolan to leave him, but we really felt it was the right thing to do. The doctors had said his dad would soon be well enough to return home, and Nolan knew he would understand his wanting to fulfill his obligation to the Mets.

We walked out of the hospital in silence, but our mood definitely took an upward swing as we stepped into the almost-empty parking lot. The Impala was impossible to miss, streaked with goofy, white-shoe-polish signs, rice spilling off the hood, and tin cans tied to the rear bumper. Giggling, we pulled into the drive-through lane of a nearby Whataburger, embarrassed but too hungry to care. The only thing we had eaten all day was wedding cake and punch, so we filled up on hamburgers, fries, and Cokes. People inside stared out the window at our car, and a few of them probably wondered if it was some kind of prank. After all, who would eat dinner at Whataburger on their wedding night?

Married to Baseball

We spent the night in the Holiday Inn on the Gulf Freeway in Houston and caught a 7 A.M. flight to Jacksonville. When we reached the apartment Nolan had rented there, we found that the electricity wasn't turned on, the room temperature was about 120 degrees, and the bed had no pillows. We immediately fled to an air-conditioned five-and-dime to buy two pillows on sale for ninety-nine cents each.

The next day, Nolan left with the team for a two-week road trip.

I remember sitting there in that little apartment after he left, feeling that everything seemed so strange. I was eighteen years old, on my own for the first time in my life, and feeling totally alone.

The day after our wedding was my mom's birthday, and Dad's birthday was two days after that. I hadn't even thought about their birthdays in all the excitement of the wedding, and as soon as I remembered, I called home.

I was in tears before they even answered.

"Are you okay?" Mom asked. "Is everything all right? Where's Nolan?"

"He's on a road trip . . . for two weeks." I tried to sound normal, but my quavering voice made me sound like a little kid. "I'm fine, Mom. Really. I'm fine *(sniff)*. How are you and Daddy? What are you doing for your birthdays?"

Suddenly I could picture them there at home, in their quiet, peaceful house. I imagined my brothers in the school across the street, and I pictured my friends heading for the beach or warming up on the tennis courts. I had thought being separated from Nolan while I waited back home in Alvin was the worst situation I could ever encounter. But I was wrong. Oh, so wrong. Being separated from him while I waited behind in a strange place was much worse!

I knew I would only be in Jacksonville until August, then I would head home to Alvin to enroll in junior college while Nolan finished the season. But suddenly those two months ahead of me seemed like a life sentence.

One story, in particular, shows just how unprepared I was for married life. It happened when Yvonne Koosman, seven months pregnant with her first child, came to visit. Nolan and Yvonne's husband, Jerry,

46

were both rookies and, in fact, shared the same bubblegum card. She had stopped by to introduce herself and to tell me which other wives were living in the building. After I talked to her for a few minutes, I asked, "By the way, do you know how to wash clothes?"

She thought that was hilarious, but I was serious. I had never run a washing machine in my life. She took me to the laundromat, showed me how to sort the clothes, how much soap to put in, where to put the coins in, and which cycles to choose on the washers and dryers. It had never occurred to me to ask my mother before leaving home, and Mom probably assumed I knew.

There were other challenges besides learning to do laundry. Looking back, they all seem pretty minor. But at the time, they appeared to be almost insurmountable. For example, I didn't want to get in the Impala and drive around because I didn't know where I was going. I was afraid I'd get lost, and I was timid about asking strangers for directions.

But gradually I built up my confidence, and I managed to cope. And when Nolan was home, life was good.

Still, there were moments when I sat down and plotted out my future, and it didn't look all that rosy. I could see a pattern emerging that wasn't the ideal way to launch a marriage. If Nolan was going to be gone two weeks out of each month from April to October, and if he had to spend two weeks in the army for summer camp and then head back to Florida for the Instructional League and spring training, I figured I was going to spend less than half of that first year with my husband.

I wanted to cherish every moment we were together, and I was really relieved when Nolan came off the road. But the day after he returned, I got upset all over again. As we walked into a bank to add my name to Nolan's account, a strange woman yelled across the lobby, "Hi, Nolan!"

She was very pretty, blonde (*somewhat hard-looking*, I thought, feeling a little catty), maybe thirty (*an older woman*) and with a good figure. I just didn't expect a woman in a strange town to be yelling at my husband as if they were best friends.

I was even more shocked when she came over and hugged him and he introduced us. He said she lived in our building.

He explained later that she was one of the so-called groupies, or "Baseball Annies," who gave parties for the players out by the swimming pool. That was all new to me, and I was totally unprepared to learn that this, too, was part of professional baseball: women hanging around the ballpark, the pool, or the local bars to meet the players.

When you're young and first married, with a lot of insecurities, it isn't difficult for the seeds of doubt to get planted in your mind. Your feelings are easily hurt, you're not yet bound together by hoops of love-hardened steel, and you don't have a long, tested relationship to cushion you.

This was my first exposure to the dark side of professional sports, but too soon the stories of infidelity and promiscuity no longer surprised me, although they always left me feeling sad. Eventually, it was almost expected for a baseball wife, going through a divorce, to talk about the process as though it were a form of vicious combat replete with yelling, fighting, and cheating.

This was a side of marriage I had never seen. My parents didn't yell or fight, and if they had any problems they certainly hid them well. The picture scared me. I found myself looking around and thinking, *Is this what we're going to be like in five years?*

But Nolan always reassured me, reminding me that we were different from most of those other people. We had different backgrounds, different values. And, he would say, "We can't live our lives worrying about other people and wondering if we're going to have the same problems they have."

I knew he was right, and besides, I had other things to think about. We both continued to worry about Nolan's arm. It was still hurt, and he wasn't pitching. We just didn't know what the future held, but we figured if the Mets still believed in him, we'd hang on a while longer. It was frustrating for both of us as the games came and went and he still didn't play. Sometimes, when I sensed that Nolan was feeling unsure of his future, I even thought about suggesting that he could come back to Alvin with me and enroll in junior college if he thought he wasn't going to pitch anymore—but I didn't say it. I was learning to be patient and let him figure out what he wanted to do.

Once in a while, when the team was in town, we'd go to the beach with another couple or round up a bunch of players and their wives to watch television and order pizza. Those were good times, but they were pretty rare.

After two months of marriage—and only about three weeks of being together—I headed home, as planned, to enroll in Alvin Junior College. In my young, idealistic state, I thought I could somehow earn a college degree while coping with a long-distance marriage. When Nolan moved up to the major leagues, I expected to transfer to some other college wherever we lived and continue my dream. I hoped to major in physical education, preparing myself to be a coach.

For a while, it almost seemed to work.

My parents had a tiny little house in their backyard, and that was where Nolan and I set up housekeeping, filling the two rooms with furniture given to us by the Topps Bubblegum Company. Instead of paying players when they put the players' pictures on baseball cards, Topps gave them gifts. They gave us a little aquamarine-and-lime-green vinyl couch and chair with metal frames and plaid cushions. It wasn't the most stylish decor, but it was functional and we liked it and used it for many years. Mother helped out, too, by giving us an old bed and dresser. We didn't have much room in that little dollhouse, but we didn't need it back then.

What we did need was money. Nolan had used his twenty-thousand-dollar signing bonus from the Mets to pay off his parents' home mortgage and to buy the maroon Impala, so our only income was his five-hundred-dollar monthly salary plus a loan we'd taken out to try to survive. I had a job working part time in the college bookstore. But after taxes and college fees, it didn't leave anything for commuting back and forth to be with each other when Nolan was away.

When Nolan came home at the end of the regular season, he worked at whatever pickup jobs he could find. Sometimes he pumped gas at one of the service stations in town. It was hard for him to find steady work because everyone in Alvin knew he would be leaving again for the Mets Instructional League in Saint Petersburg, Florida, and when that was finished he would be home only a few weeks before leaving again to rejoin the team for spring training.

Despite these financial worries—and our continuing worry about Nolan's still-injured arm—we were very happy in that little house. We really never gave a thought to what we didn't have. I always knew if Nolan couldn't play baseball anymore he could still work, and I could still work too. We would be fine.

This is not to suggest everything was perfect. I will never forget the day he got home from the Instructional League. We had been married since June, and now it was November. I was so anxious to be with him. I thought, *My husband is coming home, and we will be together full time—at least for a little while.*

But I was in for another rude surprise. As soon as Nolan walked in the door, he started getting things together to leave again. I was stunned. He was going deer hunting! He finally noticed the shocked expression on my face and stopped packing to give me a reassuring hug.

"Ruth, it's opening weekend. It's something I've looked forward to all year. I'll be back in a couple of days. Okay, Honey? Try to understand."

Since then I've endured other episodes of hurt feelings on the opening day of deer season, as I'll explain later, but now, nearly thirty years later, I've come to accept deer season as a traditional Ryan holiday. All of our kids go hunting with Nolan now, even our daughter, Wendy. But on that hurt-filled day in 1967, I *didn't* understand. I was upset, and after Nolan left with his hunting buddies I remember standing in the middle of the room, staring at the door for a long time.

When he left for spring training in February, I stayed behind to continue my classes at Alvin Junior College. It seemed we had spent the first year of our marriage saying good-bye to each other.

On April 1, 1968, Nolan made the team; he had worked his way up through the minors, and now he was playing with the New York Mets. On Easter Sunday, Nolan pitched against the Astros in Houston and earned his first major-league win, pitching six and two-thirds innings and beating Larry Dierker, 4-0, in a duel of young right-handers. He allowed only three hits, struck out eight, and walked two.

I remember thinking all that was great—but the important thing to me was not that he was pitching in the Astrodome but that he was home.

6

New York Rookies

$\mathcal{I}$n the spring of 1968 I hesitantly approached one of my teachers at Alvin Junior College and told him I was going to miss a day of class. When he asked why, I told him, "I'm going to New York to be with my husband."

I was scared to death to make the trip alone, but I was so desperately lonesome for Nolan that I'm sure I could have overcome any difficulty to make the trip. It turned out to be quite an experience, and it included an incident that was the first time a stranger ever made me cry.

I flew into La Guardia and took a cab to the nearby Travelers Hotel, which served as the team's guest quarters. Nolan had told me he would be at Shea Stadium when I arrived, but he said, "Don't worry. They'll take care of you at the hotel. Just ask someone at the front desk to get you a ride to the stadium."

I took my stuff up to my room then headed down to the lobby. When I told the man at the front desk I was a Mets player's wife and needed a ride to the stadium, he looked at me like I'd just arrived from outer space. Finally, he stepped outside and whistled, waving his arm vigorously toward the street. A cab pulled up to the curb and the man who had whistled opened the door of the cab for me. I got in, looked up at him with a polite smile, and said, "Thanks a lot."

He paused for a moment, then he slammed the door so hard my teeth rattled. It startled me so much I didn't know what to think. I was just starting to catch my breath from the door-slamming scare when the cabdriver turned around and barked at me, "Lady, I'm not taking you anywhere if you don't give *me* a tip!"

I was nineteen years old, in New York for the first time since coming with my mother as a toddler and with the rest of my family when we came to visit my grandmother when I was seven. I'd never ridden in a cab by myself. I knew I should tip the driver, but I had no idea I was supposed to tip somebody for whistling at one. I was terribly embarrassed by my ignorance—and even more embarrassed that tears were welling up in my eyes. I mumbled a promise to tip the driver, and he stepped on the gas, eager to get me to my destination and be rid of me, I'm sure.

The thought of actually living in such a hostile place was almost more than I could bear. I couldn't think of a single soul—let alone *two* people—back home in Alvin who would treat a stranger as those two men had treated me.

I spent the weekend with Nolan and watched him pitch in the next game, then returned home to finish out the semester in Alvin.

When I got back home, I realized I was living a life of contrasts. I was still a teenager living with my parents—but I was an adult with a husband in New York. I was a college student, but I no longer had anything in common with most of my classmates, who were pursuing their own careers without the distractions I faced. Sometimes when I walked by the tennis courts, I thought, *I could be living a normal life, playing tennis and competing in tournaments. How can something I want so much—being married to Nolan—make me so miserable?*

After that first year of struggling to concentrate on schoolwork while my heart was a thousand miles away with my husband, I knew that something, *someone,* had to change. And I was that someone. When the semester ended, I never went back again full time. If I was going to be married, I wanted to be with my husband, no matter where he was. I never missed all of spring training again after that year except in 1977, when Wendy was born.

Feeling greatly relieved that I'd made these decisions, I flew back to New York to rejoin Nolan. We moved his few belongings out of the Travelers Hotel and into a little apartment on the seventh floor of a twelve-story building in Elmhurst, Queens.

There were many foreigners there, and I felt like a foreigner myself. I naively expected my neighbors to come calling. In Alvin, whenever someone new moved into town, the neighbors would go over and bring a cake or even a dinner. It sure wasn't like that in New York! You could live in one of those apartment complexes for years and the only person you got to know well was the "super," the building superintendent in charge of most repairs.

One day there was a knock on the door. When I opened it I was delighted to find a little old lady standing there. I thought maybe she had brought some cookies or was finally coming to get acquainted. Instead she scolded me, saying, "Why do you make so much noise at night?"

We never played music or made noise, but we did come home late at night after Nolan's ball games. She told me she wanted us to be quiet.

I thought, *What a great neighbor.*

I wasn't the only one who was frustrated. Nolan's career with the Mets seemed to be going nowhere. One problem was that he missed a lot of pitching opportunities because of the weekend meetings he had to attend each month to fulfill his obligation to the army reserve. The other problem was that the Mets didn't seem to have the time— or the interest—to work with him. He could throw the ball faster than a lot of the finest pitchers in baseball, but too often his pitches were wild. He needed to develop more control, and the Mets weren't willing to help him.

Nolan spent game after game "warming up" in the bull pen but never going into the game. It was one of those Catch-22 problems: He needed help and experience to gain more control of the ball, but the Mets didn't play him because he was inexperienced and, as a result, ineffective.

But if Nolan wasn't getting the training he needed, I was making up for it by getting educated in a wide variety of survival techniques, starting the very first week. For example, there was the New York shopping technique, going from one store to another to fill the grocery list instead of getting everything in one supermarket, the way I'd done in Alvin. I complained about it so much that Nolan finally said he would go along with me to see what all the fuss was about.

First, we went to the dairy and bought our containers of milk. Then we went to the butcher for meat and poultry. Then we stopped at the produce stand for fruits and vegetables.

I warned Nolan not to buy too much because we had to carry everything and it was a long walk home, mostly uphill, but he didn't listen. He figured he wouldn't have to go through it again if he bought everything at once.

It was hot out, so when one of the milk containers started leaking it dripped on Nolan's shirt and very quickly started to smell bad. It also soaked the bag so that the bottom fell out, and we had to stop on the sidewalk and rebag everything. When we finally reached our building, climbed the stairs, and opened the door to the apartment, Nolan flung those bags of groceries onto the table, then turned around and walked out of the kitchen, exhausted, frustrated, and defeated. I can't recall his ever going grocery shopping with me again.

I hated the feeling of being stuck in the apartment all day and having so little control over my life, so I made up my mind to venture out and explore my surroundings. Nolan had left the Impala in Alvin, thinking we wouldn't need a car in New York. But after having to ride the subway to get to Shea Stadium, we both decided that was wrong. So we bought an old 1956 Chevy for $150, glad to have any kind of wheels.

But owning a car was a hassle too. We had no place to park but the street, and the city required car owners to move their cars from one side of the street to the other at a certain time each day so the street sweepers could clean. To folks from small-town Texas, this was about the strangest law anyone could ever imagine, but New Yorkers seemed to accept it as perfectly natural. For us, it was a daily challenge to remember to move the car so we wouldn't get ticketed and towed.

I did manage to venture out in the car, but except for this daily streetside shuffling, I didn't venture out for long. As luck would have it, I picked the worst day possible for my first exploratory jaunt in the old Chevy. It was a day when the skies opened up and the rain was as thick as a curtain—and the windshield wipers quit working. I managed to get turned around and headed back to the apartment by driving the old car at a crawl and sticking my head out the window occasionally to see if I was inside the yellow line. The other drivers honked and yelled at me all the way back to our building. I got out of the car, slammed the door behind me, and stomped up the steps to our apartment. I hated that car, hated New York, hated that apartment, and hated baseball for bringing all those other hated elements into my life.

When the Mets were getting ready to leave New York on a two-week road trip, I couldn't stand the thought of staying there alone in that place I detested. I told Nolan I thought I'd be better off in Alvin than spending two weeks alone in the apartment. "I need to go home," I said.

He answered, "Fine. Go."

So I did. While I was back in Alvin, I went to the doctor for a routine checkup. He found a lump in my breast and, trying not to alarm me, told me that it was probably a benign tumor or cyst and that it should be removed as soon as possible. Since I was only nineteen and had never even been in the hospital I was pretty naive about such things. I told him to go ahead and schedule the surgery so I could get back to New York.

The next day I checked myself into the hospital in Alvin. My parents were in town, but I told them not to worry. I said I was only having minor surgery and that I would be out the next day. I told them it was no big deal—and I believed that.

It *was* minor surgery, so I really wasn't prepared for what my doctor told me in the operating room. Just before I went under the anesthetic, he patted my arm and said, "If your tumor is malignant, I'll go ahead and remove the breast while you're still under the anesthetic so you won't have to go through this again."

I know it sounds incredible that things could happen this way, but there are thousands of women—and their doctors—who can verify that this was standard practice back then. As the anesthetic took effect and my world went black, I didn't know if I would wake up with or without my left breast. That was the scariest feeling I had every experienced.

When I came to after the surgery, the first thing I did was place my right hand over my breast to feel if it was still a part of me. It was. Luckily, my benign tumor, about the size of a large grape, was all the doctor removed.

That night I was hurting and lonely in my hospital room. I couldn't sleep because of the pain, and I didn't know enough to call for a nurse and ask for medication. As I said, I was still, in many ways, a terribly naive teenager. Luckily, one of my sister's friends was a nurse on duty there that night, and she just happened to pass my room and see my name on the door. When she came in to see why I was there she could see immediately that I was hurting, and she called in for some medication. Finally I was able to sleep.

The next day I left the hospital and went to my parents' house, and the day after that I flew back to New York. Anyone who's been through this kind of "minor" surgery knows exactly how I felt that day after a long trip and having to carry a suitcase and other stuff. By the time my plane arrived, I was exhausted, uncomfortable, and miserable—but happy to see my husband again.

In those days, the late sixties, I was taking the birth-control pill, and there was some controversy about whether the pill caused cancer and other problems. The pill hadn't been around that long, and some of the studies were inconclusive. I quit taking it about a year later because of the fear of developing another tumor.

Now I cringe when I recall this entire experience. I know much more about my body now, and I would never approach surgery in that same manner. I would have insisted on having the biopsy first with the understanding that I would have a chance to consider my choices if it were malignant. I would have used a specialist and a Houston medical center hospital, gotten a second opinion, weighed my options, and made sure I knew exactly what the surgery would consist of ahead of time.

But the experience did one good thing for me: It convinced me to have regular checkups, and now I never miss going for my mammogram once a year.

Despite this difficulty, going to Alvin helped "charge my batteries," emotionally. While I was back home with my family and friends, I gathered up enough strength, courage, and fortitude to tackle New York again. Most of all, I was anxious to see Nolan; I would have gone anywhere as long as I could be with him.

It wasn't long, though, before we were both suffering from cabin fever again. When Nolan was gone, I coped by going into Manhattan to visit the museums and enjoy some of the Broadway plays. Nolan's remedy was to drive to the ballpark. "But no matter what time I went," he griped, "there would be traffic and people getting into fights, honking, flipping people off, yelling."

Later, he sent for his black Labrador retriever, Molly, so I'd have a companion and a bodyguard while he was on the road or at the stadium.

He didn't care for New York any more than I did. There were too many people, too many buildings, too many cars, too much concrete. But all that changed, at least for Nolan, whenever it rained. He would put on his jogging clothes, snap a leash on Molly, and go running through the park in the rain. I'm not sure why he liked it so much, but he did. Years later, he would say, "That was about the neatest experience I had in New York."

Molly also went with me when I drove to Brooklyn to visit my grandmother, my mother's mother. She lived in a row house in Brooklyn with her second husband, Henry. Before we moved to New York, I had only seen her four or five times in my life; she had come to Alvin when one of my brothers was born, and we had visited her in New York two times during my childhood. Mormor was from Sweden, and she spoke with a strong accent. At first, I had trouble understanding her, but eventually we got so we could communicate with each other.

When I was planning a visit, I would call and ask, "Mormor, Nolan's game will be on television. Will Henry mind if I watch?" She would say they'd be happy to watch the game with me, but I'm not sure they ever understood what was happening. One time she was watching Nolan pitch and she asked, "Is he trying to hit that bat with the ball?" But she always watched with me, and I tried to explain the basics of the game. She would also send me things she'd clipped out of the newspapers when she saw something about Nolan or the Mets or some other baseball story that caught her eye.

Molly always went to Mormor's with me. She was the greatest dog, never rambunctious or loud. She would lie by my feet for hours. One day when I'd been there five or six hours I asked Mormor if I could take Molly outside. Henry said I was not to let her use his yard—or anyone else's yard—and she shouldn't use the street or sidewalk either. That posed quite a dilemma, which Molly solved by quickly using the nearest piece of grass she could find. I was glad Henry wasn't looking.

Mormor moved to Alvin several years later; she died there in January 1992.

I'm not sure which one of us was more miserable that first year in New York, Nolan or me. Nolan was just another struggling kid with a wild fastball and an unhappy young wife, and after he ended the erratic year with six wins and nine losses, I think he was ready to chuck it and stay put in Alvin. I knew I couldn't make that decision for him, but I told him if he gave up now, he would look back years later and always wonder if he might have made it. He didn't quit, but in the four years he was with the Mets, I don't think he had four consecutive weeks when he looked to the future with any confidence.

As the season was finally coming to an end, Daddy flew to New York to help me drive the old Chevy home to Alvin. (When we got there, we sold it to my brother for fifty dollars.) We drove straight through, taking turns driving and sleeping, with no stops except for food and gasoline. Daddy kept saying the trip reminded him of that adventurous odyssey he and Mom had made when they left New York, bound for Texas in 1948. The main difference, I thought, was that Mom was probably sad to leave her home in New York and even sadder to see Alvin.

For me, just the opposite was true.

7

Big Wins, Hard Losses

The next spring, 1969, was the first year I got to spend all of spring training with Nolan—at least I was with him when he wasn't on the road. I remember how exciting it was when we rented a small apartment above a garage overlooking the beach in Saint Petersburg. It was small, but we couldn't afford anything bigger. And besides, I thought it would be romantic to live on the beach.

That was my first mistake. That spring in Saint Petersburg had to be the coldest, wettest, and windiest on record. Sand constantly blew through the cracks around the windows and under the door. In the bathtub, you felt like you were sitting on wet sandpaper. And I felt like I could never get warm.

Mistake number two was thinking that I couldn't live without all my wedding gifts and most of our earthly goods, including pots, pans, dishes, silverware, linens, and everything else. We drove to spring training pulling a trailer. Since Nolan had to practice all day, it became my job to unpack the car and trailer and carry everything upstairs to our apartment. By the end of the day I was exhausted and had caught a cold from the bad weather. It wasn't a good way to start the year.

Married to Baseball

It seemed like a rough beginning, but some of the other wives—especially Nancy Seaver, Yvonne Koosman, and Carol Kranepool—took me in hand. They were especially helpful when reality set in as spring training ended.

It hadn't occurred to me that when the Mets broke camp to open the regular season, Nolan would fly off with the team and I would be left on my own to get the car and the trailer full of wedding gifts to New York.

At first, the thought of what I had to do was overwhelming, and I had a momentary urge to call my dad and ask him to come help me. But the other wives encouraged me, and I finally summoned enough resolve to believe I could do it. Actually, the nearer the day came, the braver I felt.

We had a new car then—a Cutlass—and we had brought along Molly, the beloved Labrador retriever. So, boldly going where no Alvin girl had ever gone before, I hooked up the trailer and followed Nancy Seaver's brown Porsche north out of Saint Petersburg, headed for New York. We had already agreed where we would spend the night, about twelve hours up the road.

Everything went smoothly until we hit Atlanta at rush hour, and I lost sight of the brown Porsche. Suddenly, surrounded by hundreds of stern-faced, fast-driving commuters, I felt completely abandoned. I was gripping the wheel tightly with both hands and thinking how glad I was to have Molly's friendly face smiling up at me when the car beside me swerved and sideswiped the trailer. I was too scared to stop in the heavy traffic—and the other driver didn't stop either. Shaking more than ever, I pulled my chin up and drove on.

I finally reached the motel where Nancy had said we would stop for the night, but she wasn't there. (When I didn't show up after she arrived, she figured I had missed the motel so she went on ahead.) I had never stayed in a motel alone, and I fumbled when I signed the form at the front desk. I was wiped out by the time I finally got to the room and didn't sleep a wink the whole night. Once again, I was glad to have Molly with me; she's probably the only reason I survived that night in Atlanta.

Nancy called back to the motel early the next morning, and we managed to meet the next night in another motel. And finally, on the third day, we neared New York. I'll never forget the sensation of pulling that little trailer up the freeway as the New York skyline appeared in the distance. I'd never seen so many roads, so much traffic, and I had to give myself a long, determined pep talk before I could actually drive into the city.

We eventually ended up at the seedy hotel near Shea Stadium that the team used as its headquarters. It was still a real dump, and it was in a neighborhood that had me checking the Cutlass's doorlocks every minute or two. The team was out of town, so Nolan wasn't there to meet me. My first impulse was to just leave everything in the trailer and get some rest, but somehow I found the strength to unload all the luggage and boxes, piece by piece. By the time I staggered into the room and stacked the last box in the last available space, I was lucky to find the bed.

I conked out immediately and was surprised to open my eyes and find it was morning. When I got dressed and went outside, the trailer had been stolen. Someone had simply unhitched it during the night and hauled it off. I was so glad I had emptied it the night before. I remember muttering as I called the police, "Welcome to New York."

We eventually rented part of a house in Bayside, Queens. The basement apartment was rented by a frail little old lady named Mrs. Raines. The first day we moved in she hobbled up the stairs, banged on my door, and demanded, "Come downstairs right away so I can show you something." She was very bossy, so I politely obeyed. She proceeded to show me an old school bell she kept next to her bed. "If you ever hear me ringing this bell, get down here fast and hook me up to my oxygen tank," she said.

Somehow, I knew I didn't want to be responsible for this old woman's life if she had a heart attack or something, but I did try to take care of her needs as best as I could. Thank goodness, I never heard the dreaded school bell ringing!

The house we shared with the old lady in Bayside cost three hundred dollars a month, twice as much as we could afford, but Nolan wanted a yard, a little breathing room, and a space where he could grow tomatoes, which he happily passed out among the neighbors. We lived there three summers, returning to Alvin at the end of each season. And gradually, New York life became a little more bearable for us, but it was never what you would call tranquil.

My brother, Larry Holdorff, visited us for a week one summer and went to the nearby park one day to play basketball. He got there just in time to see two kids mug the Good Humor man. He was breathless when he got back home and described the scene to us.

"Now you never saw anything like *that* in Alvin, Texas," he exclaimed.

It helped me a little when two of the other wives, Nancy Seaver and Carol Kranepool, took me on a "road trip" of my own, driving me to see my cousins who lived in Newton, New Jersey. I was a little nervous about going, even with these two "veterans" to accompany me, but they insisted. They said I had to get out of the city or I would go nuts. And they were right. I have always been grateful for the kindness these Mets wives showed me; they went out of their way for a young and naive neophyte.

Although we were trying to cope, Nolan and I were not happy living in New York. In fact, if we had to admit it, deep down we were still miserable. Sure, Nolan was playing with a major-league team, but in reality he was just another struggling kid looking for a break. I tried to do things to keep busy, but even trying to play tennis or take ballet lessons (two things I really enjoyed) were either too much of a hassle or too expensive—or I had to travel an hour in traffic to get to the place.

This was such a lonely time for me. I felt very unproductive, always wishing I were somewhere else. A lot of my days were spent reading or sewing or just waiting for the baseball game to come on television.

Because of his commitment to the army reserves, Nolan missed a lot of pitching opportunities, and the Mets didn't seem interested in working with him to help him make up the time he lost. Now when he looks back on those years with the Mets, he says, "I was wild and getting wilder; I had a lot to learn and wasn't learning it." He lacked control because he wasn't pitching, and he wasn't pitching because he lacked control. And the Mets didn't seem to care.

Nolan's future was uncertain, and money was scarce. He had started out with the Mets making about six thousand dollars a year—enough to live on in Alvin, but not enough to live anywhere else. More than once we had had to borrow money to make it through the winters, even though Nolan worked in the gas station or the appliance store and I worked in the college bookstore.

His salary increased when he moved to the majors, but we still struggled to make ends meet. As the Mets kept him sidelined, his frustration mounted, and so did our worries about the future.

And I had other worries of my own. I didn't always feel safe in New York. Another wife—she was from a little town in Tennessee, so we felt like kindred spirits—told me that her kids had been beaten up at school. And sometimes the Mets players' families seemed to be singled out for insults and abuse. New York fans can be wonderful when things are going well, but if things are going bad, they really get down on you. Sometimes it was good to say you were associated with the Mets; sometimes it was a big mistake.

And then there was that big worry, the one too terrible to imagine. During my early days in New York, I went out to lunch with some baseball wives, and one of them told me, "All baseball players fool around. If you think you are different from anyone else, you're fooling yourself."

I guess I was still pretty naive at that point, but her statement absolutely floored me. Being the innocent newcomer, I took her word as truth, and I went home and cried my eyes out. When Nolan called me that night, I blurted out what the other wife had said. He told me, "Ruth, all I can tell you is we have to think about *our* relationship, *our* marriage. We can't worry about what anyone else does or says. Everyone has to work at being married, and that's what we're going to do. That's about all you can do."

I'm not saying Nolan's words eased my mind that much, and I can't say I never thought of the other wife's words again. That's just not true. But it's like Nolan says: You can't just say, "Okay, I trust you." You have to work at building trust, and you have to work to keep it. Until someone betrays you, you continue to trust that person. And if you're betrayed, then you've got to start over, one way or another.

No, I can't say I didn't worry. But I tried hard not to focus on those things. Instead, I focused on being the best person I could be in difficult circumstances, and I tried to be the type of wife Nolan could love and respect and be proud of.

A lot of the time in New York, I focused simply on getting through one day at a time.

One of the ironies of Nolan's situation with the Mets was that Nolan wasn't pitching because the Mets had plenty of stronger, more experienced pitchers, including Tom Seaver and Jerry Koosman. And as a result of that strong pitching—and because the Mets had a strong team as a whole—they won the World Series in 1969.

Even though Nolan didn't feel he had contributed much to that title, it was still thrilling to be a part of a World Series team. To ride through Manhattan in a ticker-tape parade was a thrilling experience. Sitting on the back of that convertible, waving to the crowds lining the streets and throwing confetti from the skyscrapers, I couldn't help but think of my brother Larry's remark in a different light. *You never saw anything like this in Alvin, Texas, either!*

New Yorkers opened their hearts to the Mets when the team won the series, and they included the Mets' wives in their largess. I remember someone giving me some beautiful dresses just because I was a Mets player's wife. If we went into a restaurant and someone recognized us, champagne would be sent to our table or our tab for the whole meal would be paid. The team gave all the wives gold charms. Mine had Nolan's name and number on it, and on the back it said, "to Ruth from Bill Shea." After the series, the entire team was on the Ed Sullivan television show.

That year was a remarkable time in other ways also. In July, man first walked on the moon, and soon afterward the three astronauts were being showered with ticker tape too. The summer was filled with anti-war demonstrations; I remember being amazed by the "Peaceniks" in

Greenwich Village; watching them, I thought it was good that people could say what they believed—and I'm a peaceful kind of person, so I admit I sometimes connected to their feelings, their desire for peace. But I felt different from them, somehow. I believed I couldn't—or shouldn't—express my feelings so publicly.

It must have been hard for Nolan's brother Robert to come back from the war to be greeted by apathy and even derision while his baseball-player brother rode through the streets of Manhattan in a ticker-tape parade. Even though it took a long time, I was glad when America finally started realizing how it had turned its back on the Vietnam vets. They deserved a parade too.

But I'm quick to point out that Nolan also paid his dues. No, he didn't go to Vietnam. But his tour in the army reserve lasted six years, and he had to attend weekend training sessions each month and spend two weeks each summer at training camp. It wasn't easy in a career like baseball to give up that kind of time, but the Mets had almost demanded it, and Nolan did it without complaint.

So the summer of 1969—as well as our next two summers in New York—had ups and downs. You would expect that after the Mets had won the World Series, our lives would get rosier—and I have to admit they did. I actually started venturing out more in New York and visiting some of the fascinating museums and galleries there. Some days I would drive the Cutlass to Shea Stadium, take the subway to Manhattan, and then take a cab to see a Broadway show or go to a museum.

Another highlight was my dad's visit one summer. He was on the school board in Alvin, and he came to attend some kind of national school board conference in the city. I remember feeling happy and very proud of myself as I drove to La Guardia to pick him up.

One of the dark days came in 1970 when Nolan's sister called to say their father had died. Nolan's dad, Lynn Ryan, had smoked since he was a boy, and he suffered terribly with the lung cancer that afflicted him the last years of his life. He had been in and out of the hospital since he had been admitted on the day of our wedding, and we knew he couldn't last much longer.

Married to Baseball

Shortly before his dad died, Nolan had been home to see his folks while the Mets were playing in Houston. He spent three days with his dad in the hospital then, and when he had to leave, it was one of the saddest days of his life. He knew it was the last time he would see his dad alive.

When the call came, we left immediately for Alvin. The closer we got to home, the more we realized what a strong legacy this wonderful man had left us. He had taught his six children the value of honest labor, and he had shown them by example how to live a life above reproach. He was proud of all his children and grandchildren, and they all worked hard to live up to his expectations. We were happy he had lived to see Nolan pitch in the playoffs and be part of the team that won the World Series in 1969. That had been a special pleasure for him.

The months after his dad's death were hard for Nolan. He was grieving for his dad, as anyone would, but he wouldn't let it show. And he wasn't just mourning the death of his father; he was grieving for the loss of a trusted mentor, a favorite friend, a beloved companion.

Frequently when he had faced a decision in the past, Nolan would first talk it over with his dad. So it was perfectly natural that, for a long time after his dad died, Nolan would start to pick up the phone and then realize his dad was gone. It was a struggle for Nolan, and I knew he was miserable much of the time.

His pitching suffered as a result. When he was on the mound he was either hot or cold, and he didn't think he would ever get a chance to stay in the pitching rotation long enough to work through his problems and gain any consistency. In addition, Gil Hodges, the manager, always seemed to be down on Nolan.

In 1971, he pitched a little more but still completed only three of twenty-six starts and wound up with a 10-14 record. He had 137 strikeouts—and 116 walks—in 152 innings. He obviously had potential, but he still wasn't consistent.

And he still wasn't happy.

There was one bright spot in that season, however—at least for me. One of my happier moments came when I was surprised with a baby shower in my honor at Nancy and Tom Seaver's house in Connecticut.

Most of the Mets wives were there to wish me good luck and give me gifts for our first baby, due in December. In those days, we didn't know the sex of the baby ahead of time, but one wife gave me a cute little blue-and-white outfit, knowing we were hoping for a boy. It was a fun day for me, and when I showed Nolan my gifts when he got home, the reality of our impending parenthood definitely set in.

It was the happiest moment in a dismal summer, and we were both glad to see it coming to an end. I can remember the last night of the season so vividly. I was six months pregnant by the time the season ended, and that last game seemed to go on forever. I was so completely exhausted I can't even remember now if the Mets won or lost; I can't even remember if Nolan pitched. All I can remember is what happened when we got home after the game.

As we walked up the steps, Nolan said abruptly, "We're leaving."

I said, "Leaving now? Nolan, it's midnight, and we're so tired. Can't we wait until morning when we're rested?"

"No," he said, his mind made up. "We're going now. I know I'll never be back to this place."

Stumbling through our weariness, we packed up all our stuff and left for Texas. We rode until Nolan couldn't keep his eyes open any longer, then stopped and dozed for an hour on the side of the road. Then we drove on until he had to stop again to rest. My back ached, I was worn out, and the baby inside me seemed to be turning somersaults. It was a long, torturous journey home.

We didn't talk much during the trip; Nolan seemed a thousand miles away. His eyes straight ahead, his hands gripping the steering wheel, he drove fast and said little. But somewhere near the Texas line, he nodded his head resolutely as if he'd just made a hard decision.

His voice as determined as it had been back in New York, he told me, "Either they trade me or I'm quitting baseball."

Part Three

. . . .

The Angels

8

. . . .

A New Beginning

My water broke at 9 A.M.

It was the Sunday before Thanksgiving, 1971. My sea-captain grandfather was in town, and we were looking forward to the big family dinner my mother was having after church. Everyone was supposed to bring something, and since I didn't have the best reputation as a cook, my assignment was salad.

With our first baby due on December 10, I was deep into nest-building as Thanksgiving approached. Nolan's twenty-thousand-dollar World Series bonus in 1969 had allowed us to buy a little house on eight acres outside of Alvin. It was an old pier-and-beam house—meaning it sat on pilings of concrete blocks—with two bedrooms, a living room and kitchen, a bathroom, and a little front porch. We had painted and wallpapered, my dad and brother had helped us install some cheap carpeting, and as the birth neared, my sister had helped me fix up the "nursery." It was humble, but it was home.

Like all first-time parents-to-be, we were excited and anxious, but we felt confident we would know what to do, and anyway, the hospital was just a half-hour drive away in Houston. There were no birthing classes back then, at least not in Alvin, but I had read lots of magazine articles and a book or two, and Nolan had been around farm animals enough to know how Mother Nature worked. So when my water broke that Sunday morning, we realized *Today's the day!* but we managed to stay fairly calm.

I called my doctor, and he was laid-back too. He said, "Well, just keep track of the contractions and call me when they get closer together."

My next call was to my mother, to tell her I wouldn't be there for dinner. When my sister Lynn heard the news, she said she would make the salad. Then she quipped, "That woman will do anything to keep from cooking!"

I took a shower, washed my hair, packed my suitcase, and tried to fix some things Nolan could eat while I was away. Nolan climbed on the tractor to mow the field. By noon the contractions were five minutes apart. I called the doctor again.

"Well, you can come in if you want," he said nonchalantly, "but there's no big hurry."

I hung on until a little after three o'clock, then told Nolan we'd better go. We loaded my suitcase in the car, pulled out of the driveway—and suddenly the baby was on the way!

"Nolan, hurry!" I probably said it louder than I meant to, but I was quickly losing control. I wasn't actually scared. I knew Nolan would know what to do. (After all he had helped his veterinarian friend "pull" calves several times, I reasoned.) But I had visions of giving birth on the front seat of the Cutlass with unknown passersby gathered around, watching, on the side of the road. I could just see the headlines the next morning . . .

With Nolan driving like Mario Andretti, we got to the hospital in record time. The emergency-room nurses whisked me off to the delivery room and sent Nolan to a waiting area. The contractions were coming hard and fast, and the pain was excruciating. I remember lying there on that hard table, thinking I was going to die. Drenched with sweat, consumed with agony, I felt completely alone.

Just as I thought I was nearing death's door, the anesthetist administered an epidural, and the lower half of my body went numb. The nurse finally appeared, and I thought she was going to ask if there was something she could do for me—rub my back, perhaps, or put a cold compress on my forehead. Instead she leaned down to my ear, smiling anxiously, and said, "Oh, Mrs. Ryan, do you think your husband would give me an autograph?"

I guess the look on my face told her I had other things on my mind. Luckily for both of us, a contraction just then took my breath away and prevented me from saying something I know I would have regretted later.

The next thing I knew, the baby was there. Reid (named after Nolan's brother, Robert Reid) was born less than two hours after we arrived at the hospital. From the first moment he was a live wire, a vigorous, loud-voiced, fist-flailing rounder. I remember how happy I felt when Nolan appeared beside my hospital bed wearing a hospital gown over his blue jeans and a grin as wide as Texas—and holding Reid in his arms. My mom and dad and sister showed up next. The pain and misery I'd just gone through were instantly replaced with the greatest feeling of happiness and contentment I'd ever known.

Reality returned on Thursday, Thanksgiving Day.

My first rude awakening occurred when I started to get dressed to go home from the hospital. Being a first-time mother, I had brought along my regular nonmaternity clothes to wear home. I reasoned that when the baby was born, I would no longer be pregnant, so I would no longer need maternity clothes. I suppose there *are* women out there somewhere who do that, but I've never met any of them. However, I have talked to a lot of other moms who did the same thing I did when they went to the hospital to give birth for the first time—took along their regular clothes, planning to wear them home. Somehow, we just didn't stop to do the math: twenty-five pounds gained during pregnancy minus an eight-pound baby does not equal twenty-five pounds lost!

So that was the first strike in my postpartum-blues count. As I got dressed that Thanksgiving morning, I nearly killed myself squeezing into that skirt so I could leave the hospital in something other than maternity clothes. But as soon as I got home, I took the skirt off, and I didn't wear regular clothes again for weeks.

The Angels

The next dose of reality came when I foolishly disregarded my mother's advice not to overdo when Nolan brought Reid and me back to our house. After all, I felt fine. I was so thankful that Reid had been born in the fall so Nolan could be there for the birth and we could be a real family during those first few weeks. I remember seeing Nolan sitting in the rocking chair, holding the sleeping Reid in his arms, and thinking, *This is as good as it can get.*

While Reid napped that first day, I did laundry and cleaned the house. Several friends and relatives came by to ooh and ah over the sleeping baby. It really seemed like my life was going to be perfect.

Then came the night.

Reid, who had slept almost all day, cried all night. I got no sleep. I fumbled with bottles and pacifiers and diapers and flipped through *Dr. Spock* trying to find something—anything—that would restore peace to my household and let me get some rest. Nolan occasionally woke up and offered to help, but in my perfect-household mentality, I said, "No, it's okay. Just go back to sleep." I didn't want to inconvenience him. I wanted fatherhood to be a pleasant experience for him, I guess, and I was learning firsthand that this middle-of-the-night stuff was *not* fun.

Sometime around dawn on Friday morning, Reid and I both collapsed from exhaustion. A few minutes later, Nolan's alarm clock went off.

For a moment I thought, *Why on earth did he set the alarm?* Then I remembered: It was the opening day of deer season. How could I have forgotten?

Bleary-eyed, I stood in the doorway in my nightgown, watching as Nolan packed the pickup for his trip to the deer lease, some hunting land three hours' drive away that he and some friends had leased for deer season.

"Ruth, if you don't want me to go, I won't," he said, leaning down to kiss me. His hands were full of gun cases.

"Oh no. You go on," I told him, smiling weakly. "We'll be fine."

Looking back on it, I wonder why I didn't admit the truth. Why didn't I say, "No! Don't go! I need you!"? Instead I thought, *I can handle this. I've been through a lot. I can do this too.*

Twenty-four hours later I was ready to admit defeat. I called the deer lease in tears. My voice wavering pitifully, I told Nolan, "Can you please come home? I can't handle this!"

"Sure, Hon," he said. "I'll leave right now."

That whole year I thought of nothing but sleep. Nolan did what he could to help, but since I was always reluctant to ask—and since he had no idea what I needed—I was left to fend for myself much of the time. It was the same with my mother. She would have been glad to come and watch Reid for a few hours so I could get some sleep, but for some reason I never asked her. There was this defiant, stubborn, little-red-hen part of me that kept insisting I could do it all myself.

During that first year I think I only left Reid once or twice. The most memorable time was when my sister Lynn volunteered to keep him so we could go out for the evening. We all agreed it would be better if Reid stayed all night so that Nolan and I could stay out late and we wouldn't wake up Lynn when we got back.

That turned out to be the joke of the century. Reid slept soundly until midnight, with Lynn hovering over him, thinking he was going to wake up any minute. By midnight, she was ready to crash. Reid, on the other hand, was ready to party. Lynn managed to get through the night, but she called us early the next morning and said, "I didn't sleep more than five minutes all night! I'll *never* do this again!"

I've always wondered if that early baby-sitting experience with Reid could be the reason Lynn still has no kids today.

It took a long time to recover from this first brush with motherhood. I moved through the days in a blur, responding automatically to Reid's cries and longing for sleep. This was the state I was in when the Mets general manager called and told Nolan he'd been traded to California.

Nolan said, "Oh, the Dodgers?"

"No," the general manager replied, "the Angels."

9

Soaring with the Angels

*W*elcome to Holtville, the Carrot Capital of the World."

Despite the welcoming sign, I felt very unwelcome in the Angels' spring training camp in Holtville—and for good reason. The team made it perfectly clear: Wives *weren't* welcome at spring training. If a player chose to bring his wife and family, the team refused to pay for living expenses.

Still, I wanted to be with Nolan, and I was willing to put up with a little temporary hostility to do it. By now I had overcome a marital lifetime of personal hurdles. Given what I had already endured, I believed I could do anything I had to do to be with Nolan.

But that was before I saw Holtville.

The Angels' spring training facility reminded me of the Little League field in Alvin, except that the Angels' stands seemed rattier. The facility was run-down and sad-looking. After coming from the Mets' high-caliber facilities, the rickety Holtville stadium seemed like the end of the line.

Although we had welcomed a trade, the Mets' decision had surprised both of us, especially since it involved a move from the National

League to the American League. I think Nolan's feelings had been bruised a little, too, when he read the Mets' Gil Hodges's quote in the newspaper saying Nolan was the starting pitcher he would miss the least. He was anxious to make Hodges regret that statement, and he was pleased that the move bumped up his salary a little, from twenty-four thousand to twenty-seven thousand dollars a year. That was 1972.

The only downer was the team's attitude toward families, and as I stood there looking at the grungy stadium, I couldn't help but think, *What have we done?*

We found little motels near the facility, but since we had to foot the bill, we couldn't find anywhere we could afford to live for three weeks. So Nolan called his sister, Mary Lou Williams, who lived in Chatsworth, California, and asked if we could borrow their travel trailer. She quickly agreed, and the next thing I knew we were backing it into a campsite at a nearby KOA campground. It wasn't ideal, but I believed I could stand anything for three weeks if I could just be with Nolan.

It was a hundred degrees in the campground the next day, and although I didn't actually measure it, I suspected the temperature topped three hundred degrees in the trailer. There was no shade, no air conditioning, and no television, and Nolan had the car all day.

To survive, I scooped up Reid and sat outside in a lawn chair, dragging the chair around the dirt so I could stay in the shade of the trailer as the sun moved across the sky. High noon was unbearable. The only shade then was *beneath* the trailer, and I wasn't about to crawl under there!

You might think I would at least read books, but I didn't. Surviving the heat and taking care of four-month-old Reid, who continued to be a very fussy, active baby, were the only things I could manage. Nolan left each morning at 8:30, and I spent the day holding Reid in that lawn chair outside the trailer. Sometimes when Nolan got home at night, we would go out somewhere to eat, but even that proved to be a disaster more times than not. Just as the food would arrive, Reid would start fussing, and one of us would end up gobbling down the meal while the other sat on the opposite side of the booth trotting the crying baby wearily on a knee or bouncing him on a hip outside in the parking lot.

There are certain images that pop into my mind when someone asks me about the "glamorous life" I've led as the wife of a major-league pitcher. There have been glamorous times, I'll admit. There have been times of sheer hell too. Holtville was one of them.

When the team moved to Palm Springs for the exhibition games, I thought, *Okay, this will be better. At least there will be baseball games I can go to.* But in Palm Springs everything was even more expensive than it had been in Holtville, and once again the Angels' rules forbade wives from staying in the team hotel. It always burned me up to think that girlfriends of single players were allowed there, but wives were not.

Knowing we would be moving on to Anaheim in a few weeks, we went ahead and rented a house there, a nice split-level that was just a ten-minute drive from Anaheim Stadium. But until the regular season began, Nolan would have to commute back to Palm Springs each day. It was lonely for me and a hard, two-hour drive each way for him, but at least we could still spend our evenings together. He was gone from 6 A.M. to 6 P.M., and he never complained. The Angels did, though. After one of the players was killed in a car crash that year, they said they didn't want Nolan driving so much. I was furious, thinking, *Those guys are out running around all night, and you don't want Nolan to come home to his family?*

In addition to the official rule about no families staying in the team hotel, there was an unwritten rule that said ballplayers did not take their wives into the bar in the team hotel or wherever the guys hung out. Some of the players seemed to think the wives would "tell on them" if they saw the players in one of these places with another woman. But Nolan was good about it; he believed we could go wherever we wanted to go—and we did. When some of the older players complained, he told them, "I'll take Ruth wherever she wants to go. I'm not the one who has to worry about where I'm seen."

I *have* seen players with women other than their wives, but I would never tell someone's wife that—I would never do anything that would wreck a marriage. But wives would ask, rather cryptically, and it would be very awkward to know what to say. I don't know what I would say if one came right out and asked me point-blank.

I expected our lives to finally ease into something resembling normalcy when the regular 1972 season began. Instead, in April, the players went on strike for the first eight games of the season. With no paycheck coming in, we had to borrow fifteen hundred dollars against our 1971 tax refund to pay our rent and other bills.

Looking back on it, Nolan said, "If they hadn't settled the strike by the time the fifteen hundred dollars was gone, we'd be gone too."

Despite our rather rocky beginning in California—at least it was rocky from my point of view—our eight summers with the Angels turned out to include some of our favorite memories. Best of all, Nolan's pitching finally started showing signs that his control could match his speed. The 1972 season was a real turnaround for him and a happy time for me. I was enjoying being a mom in the relaxed atmosphere of California, and several neighbors (including the Hernandez family and Vel and Joe Smith) welcomed me warmly and even helped baby-sit Reid when I needed to get out by myself. The neighborhood was more like what we had been used to in Texas, and I felt fairly comfortable finding my way around Anaheim.

The next year, 1973, was even better—one of our happiest. Reid was two, and the moves between Alvin and California didn't seem as difficult. One difference, though, was the image of the Angels compared with that of the Mets. The Angels were the poor relations of the Dodgers—about the only celebrity they attracted was Richard Nixon, soon to be forced out of the White House by the Watergate scandal.

We both were really fond of Angels owner Gene Autry, the old "Singing Cowboy" and surely the most humble person who ever owned a baseball team. Nolan's family and mine both had seen Autry perform at the annual Houston Livestock Show and Rodeo when we were little kids. Nolan had even gotten to shake his hand one year as Gene circled the arena on the back of his great horse, Champion.

When Nolan joined the Angels, he and Gene really hit it off. They were both a kind of rare breed—quiet, modest Texans—and Autry had a nice, self-effacing sense of humor. People were often surprised to discover how rich he was, probably worth twenty or thirty million even before the value of the franchises sailed into orbit.

Suddenly everything seemed to have changed for the better. Nolan's skill and reputation took off, making 1973 and 1974 the best of his career as he racked up a lot of wins, a record number of strikeouts, and an ERA of less than three.

And in 1973 he pitched his first no-hitter.

I watched the game against the Royals in Kansas City on the neighbors' (the Smiths') television in Anaheim—theirs had a larger screen than ours. By the middle of the game, most of the neighborhood had dropped in, including the Hernandez family with their five children. One of their daughters was Reid's favorite baby-sitter.

As we realized what was happening, the excitement suddenly burst over us. We were all giddy, absolutely beside ourselves, because no one— not even Nolan—had ever dreamed he would pitch a no-hitter this early in his career with the Angels. Sure, he had won nineteen games in his first season with the Angels in 1972, and he had struck out 329 batters and led the league with nine shutouts. But he had also led the league in walks, hit batsmen, and wild pitches. We both believed he was still finding himself as a pitcher after wasting four seasons with the Mets (where he had won a total of twenty-nine games and lost thirty-eight).

In the neighbors' living room, we sat on the edge of our chairs, watching Nolan's every move and speaking encouragingly to the television. By the bottom of the ninth, all he needed was to retire one more batter, Otis Amos, who had been his teammate with the Mets.

The first pitch was a fastball. Otis swung and missed. Then, as we all held our collective breath, the batter drove a long fly to deep right field. Ken Berry, one of those outfielders who climbed walls like a human fly, leapt from the turf and caught it on the warning track for a heartstopping ending. The Angels won 3-0, and Nolan had his first no-hitter, striking out twelve and walking three.

I hurried home, hoping Nolan would call before the team had to rush to its plane, and of course he did. When the phone rang, I didn't even wait for him to say anything. I blurted out how we had all watched the game at the neighbors' house with the bigger television, how we had cheered for him until we were hoarse, and how ecstatic everyone was. Finally, I stopped for a breath and said, "You pitched a great game, Nolan."

He responded in his typical, understated way. "Yeah, I guess I pitched pretty good," he said with the same tone he might use to describe the weather. "But to tell you the truth, I'm just glad it's over."

But it wasn't over. Just two months later, Nolan would do it again.

It was July 15, 1973, less than two weeks after Nolan had registered his one-thousandth career strikeout, a fairly astonishing mark when you consider that Nolan hadn't been in the starting rotation in New York until 1971, his last season there, when he won ten games for the first time and lost fourteen.

Despite this achievement, it seemed unlikely that this would be a no-hitter, because the Angels were facing the Tigers in Detroit, and the Tiger lineup featured a cast of tough hitters that included Norm Cash, Gates Brown, Jim Northrup, Mickey Stanley, and Dick McAuliffe. All had played on Detroit's World Series champion team in 1968.

Actually, it might have seemed unlikely to *everyone else* that Nolan would pitch a no-hitter this day, confronted with this crew of dangerous hitters. But as the game got under way, Nolan actually predicted he would do it. He said later he thought he was throwing "the best fastball and curveball I ever had in any game."

I had no way of knowing this, since I had stayed behind in Anaheim and was once again part of the neighborhood gang that had gathered in the home of the neighbors with the largest television screen. Still, in the little pregame glimpses of Nolan I managed to see in between the announcers' interviews with managers and various commercials, I thought I caught a hint of something new. It wasn't greater confidence, really, because Nolan has always played in a very self-sure manner. But it was some unspoken feeling—a sense of anticipation, maybe—that something special was about to happen.

Later he told me he had so much velocity and such a hard curve while warming up that he told pitching coach Tom Morgan, "With the kind of stuff I have right now, if I ever have a chance to pitch another no-hitter, it'll be today."

His catcher, a colorful character named Art Kusnyer (the players nicknamed him "the Caveman" because of his appearance behind the plate), caught the magic that seemed to hover over the mound that night. After the game he told a reporter he had sensed what was about to happen. "I thought to myself, 'The Cavemen has got a chance to catch a no-hitter.'"

As the game got under way, Nolan decided to call his own pitches because the Angels thought the Tigers were stealing their signs. Although it was a wise decision, it probably made both Nolan and the Caveman a little nervous, due to their history of miscommunicating.

They had met each other for the first time in spring training in 1972 and had been roommates when the team traveled. Their history of crossed signals had started one day during an intrasquad game, when they got their signs mixed up and Art had stormed to the mound and thundered, "Hey, Huck-face, whose signs are you using?"

Knowing they had had problems before, they decided to keep things simple in the game against Detroit. The Caveman would just put down anything he wanted, and Nolan would nod and pretend he was taking it. In reality, Nolan would call the pitch himself, touching the back of his cap to indicate a fastball was coming and the front of his cap if he planned to throw the curve.

As simple as it seemed, they got confused right from the start. Art was looking for a fastball, and Nolan threw a curve that broke a foot out of the batter's box and went right down the middle of the plate, past Art's glove and squarely into the knee of the umpire, Ron Luciano. He called it a ball.

Luciano was just so surprised at being hit that he blew the call. After that, Nolan decided to go mostly with his fastball. But Luciano could see what was coming. "From the first pitch Nolan threw," he said later, "there was no question the batters would have no chance. When Nolan wanted to hit an inside corner, he hit an inside corner. When he wanted to throw letter-high, he threw letter-high. It was the most perfect pitching I've ever seen in my life."

The Angels

Even watching from hundreds of miles away, I was stunned by the power of Nolan's pitching that night, and I wasn't the only one who was awestruck by the extraordinary skill he showed, beginning with that game in Detroit. As Tom Seaver said years later, "There was more than power to Nolan. Yes, he had this great God-given ability, but he had a lot of other things too. He had an understanding of what pitching is all about, and he had a great work ethic."

The late Billy Martin was managing Detroit then, and he spent most of the night haranguing Nolan, trying to rattle him. He kept reminding him about the no-hitter, as if that might jinx him. Once he shouted, "Aurelio Rodriguez is gonna homer off you now! You lose the no-hitter on the next pitch."

Nolan looked right at him and said, "No way, Billy." Rodriguez struck out, and Martin turned his back in the dugout so he wouldn't see Nolan's grin.

By the time Nolan had struck out sixteen batters in the first seven innings, we were going crazy back in the neighbors' living room. Still, the game was close, just 1-0, until the top of the eighth, when the Angels scored another five runs. We thought we were home free.

But a problem had developed while all the scoring was going on. Nolan's arm had tightened up a little as he rested in the dugout, and he didn't have quite the same arsenal when he went back out to the mound. That became obvious as the Tigers started making contact. Mickey Stanley grounded out to lead off the ninth. Then Gates Brown, the designated hitter, hit a hard line drive to the left side, right at Rudy Meoli, who had made a key fielding play in the first no-hitter—and did it again that night.

With the Tigers down to their last out, Norm Cash came to bat. Nolan always liked Cash, an outdoorsy guy like Nolan who loved to hunt and fish. He was also a showman and a free spirit. He had already struck out twice, and when he stepped up to the plate for the third time, Nolan did a double take when he saw what Cash had in his hand.

"Hey, Ron," Nolan called to the umpire, "what's he got?"

Luciano hadn't noticed. "What are you talking about?" he yelled back.

"Check his bat," demanded Nolan, who couldn't keep from grinning. "Check that thing."

Luciano lifted the wood from Norm's hand and examined it. Nolan found out later Cash had ripped off the leg of a buffet table in the clubhouse. Luciano threw it out, and Cash, a broad smile plastered over his face, trotted back to the dugout for a real bat. He may have been trying to distract Nolan or unsettle him, or it may have been his way of simply saying he had no chance. At any rate, everyone in the ballpark was laughing, including the television announcers and Nolan. Ironically, that prank broke the tension, and it may have helped Nolan muster his strength for what had to be done.

Cash had won batting and home-run titles in the American League, and Nolan worked on him carefully. With a 1-2 count, Norm lifted a pop fly to short left. Meoli went back to catch it, and Nolan became only the fifth pitcher in history to throw two no-hitters in the same season.

I couldn't wait to talk to Nolan. I was so eager to hear about what had happened after the game. He told me the Caveman had gone all around the clubhouse, showing off his bruised fingers and the swollen palm of his left hand, worn out from catching Nolan's lightning-fast pitches. Someone told him later that as the Tigers came out of their clubhouse, some kids asked Duke Sims, the Detroit catcher, for a cracked bat. "Did you watch the game?" Sims asked them. "We didn't hit the ball hard enough to crack any bats."

When Nolan came home from that road trip, the Hernandez family had painted a huge banner that said, "Congratulations, Nolan!" and hung it across the front of our rented house. It was a good feeling to have friends and neighbors who cared about us and were excited about Nolan's achievements (quite unlike New York).

I was glad Nolan's next start would be in Anaheim against the Orioles. Along with everyone else, I wanted to be there to see if Nolan could duplicate Johnny Vander Meer's feat of throwing two no-hitters back-to-back. A part of me tried not to think about it, and I certainly didn't talk about it to Nolan. The reporters were doing enough of that; he didn't want to hear it at home too.

The Angels

Nolan told the reporters what he honestly thought: "It will be easier for me to strike out twenty in one game than pitch another no-hitter."

The writers kept pressing him about it, though, and that got him to thinking it just might be possible. So when he went into that game against the Orioles he decided to try. It was the first time he ever approached a game with that kind of goal in mind.

And it was the last time.

"Going for a no-hitter puts added pressure on you," he told a reporter later. "It makes you work harder than you usually do because each pitch has the potential to extend the no-hitter."

Nolan concentrated so much on each batter, he was worn out before the end of the game. The Orioles were aware of what was going on, and their manager, Earl Weaver, kept asking the umpire to check the ball for pine tar or Vaseline. Nolan had never used anything like that and Weaver knew it, but it was an attempt to break his rhythm or upset him.

At the top of the eighth inning, the score was tied 1-1, and the no-hitter continued. (The Orioles had scored on a walk, a stolen base, a wild pitch, and a ground ball.) Nolan's fastball was exploding, but he was tired now, and his pitches were going wild.

Come on, Hon. You can do it. I sat in the stands with my hands clinched into tight little fists, my lips bitten mercilessly, and my stomach churning like a washing machine. Nolan hadn't given up a hit in sixteen innings. He had pitched two no-hitters in half a season, and now he was six outs away from a third. I was beside myself. It was as if Nolan had suddenly become untouchable; it was an unbelievable and dramatic effort to watch.

Brooks Robinson led off the eighth for Baltimore, and Nolan hit him with a wild pitch. That put Robinson on first and brought up Mark Belanger, a slick-fielding shortstop who was barely hitting .200. He was choking up on the bat, trying to bunt Robinson to second. Unbelievably, as Nolan jammed Belanger with an inside pitch, he tried to duck away from it and the ball hit his bat and blooped into left center field. Ken Berry charged in from right center, but the ball was just out of his reach for a hit. The Orioles went on to beat the Angels 3-1 in eleven innings. By the end of the game Nolan was exhausted. And so was I.

As always, he was easygoing and philosophical about his near brush with glory. He told reporters the madcap play was a "pretty good example of why no-hitters are hard to get."

That year, 1973, was when the hitters began talking about Nolan in their interviews with the press. I still chuckle when I remember what Reggie Jackson told one reporter. He said, "I love to bat against Nolan Ryan, and I hate to bat against Nolan Ryan. It's like ice cream. You may love it, but you don't want it shoveled down your throat by the gallon."

By all accounts, 1973 was a spectacular season for Nolan. He struck out ten or more batters in a game twenty-three times, breaking another Sandy Koufax record. Sandy had done it twenty-one times, and one of them was in a game Nolan had watched in the Astrodome when he was a high school senior.

I doubt that any pitcher ever had a more sensational season without making the All-Star team. Nolan wasn't all that upset when Dick Williams left him off the All-Star squad, but a lot of other people were. In fact, it caused so much controversy that the commissioner of baseball, Bowie Kuhn, stepped in and announced the addition of one player to each team—Nolan in the American League and Willie Mays in the National League. It was a nice gesture, both to recognize Nolan's achievements and to get Mays into the game at the end of his career.

The Angels didn't give Nolan any extra reward for his no-hitters, either, and that taught him a lesson. He made sure an incentive clause was included in his next contract that promised a three-thousand-dollar bonus for any more no-hitters he might pitch.

Nolan didn't talk about it, but I think part of the reason he made such a strong turnaround was his steadfast determination to prove the Mets wrong. They had traded Nolan, outfielder Lee Stanton, and a couple of prospects for the Angels' third basemen, Jim Fregosi. Even though Nolan wanted out of the New York team, I think the way it was done hurt his pride quite a bit.

The Angels

But what goes around comes around, as they say. Fregosi was overweight and was declining as both a hitter and fielder; his career as a player was coming to an end. Later, in one of those ironies that keeps the game of baseball so interesting, Fregosi returned to manage the Angels, and Nolan played under him his last two years with the club.

Another reason for Nolan's turnaround was that he had Angels pitching coach Tom Morgan and a discerning catcher, Jeff Torborg, to work with him. They drilled him not to rush his delivery; they kept telling him he didn't need to throw every pitch a hundred miles an hour. The other major factor was that he had completed his military obligation, so he could be part of a regular pitching rotation, taking his turn each time it came up. As all these components fell into place, Nolan began to find the consistency that had eluded him in New York.

Recognizing his improvement—as well as his continuing potential— the Angels nearly doubled his salary to fifty-four thousand dollars in 1973. For the first time in our marriage, the future was starting to look a little more stable, a little less rocky.

Nolan had learned the strike zone, perfected his curve, and added a changeup. The only thing he couldn't learn was how to be lucky. That's why, when one of his foes knocked him for going after strike-outs—as the guy put it, "for being in love with his speed"—Nolan said coolly, "He never stood on that mound with a bad team and no runs and knew if he threw one bad pitch, he'd be beat." Nolan never stopped throwing hard.

In 1973 Nolan pitched twenty-six complete games, more than the total of his previous eight seasons combined. He broke Sandy Koufax's major-league single-season record with 383 strikeouts. He had two no-hitters and a 21-16 record with a weak-hitting team; his earned run average was 2.87. He won his last seven games, and the Angels increased his annual salary to one hundred thousand dollars.

Overall, our early years with the Angels were pleasant, and Nolan was beginning to make a name for himself. We enjoyed having Nolan's sister, Mary Lou, and her family come to his games, and we spent time taking Reid to Disneyland and just enjoying the California lifestyle.

But it was still difficult to pack up and move our belongings every time we (a) left Texas for Holtville, (b) left Holtville for Palm Springs, (c) left Palm Springs for Anaheim, and (d) left Anaheim for Texas. Every year seemed like a constant shuffling of belongings, especially now that we had a child. We had to carry everything but the kitchen sink everywhere we went.

Years later I ended up owning four cribs at once—two in Texas and two in California. We also began to take our dogs with us when we moved from one home to the other. I'm sure at times we looked like the "Beverly Hillbillies" as we moved in and out of the neighborhood.

Still, it was a fun, lighthearted time for us, and that 1973 season was one of the best. I don't claim to be objective, but I felt Nolan deserved to win the Cy Young award that year; instead, it went to Jim Palmer of the Orioles.

Of course, there are things a lot worse than losing a Cy Young award . . . as we would find out all too soon.

10

Expansion

$\mathcal{W}$e didn't try to plan when our children would be born, so it was only luck that let Reese arrive in January 1976—before spring training and after hunting season.

We were back home in Alvin, and I was nearing my due date. But I'd been to see the doctor that morning, and he had assured me it would be "at least another week or two." I was in a happy mood, anxious for the baby to arrive but also content with the way our lives were shaping up.

Nolan had continued to thrive with the Angels—at least for a while. He'd had a tremendous scare in April 1974 when he threw an inside fastball that hit Boston's Doug Griffin above the left ear. Griffin had squared around to bunt and did not react quickly enough as the pitch, high and tight, spun toward his head.

As Griffin collapsed in a heap, Nolan headed for the batter's box. "I didn't know how bad he was until I got up to the plate," he told me later. "He wasn't moving, and his eyes were rolled back up in his head. I thought I'd killed him."

Griffin recovered, but he missed fifty-one games. Nolan was rattled by the accident, but he regained his confidence quickly, and later that year he threw his third no-hitter.

And once again I wasn't there to see it in person.

It happened on September 28, 1974, when the Angels were playing the Minnesota Twins in Anaheim. I couldn't believe my rotten luck. I was beginning to think there was some kind of curse that was keeping me from seeing him throw a no-hitter in person.

I had returned to Alvin with three-year-old Reid just before the end of the 1974 season. I had never missed one of Nolan's home games since he had been in the major leagues, but this was just two days before the end of the season, and it was just one game, I told myself. I wanted to get a headstart on unpacking our things and getting the house in order in Alvin so it would be less work for Nolan when he came home.

I couldn't get the game on television or radio, so I called the stadium less than an hour after the first pitch, just to get a score. At first, the switchboard operator said she couldn't give it to me. I thought that was odd, but I asked, "What inning is it?"

She said, "Bottom of the fifth."

I asked, "Are we winning?"

She drew in a slow breath and said, "Yes-s-s-s." Then there was a pause and she whispered in a rush, "Ruth, I'm not supposed to say anything, but Nolan is pitching a no-hitter!"

I suppose she thought that saying anything would be a jinx—there's a lot of superstition in baseball, especially concerning a no-hitter.

I didn't know whether to get excited or to feel sorry for myself, so I did both. I started calling back every fifteen to twenty minutes. It probably would have been cheaper to just stay on the line, but I needed to move around and work off some of my nervous energy. I probably called half a dozen times, and on the last time I got through, as soon as I'd said hello, the switchboard operator yelled, "Ruth, he did it! He did it!"

I was both elated and angry, thinking, *Of all the luck! After all the games I've been to, I have to miss this one. Why couldn't I have waited? Why was I in such a big hurry to get back to Alvin?*

At least I knew Nolan wouldn't be going home to an empty house. His sister, Mary Lou, lived in the San Fernando Valley and drove down with her kids for all his games. I knew she would be there, and I knew all the neighbors would come over to help Nolan celebrate. But I was heartbroken, thinking they would all be at *my* house in Anaheim, and I wouldn't be there. To this day I've never even seen a videotape of the game.

For Nolan, that third no-hitter is a bittersweet memory; while he had continued to do well, the Angels, as a team, had continued to decline. The game against the Twins came at the end of yet another forgettable season for the Angels. The irony was that Nolan had won twenty-two games for a team that finished last in scoring runs. The fans were less than enthusiastic; some of the spark seemed to be dying. Attendance on the night of Nolan's third no-hitter was only 10,872.

And even though Nolan was proud of pitching a no-hitter, he knew it hadn't been very artistic. He had been wilder than usual, but for once that seemed to work in his favor. "I was all over the place, and they couldn't establish a pattern on me," he said.

After missing three no-hitters, I was afraid I'd missed my chance to see Nolan pitch another one, although my heart started pounding in a lot of games as the innings mounted and no hits were scored. But it wasn't until June 1, 1975, that my dream actually came true, when the Angels played Baltimore in Anaheim.

The game was played on a sweltering Sunday afternoon. Once again, there was no reason to think this game would be anything special. And neither one of us felt all that well that morning. I had just found out I was pregnant and was feeling a little queasy, and Nolan had suffered several minor injuries during the season, including two groin pulls and bone chips in his pitching elbow.

He was hurting with every pitch, and since he sometimes threw more than 200 pitches in one game, he could end up in sheer agony as the final innings neared. In an earlier game that season he had gone fifteen innings and thrown 229 pitches in one game; three days later, he had started again and pitched a shutout.

The Angels

Before he left the house that Sunday morning, Nolan had trouble lifting his pitching arm to comb his hair. He didn't say anything, but I could tell he was worried. I wanted to say something, do something to take away the worry and the pain. But Nolan wasn't one to be fussed over. So all I could do was give him a kiss and wish him good luck.

He faced another bad omen when he got to the clubhouse and found that his catcher, Ellie Rodriguez, had a head cold and was feeling pretty bad. Nolan tries hard to keep his mind off his problems, and he "helps" others do the same. On this day he "helped" his catcher by bouncing a Ping-Pong ball off poor Ellie's sore, congested skull. It was Nolan's way of perking him up.

"See this?" he said to his chunky catcher, flipping another Ping-Pong ball at him. "This is what I'm gonna be throwing today."

I took Reid to the game with me, and it wasn't long before the old familiar flock of butterflies started fluttering in my stomach as the innings passed without the Orioles' getting a hit off of Nolan. I kept trying (unsuccessfully) to contain my emotions, trying not to build myself up for yet another disappointment, especially since I knew Nolan was pitching with a sore elbow. *How could he possibly pitch a no-hitter when he couldn't even raise his arm to comb his hair this morning?* I reasoned to myself.

But what I was seeing defied all logic. As I mentally charted his pitches, I could see that after the sixth inning he actually seemed to be getting stronger. Suddenly the old magic was dancing over the mound again. By the time we stood up for the seventh-inning stretch, I had Reid standing in his seat, and we were doing an excited little cha-cha.

Still, I kept trying to tell myself, *We've been this far before, and nothing came of it.* But not this time. An hour or so later, Nolan threw a change-up on a 2-2 count to strike out Bobby Grich, and the game was over. The Angels beat the Orioles 1-0, and Nolan had his fourth no-hitter and was tied with Sandy Koufax for the career no-hitter record.

"It was one of those deals when I warmed up just hoping I could get through the game," Nolan told reporters later. "The last thing that went through my mind was having a game like that."

When it was over, I couldn't wait to see him. Having missed the first three no-hitters, every pitch of this one felt precious to me. I wanted to replay the whole game in my mind, inning by inning, batter by batter.

When he finally came out of the clubhouse, Reid and I rushed up to him for a happy family hug.

Once again a huge crowd turned out for Nolan's next start, hoping for that elusive back-to-back no-hitter. And once again, he started off strong and held the Milwaukee Brewers scoreless, until Hank Aaron's single in the sixth inning killed the Angels' magic.

After that game, Nolan's rising star seemed to dim a little. The pain in his elbow grew worse, and the effect was obvious. He lost eight games in a row and eventually agreed to undergo surgery late in the season to have the bone chips removed.

I can remember going up to his hospital room in Houston to visit him. I was pregnant and had sprained my ankle on the sidewalk just outside the hospital. After the surgery, Nolan finally consented to let a few reporters into his room for an interview. Being pregnant with a sprained ankle didn't help my disposition, but I really became annoyed when the first question was, "Nolan, what are you going to do when you can't pitch anymore?"

Because our future was uncertain anyway and our family was growing, I wanted those reporters *out* of that room so Nolan could recover in peace. His mood was not helped by the nausea he was experiencing from eating a bowl of grapes the nurse had specifically told him *not* to eat (stubborn guy!).

Even after he came home from the hospital he could not sit still for even a day. He went out on his tractor (arm in a cast) to mow the pasture, even though his doctor had told him to take it easy. That night he experienced throbbing pain and refused to take the pain pills the doctor had prescribed. I can remember trying to take care of myself and my sprained ankle, our four-year-old dynamo Reid, and my stubborn patient. I was quite overwhelmed!

During his recovery, the sportswriters continued to have a field day, speculating on what had gone wrong. The ones who really got to us were those who suggested Nolan had simply grown lazy or that he had given up. I consoled myself by saying those writers simply didn't know the real Nolan Ryan; still, it was hard to see their harsh ideas were accepted by a lot of fans.

But by January 1976 we had tried to put all that behind us, and things seemed to be looking up again. Nolan was in the middle of a two-year contract at $125,000 a year. We were living in a nice brick house we had built a couple of years earlier after we had moved the little old house off our eight acres of property. Nolan's arm had recovered well and felt good after having been immobilized for several weeks following the surgery. He was building himself up for a strong comeback.

So our mood that cool winter day was easy and pleasant. I decided to ride along in the pickup when Nolan went to check the cattle. As we bounced over the rough hills and pastures, we were happy just being together, anticipating the birth of our second child and looking forward to a productive baseball season.

I was in such a happy state that when a sharp pain streaked up my back after one especially big bump I dismissed it as a consequence of the rough ride. But when the pain came back a few minutes later, followed by another pain shortly after that one, I realized I was in labor.

"Nolan, this may be it," I told him, sucking in a sharp breath as another contraction ripped up my spine.

"This may be what?" asked Nolan, looking around to see where I was pointing. He thought I was talking about something outside.

"The baby! I think I'm in labor," I told him.

"Oh!" was all he said. He turned the truck around and headed home. By the time we got there it was almost dark. My contractions were getting stronger, but like many women I didn't think I could have the baby until I had taken a shower and washed my hair. Nolan's mom came to stay with Reid, and we headed for the hospital. Our second trip to the emergency room was a little less frantic than the first, but we still didn't end up with a lot of time to spare. Reese was born at 11:30 P.M., and once again I cherished the sight of Nolan standing there in his surgical scrubs, holding our newborn son.

Reese was a joy. The difference between my first days at home with Reid and then with Reese were like night and day. Reese slept and ate on schedule, and he was rarely fussy. He was just a great baby. Reid, on the other hand, continued to be a handful. He would stay up until all hours and still be the first one up in the morning, and Reid *never* took naps. He just didn't need as much rest as other human beings; he was, and is, an exuberant person. In contrast, Reese was always a sensitive boy who took his time thinking things through and didn't like to be rushed.

While Reese was an easy baby, having an infant and a preschooler did tend to make my life a lot more hectic. So on that morning when Reese was just five months old and I woke up enveloped in a wave of nausea, I thought, *Uh-oh. I know this feeling, and it's not good.*

I was pregnant again, and while we weren't upset to think a third child was on the way, I was depressed when I counted up the months and realized the baby would be born during spring training. Another problem was that I felt terrible all the time I was pregnant, and I had no energy to do anything—not a good situation when you factored in an infant and an animated four-year-old. I lived on Cokes and crackers, and I dreaded the fact that Nolan might not be home for the birth.

Sadness consumed me on that day in late February 1977 when Nolan left for spring training in California without the boys and me. Somehow the house seemed quiet without him, despite the boys' chattering and playful antics. I felt big and cumbersome in my pregnancy, as well as constantly nauseous, and I felt sorry for myself and the boys and for Nolan too. I knew he would miss us just as much as we would miss him—at least I hoped he would miss us. It was the only time throughout Nolan's career that I missed spring training completely.

This was another difficult time for me because we had decided to purchase eighty acres of land outside of Alvin and move from our fairly new brick home to a sixty-year-old frame house that we would renovate and enlarge. Nolan loved this piece of property with its huge, old live oak trees. In fact, he had camped out there as a young boy with his Boy Scout troop and his mother, the den leader. He felt it was an opportunity we should not pass up. I agreed and thought it was a good idea to buy the land—but the timing seemed ominous. I was pregnant, I had a baby and a four-year-old, and my husband would be away playing baseball in California. I felt an overwhelming feeling of *I can't handle all of this and build a new house at the same time!* To make it worse, we would have to move into a small rent-house and temporarily store our belongings while we undertook the project.

When I look back on it now, I think it was one of the most trying times of my life. My depression wasn't helped when Nolan, staying with the team during spring training since his family wasn't with him, called me from the Gene Autry Hotel in Palm Springs, giggling merrily.

"The funniest thing just happened," he said between guffaws. He told me he was in his room on the ground floor when a woman stepped between some bushes and the big window in his room. "She must have been Swedish," he said. "She wanted to change out of her swimsuit top and put on a T-shirt. So she stepped behind these bushes, thinking no one could see her, but she didn't realize she was standing right in front of my window."

I was getting the drift of this story, and it wasn't shaping up to be as funny as I had expected.

"She just stripped off her top right there in front of me," Nolan said. "And man! She had a great figure. I couldn't believe it."

I stood there silently in the kitchen, surrounded by dirty dishes, a toy-littered floor, and two screaming kids, and tried to control my temper. Nolan couldn't understand why it would upset me, enormously pregnant and feeling as big as a barn, to be told he'd just watched a woman with a terrific figure change clothes right in front of him!

During a checkup a few weeks later in March, the doctor told me if I didn't go into labor that night he would induce me the next morning. I called the Angels office in Palm Springs and told the secretary what the doctor had said, but I guess she got excited and misunderstood, because she ran out onto the practice field and told Nolan I was having the baby *right then.*

He immediately caught a plane, thinking I was already in the hospital. During a layover in Dallas, he called the house, hoping someone would be there to tell him what was going on. When I answered the phone, he said, "What are *you* doing there?"

I answered, "Where else would I be?"

I was so glad he was coming home, and I felt so lucky he could be with me for the birth of our daughter, Wendy, that I tried hard to concentrate on those feelings of thankfulness and not think about how sad I would feel when he had to leave again.

We were so happy to have a baby girl, and there was absolutely no doubt that she was my child. I could have picked Wendy out of a crowd of newborns anywhere in the world with no hesitation because her nose is little and her ears are exactly like mine: one rounded, one pointed with a little indentation. She was perfectly bald when she was born; in fact, she didn't have anything but fuzz for hair until she was almost two. Meanwhile, fourteen-month-old Reese had this crop of beautiful blond curls. He looked like the girl, and Wendy looked like a boy.

Nolan flew back to rejoin the team the day after Wendy was born. My mom and dad drove me home from the hospital, and Mom stayed most of that day to help me get settled in and introduce the baby to the two boys. Then Mom left, and once again I found myself starting to feel overwhelmed by what I faced.

Wendy was a pretty good baby—or maybe she was just a normal baby. Having Reid first had forever indoctrinated me to think that babies are expected to be fussy and colicky and difficult and any baby who isn't is a miracle child. Wendy didn't cry a lot, but she wanted to be held all the time (and this was in the days before those convenient baby-carriers parents use today). Meanwhile, Reese had reached the stage of toddlerhood, and at fourteen months he needed lots of attention, especially when the new baby seemed to be stealing all the limelight. He often tried to push her away when I was feeding her. And then there was Reid, now five, who was as busy as a whirling dervish, constantly looking for mischief to get into. It was, to put it mildly, a constant challenge.

I tried to find someone I could hire to come over during the day and help, thinking maybe I could get some sleep or even run a few errands by myself. I interviewed five or six people, but somehow I just didn't feel comfortable with any of them. I guess it was the little-red-hen attitude coming back to haunt me. I just didn't think anyone could take care of my kids as well as I could. So I did it alone.

Meanwhile, Nolan was getting antsy in California. We had decided to buy a house out there because of the problems that went with renting each year—trying to find a yard for the kids and the dog and privacy for Nolan. It seemed we were always looking for impossible places at impossible prices, up to five thousand dollars a month. He was anxious to get us out there and get settled, so I finally said, "Nolan, just go ahead and buy one. You know me well enough to know what I like. I trust your judgment. Just do it."

He went house-hunting and eventually found a lovely home on a corner lot in Villa Park, near Anaheim, next door to Marilyn and Rod Carew. He sent photographs and we talked a lot on the phone, and finally he made an offer and we became a two-home family. He did a good job; I knew from his descriptions that I would love the house, and I knew we would enjoy having Marilyn and Rod as neighbors.

"Now," I told him, "you need to go get us some furniture." So once again, Nolan went shopping. And once again, he chose well. I was surprised, since he'd never shown much interest in decorating and he'd never gone with me to pick out styles or colors. But I guess he'd been paying more attention than I realized because he chose things we both liked and enjoyed. In fact, we're still using some of that furniture he bought eighteen years ago.

All he needed now was his family. He kept calling and saying, "When are you coming out?"

I was as anxious to get there as he was to have us there, but the thought of actually making the trip alone with a five-year-old, a toddler, a newborn baby, and all our luggage was more than I could handle.

Finally, though, I set the date, and each day I prayed for the strength and fortitude to actually make the trip. I knew I could do it, but I also knew it was going to be very, very hard.

Just getting all of our clothes and toys and bottles and diapers packed was an accomplishment. Mom and Dad took us to the airport and helped hold the kids while I checked all our luggage. After they kissed us good-bye at the gate and I managed to get us seated on the plane and my purse and big diaper bag stowed, I felt absolutely triumphant. But it turned out the hard part was still ahead.

I sat in a row of three seats with Reid on one side of me and Reese on the other and Wendy in my lap. Things were pretty peaceful until we were airborne. Just as I was leaning back, thinking all three of them might actually sleep, Reid said, "Mommy, I have to go to the bathroom."

Reese was in that clingy, mama's-boy stage as he approached age two, so where one of us went, all four of us went—and that included the bathroom. I've often thought how kind it would have been if one of the flight attendants had said, "Could I hold the baby while you take your son to the bathroom?" but none of them did. As I struggled down the aisle with all three kids, I also couldn't help but imagine what it would have been like if Nolan had been there instead of me. *The flight attendants would be falling all over him, trying to help,* I fumed.

While Reid, at five, was capable of using the bathroom, both Reese and Wendy were in diapers, and it was a long flight. The inevitable happened, and looking back, I wonder how I ever got those diapers changed on that plane. I do remember struggling down the aisle to the bathroom more than once.

When I think of that, I can't help remembering another flight a year later. Once again I was alone with the kids, this time on a 747, the kind of plane that has the curving stairs and the lounge area. I took the kids into the lounge, thinking they could move around a little and burn up some energy. The kids were one, two, and six then, and we'd just begun potty-training Reese. After we'd been there awhile I looked around and couldn't see Reese. Just then, I heard people chuckling and twittering behind me, and I turned around to see Reese shuffling down the aisle with his pants around his ankles.

"I went potty, Mommy!" he proclaimed loudly.

Bless his heart, he'd gone all by himself, but he couldn't get his pants back up. It was one of those moments when you feel proud and mortified all at the same time, and you aren't sure which feelings are showing. I just said, "Oh, Reese, that's good. Now let's go sit down."

The Angels

But on that first flight to California in 1977 Reese was not yet potty-trained, and there wasn't much to laugh about. Our plane was late getting in, so Nolan had had to leave for a game. He had asked someone who worked in the clubhouse to pick us up. When we landed, Reese had just fallen asleep, and when I tried to wake him up, he started fussing and crying, and I finally just let him go back to sleep. Somehow I carried Reese and Wendy as well as my purse and diaper bag off the plane, with Reid ordered to hang onto my skirt so he wouldn't go streaking off down the corridor as soon as we got into the terminal. Thank goodness the man from the clubhouse was there to carry Reese to the car.

What an ordeal it all was!

Since that flight, I've tried to be more careful to watch for opportunities to help travelers in similar circumstances. If I have a free hand, I help people carry stuff off the plane, especially moms with kids. Even if they just have one bag and one kid, I sometimes offer to help because I know what it's like to be a mom traveling alone with little ones. Even when it looks easy, it's not!

A few days after we got settled in California, one of my Alvin High School classmates called to say the class was planning a tenth-year reunion the following month.

"I'd love to come," I told her, "but I just got out here with these three babies, and there's no way in the world I could do it again for a long time!" I was disappointed, but the memories of that trip were just too fresh. And although I was happy to have our family together again, my life still wasn't easy. In fact, sometimes it was all I could do to find the energy to keep going from one day to the next.

I've heard other mothers agree that when you have little kids you sometimes think, *If I could just get some sleep* . . . When your kids are little, there's just no way to explain the fatigue that consumes your life. No one but another mother can understand what it's like. Just as Reese got so he could sleep until six in the morning, Wendy was born, and she would sometimes be up all night, or several times a night, just wanting to be held. I wasn't the kind of mom who could let a baby lie in that crib and cry. As a result, I walked around in a fog of exhaustion for months.

Nolan would get up if I said, "I just can't do it this time," but if he had to pitch the next day or if he had to leave on a road trip early the next morning, I hated to ask him. Or sometimes he would get home from a road trip at six in the morning, and I knew he needed sleep as badly as I did, so I rarely asked him to help.

Other times, he would come home from a road trip in the middle of the night, and instead of going right to bed, he liked to sit down and talk awhile, catching up on everything that had happened while he'd been away. I was always so glad he was home and I wanted so much to curl up beside him and hear about the games and all the funny things that had happened in the clubhouse. And I was anxious to tell him what the kids had done while he was away. But more often than not, as he talked, my head would start bobbing and my eyelids would start sagging, and before I knew it, I was sound asleep.

11

Turnaround Years

$\mathscr{I}$ had agreed to a telephone interview with a reporter from one of the California papers, but when she called I was momentarily stumped by her first question.

Nolan was out of town, and I was alone in the house, as usual, with the three kids. I had carefully planned my day around the reporter's scheduled call so that Wendy and Reese would be napping. I'd bought a new toy for Reid, and my plan was to give it to him just before the call so he would have something new to distract him while I talked to the reporter.

But just before the call, Wendy woke up fussing and fuming. Her crying woke up Reese, who toddled crankily out of his room just as the telephone rang. The only way I could talk was to take Wendy, her bottle, and the phone into the bathroom so that when Reese started beating on the door maybe I could still hear.

So that's where I was, sitting on the bathroom floor with my fussy infant on my lap while my toddler banged on the door, as the reporter asked, "Mrs. Ryan, I was hoping you could tell me some things about the glamorous life of a major-league baseball player's family."

The Angels

I remember laughing into the phone as I thought, *If you could only see me now.*

When another baseball wife was told, "Oh, you must lead such a glamorous life," she laughed and said, "No, we're really just glorified Gypsies."

And she was right; baseball families *are* a lot like Gypsies. Nolan and I tried hard to give our kids roots, but when your life revolves around baseball, it's a very difficult thing to do. I really admire baseball wives who stick it out; the emotional ups and downs are the real challenges. Sometimes you live day to day or week to week, not knowing where you are going to live next. It could drive anyone crazy. I knew a wife with small children who moved eight times during the course of a single season, including moves between the minor-league and major-league cities when her husband moved up and down within the system. It's not only an insane situation, it can also be very expensive. It's hard to rent a place to live one day at a time!

And even if you don't feel the threat of being moved between the minor and major leagues, it can be expensive. If you want to maintain your permanent residence somewhere besides where the team is based, you have to buy a second home in the city where the team is headquartered—or find a suitable rental, as we did those first few years in California. And if you rent, you'll probably have to sign a year's lease. That means you either have to find someone to live there during the off-season, or you end up paying double rent (or rent plus a mortgage) when you move back "home." And even with two homes, there's still spring training, when you have to pull up roots and move again if you're going to keep your family together.

No, there was very little glamour in our lives at that point, at least in mine. Sure, we were doing well financially. Nolan had signed a three-year deal with the Angels at three hundred thousand dollars a year, and his star was continuing to rise. In 1977 he would lead the American League in strikeouts for the fifth time in six years and be named American League pitcher of the year by *The Sporting News*. We were together, and we were happy, but we were definitely *not* glamorous.

And it wasn't just baseball; it was the little everyday matters that can make any mother nuts. Just taking a shower was a challenge. I knew I had fifteen minutes max before pandemonium set in and at least one of the three kids started screaming. Going to the beauty shop was a major production. I had to look long and hard before I found a shop where the operators were fast—and tolerant of children.

I had always tried to keep myself in good physical condition, but with three kids, I often felt too busy and too tired to work out. I had lost the extra weight I'd gained with each pregnancy, but I worried because I knew I just didn't feel like I had felt before. I wasn't overweight, but I didn't like the way I looked and I knew I wasn't fit. But I just didn't know what to do about it. And in the back of my mind was the unspoken threat that I would become like other wives of athletes or celebrities who, preoccupied with kids or the hectic lifestyle, seemed to let the aging process show a little too much or gained a little too much weight.

I have the greatest sympathy for these women; I know these conditions shouldn't affect a couple's relationship. But I also know that when you're in the public eye and you let yourself slip even a little bit, you start hearing those inevitable whispers: "What does he see in her?" Too often, such thoughts seem to be contagious, and before long the husband (or wife—I'm sure it works the other way too) starts wondering the same thing.

I was determined that that wouldn't happen to me, but I couldn't think of a way to exercise and still be a mother. Part of the problem continued to be the little-red-hen syndrome. I worried about leaving my kids with anyone else. A friend offered to keep my kids, but she had three of her own, and I didn't think I could leave them with her for very long because how could anyone manage six little kids at once? And for a long time I hesitated to hire a baby-sitter because the house next door had a swimming pool (we didn't at the time), and I always worried the children would somehow get away from the sitter and fall in the pool.

Just as I was coming to think of myself as over the hill in 1978, Nolan was also feeling his age. At thirty-one, he was considered one of the "old men" of baseball and was the ranking veteran on the Angels team. Various injuries made him miss several starts that year, and he ended up with a 10-13 record, his worst year since leaving the Mets. Still, he led the American League in strikeouts and had pitched three shutouts—not bad for an "old man."

Nolan seemed to come out of his slump on his own the next year; 1979 turned out to be a much better season for him. He continued to lead the league in strikeouts, averaging a strikeout an inning for 223 innings.

I, on the other hand, needed help.

I'll be forever indebted to Nolan and my wonderful sister, Lynn, for helping me conquer my slide into self-doubt and self-pity that had begun just as I was approaching thirty. I had been married almost a dozen years, I was concerned about my physical condition, and I had started wondering what I had accomplished with my life. Sure, I was raising three well-adjusted kids and I was coping with the rigors of daily life, yet I felt like a brain all dressed up with no place to go. I told Lynn, "I'm all right during the day, but sometimes at night I get depressed and I don't know why. Maybe I ought to get a job or something."

Lynn is a world-class big sister, and she has a sixth sense about being there when I need her help, her ear, her humor, and her affection. I like to think I'm there for her, too, but I know that as scattered as I am, as many directions as my mind goes, I'm sometimes off in my own little world when I should be there to give her the kind of support she's always given me.

She has always been a confident, upbeat, dependable person, and she has a way of making everyone feel special. She tells people, "Ruth is as tough as nails," and then she tells about the time I had four wisdom teeth pulled one afternoon and attended a banquet that night. Lynn is tender-tough, big-hearted, and reliable. She has been married almost as long as Nolan and me, without children, and she has always been there for my children and me.

So it was no surprise when she reacted to my blue mood in her usual direct and decisive way. She went out and ordered five hundred business cards for me that read, "Ruth Ryan, Coordinator of Internal Affairs, Ryan Residence," followed by an address and phone number.

Nolan helped too by going out of his way to be thoughtful and caring. "All mothers surely go through this," he said. "Before you know it, the kids will be out of school, and you'll be able to do whatever you want to do. Right now, they're your priority. It's like investing in the future; it's hard now, but it's going to be worth every minute of your effort. If you had an outside job, you'd just come home at night exhausted and still have all these problems to deal with too. I know how hard it is for you, and I know you need to feel appreciated, and I'm going to work hard to make sure you do."

Nolan not only helped me renew my self-worth, he also helped me get started on an exercise routine that pulled me the rest of the way out of my slump. One day when I complained to him that I didn't like the way I felt, he sat at the kitchen table and listened—really listened—to what I was saying. I had been a strong athlete as a girl, I reminded him, and now I had three kids and felt like a marshmallow. Suddenly the tears were flowing, and I was crying as if my life had ended.

In typical Nolan fashion, he pulled his chair around next to mine, handed me his handkerchief, and rubbed my back with his hand. "If you're so unhappy, why don't you do something about it?" he asked gently.

"I can't!" I wailed. Then I explained how hard I'd tried and how unsuccessful I'd been in trying to find a baby-sitter I trusted and how impossible it was to try to exercise with the kids around.

"Well, why don't you just start right now? I'll watch the kids. You can run around the block."

It's almost impossible now to imagine myself saying it, but the next excuse out of my mouth was the most pitiful of all.

"I don't have the right things to wear! My warmups are back in Alvin," I whined.

I know there are other husbands in this world who would have said, "Are you crazy? You need a psychiatrist instead of an exercise program! You're just wallowing in self-pity, and all you want to do is complain and make excuses. You don't really want to do anything about your problem or you would know you don't have to wear special clothes to jog around the block!"

But the people who say such things aren't Nolan Ryan. He listened to my tirade, then answered patiently, "You have shorts. You have tennis shoes. You can wear anything. It doesn't matter. Who are you doing this for, yourself or the neighbors?"

Finally I was out of excuses. I pulled on my shorts and one of his T-shirts and headed out the door. I only made it past our next-door neighbor's house—less than a hundred yards—before I was huffing and puffing, my shoulders heaving with each breath. I turned around and came back, defeated. I had been gone less than five minutes.

Red-faced, still trying to catch my breath, I told Nolan what had happened. "I got so out of breath, I only made it to the neighbor's driveway," I said between gulps of air. "I had to come back. I can't do it, Nolan!"

He patted my hand. "Well, the lots out here are pretty good sized. If you made it all the way to the neighbor's driveway, that's a decent start. Just add a house each day, and don't give up. Give yourself three days of feeling bad. Your legs are gonna feel weak at first, but after that, you'll be able to pick up the pace."

To this day I'm grateful to Nolan for not making fun of my first weak attempt to get myself back into good physical condition. He wanted me to succeed, and he was willing to help me do it. It took me six weeks of working at it before I could run one mile without stopping. I will never forget that day; I ran a circle completely around the neighborhood, and when I got home I felt like Rocky dancing at the top of the steps at the Philadelphia Museum of Art.

Since then I've used that approach in countless other ways. When something seems insurmountable, I visualize myself back in that California suburb, winded and defeated as I turned around in front of the neighbor's driveway. Then I remind myself, *Just add one house a day—take one step at a time.* I guess it seems overly simplistic, but it's become a philosophy of life for me. I don't try to accomplish too much at once. I accept where I am, then work toward a goal a little bit at a time, celebrating every little improvement.

This is not to say my life suddenly became easier with this new attitude and my exercise routine was now a piece of cake. I was still married to a major-league baseball player who was away from home much of the time. And I certainly wouldn't leave the three kids alone in the house while I jogged around the neighborhood. I came upon a solution to this problem one day as I was driving home from the grocery store and noticed the track at the high school. It was just a few blocks from our house, and since it was summertime, school wasn't in session. So the next day I packed up the kids—they were probably about one, two, and six then—and took them to the school. I settled them into the sand in the broad-jump pit, then I stretched out and started jogging around the track.

It became a regular routine for us. And although it didn't always work perfectly—sometimes the kids would cry when I left them in the sand pit and come running or crawling after me—I kept at it. Usually I would jog or run for thirty to forty-five minutes; then I would play with the kids and have some fun with them as a reward for all of us. The next year, I added another step to my workout and started taking ballet lessons again; by that time I'd found a baby-sitter I felt comfortable with—the daughter of the Angels team doctor.

That summer was a turning point for me. I seemed to gain some much-needed insight—as well as physical endurance—as I worked to get myself in shape. After that, I never looked back, and I've never stopped exercising. Many times, I've thought that exercising has been the only thing that has kept me from losing my sanity!

When our kids got older and got involved in soccer or Little League, I'd wear my running clothes and walk or jog around the field while they were at their practices. The kids may have been embarrassed sometimes—most of the other moms would just sit and watch, and kids go through a stage where they want their mom to be like everyone else's mom—but it worked for me, and the kids eventually came around to the idea, especially when I had more energy to play with them or keep up with their hectic schedules.

Looking back now, I believe my turnaround and my resolve to rebuild my physical condition in 1978 were nothing less than gifts from God—because I would need all the fortitude and all the strength I could muster in 1979.

12

Disabled

Reid was seven years old in May 1979, as active and rambunctious as ever. He had just gotten his new uniform for his team in the Orange County T-ball league, and he was anxious to show it off to his pals who lived across the street. So while Marilyn Carew and I talked in our yard as the younger children played, Reid ran over to find his buddies.

As he was showing his shirt to his friends, some other kids, a couple of youngsters we thought of as the neighborhood bullies, overheard Reid's proud descriptions of his team. They threatened to take his new shirt away from him and rip it to shreds.

Reid immediately headed home, running full speed while nervously looking back over his shoulder to see if the bullies were following him. During one of these backward glances, he stepped off the curb, directly into the path of an oncoming car.

Even now, sixteen years later, I can still hear vividly the sounds of that collision—the tires squealing, the sound of the impact, a car door slamming, voices yelling.

Reid screaming.

"My leg! My leg! Mama, I'm going to die!"

The Angels

As I flew down the sidewalk I could see Reid's short little body sprawled in front of the bumper. The driver, one of our neighbors about eighteen or nineteen years old, had been slowing to turn into her driveway when Reid had stepped off the curb directly in her path.

"I'm so sorry, Mrs. Ryan!" she said, trembling. "He ran right in front of me!"

Without thinking I rushed to Reid and immediately reached down to pick him up. But a neighbor shoved me aside and kept me from touching him. "Don't move him!" she shouted. "We've called the ambulance; wait 'til they get here."

Another neighbor had brought a blanket, and she spread it over him as I knelt beside his head and looked him directly in the eye.

"My leg!" he cried frantically. "Mama, they're gonna cut off my leg!"

His femur, the bone connecting the hip and the knee, was pressing outward, nearly puncturing the skin, but I was relieved that there was no blood coming from his mouth or ears; I knew that would really be a bad sign. His face, arms, and legs were covered with scratches, and his tennis shoes were twenty yards away.

"Reid, you're going to be okay. You're not going to die, and they're not going to cut your leg off. You're going to be okay. Do you hear me, Reid? You're going to be okay!"

I kept talking softly and steadily into his ear, trying to convince both of us.

"You're going to be okay, Reid."

The ambulance arrived in about fifteen minutes—fifteen minutes that seemed like fifteen years. Tearfully leaving the two younger kids with Marilyn, I climbed into the ambulance with Reid. By the time we reached the emergency room, we were both showing signs of shock. It was about 7 P.M. in California—and three hours later in Boston, where Nolan's team was playing the Red Sox.

I desperately wanted Nolan to be there with me, and yet, in 1979, the baseball code and the allegiance of a player to his team were so rigid that I actually hesitated about calling him. The doctors had confirmed that Reid had suffered a broken left femur. He was in so much pain that I thought he must have another injury, but the doctors couldn't tell from their examination. More tests would be needed. They might have to do surgery.

I knew Nolan was at Fenway Park, but he wasn't pitching that night, so I called the stadium from the emergency room. The switchboard operator at Fenway was disturbingly rude; I know now that was probably a blessing. I became so focused on getting through to her that for a moment I actually forgot how scared and upset I was. I told her steadily, "This is an emergency. I *have* to talk to him."

"Well, we can't call players during a game," she replied in a monotone. "That's a rule."

By then I was yelling at her, and I guess the urgency in my voice finally persuaded her. I waited for what seemed like an eternity, holding the silent telephone receiver to my ear and aching to hear Nolan's voice. But as soon as he came on the line, I broke down. Everything just hit me at once, and I couldn't talk.

All he could hear was my sobbing, and he was getting frantic, unable to understand what had happened but knowing it was something terrible. Finally, one of the doctors took the phone from me and explained the situation to Nolan.

I caught my breath and took back the phone. I asked him if he could come home.

"I'm leaving right now," he said.

He changed clothes and left the stadium immediately, heading straight to the airport without even checking any airline schedules. When he got there he found out the next flight wouldn't leave until early the next morning, but he still didn't leave. Instead, he spent the night in the airport.

Meanwhile, Reid was transferred to Children's Hospital. During the ambulance ride across town, my old determination and resolve came back to me. After I'd let it all out with Nolan on the phone, I didn't cry again throughout the whole ordeal that followed.

When we got to Children's, I called my mom and dad, and as always, just hearing their voices helped calm me and give me new strength. Hearing my dad say that everything would be all right was reassuring to me. I was exhausted, yes, and scared too, but with God's help I knew I could get through whatever lay ahead.

The Angels

I spent that night curled up in a chair beside Reid's bed, wearing the old, saggy-kneed double-knit slacks and wrinkled white cotton shirt I'd put on that afternoon to work in the yard and play with the kids. All I knew at that point was that Reid had a badly broken leg and that he was in a lot of pain. As the night wore on, I kept hoping for more information, but the doctors were still unable to make any judgments based on the x-rays. At five in the morning, they said they needed to do exploratory surgery. They suspected that Reid's ribs had been smashed and had severed his spleen, but they couldn't know until they looked inside. If their suspicions were correct, the spleen would have to be removed; there was no way to repair it. The surgery was scheduled for about noon.

"Are you gonna be all right?" the doctor asked after he'd delivered this news. "Is your husband coming?"

"He'll be here," I answered. "He's on his way."

Although Reid was sedated, he still seemed restless, often calling out from his sleep or shaking his head slowly and moaning. Sometime near dawn, he finally seemed to settle down, and I too dozed off. A short while later I felt a hand on my shoulder and looked up to find my dad leaning over Reid's bed, one hand stroking his grandson's head and one arm stretched out to pull me toward him.

"Dad!"

I hadn't asked him to come, but I wasn't surprised that he did. He told me, "As soon as I hung up from your call, I called the airline and got the first flight out. I just felt like I needed to be here."

Dad was the perfect person to be with me that morning. As an elder in our church in Alvin, he'd had lots of experience visiting friends and church members in the hospital. Still, it was hard for him to stand at Reid's bedside; each time Reid moaned, Dad grimaced with worry. Reid's broken leg had not yet been set, and his stomach was distended and tender. It was obvious the little guy was in bad shape.

Having Dad there was a blessing, but my eyes still kept watching the doorway, and I kept praying that Nolan would arrive soon. Finally, about midmorning, when I had dozed off briefly, I looked up and he was there, his face drawn and pale, his eyes red, exhaustion weighing down every move.

ABOVE: *Christmas 1951.*
The baseball and glove were for
me, not my new baby brother.

Lynn and I often dressed in
matching outfits that my mother
loved to sew.

Nolan was in my sister Lynn's class. He knew me as "Lynn Holdorff's little sister."

A rite of passage for Texas children...me dressed as a cowgirl.

Dad and I shared a real
passion for tennis…

…but he missed watching me in this tournament in Florida, during Nolan's 1969
spring training.

October, 1965. In simpler times, on my parent's back porch in Alvin. Nolan brought me a Mets sweatshirt.

BELOW: *June 26, 1967. Who would have thought this storybook day would end with a wedding night dinner at Whataburger?*

ABOVE: *I used to get all dressed up for the games and sneak Nolan little snacks.*

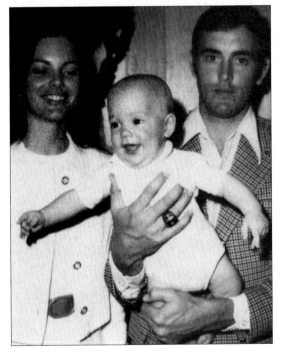

With our firstborn, Reid, in California 1972...the nurse at his delivery was more interested in getting Nolan's autograph.

ABOVE:
*Horsing around
with Reid before
heading off for
another spring
training.*

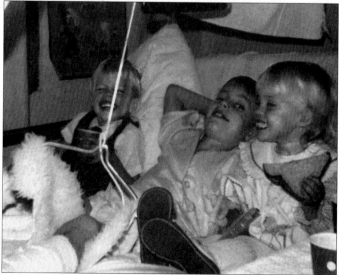

*Reese and
Wendy cheering
up Reid in the
hospital, when
we all learned
what really
matters.*

We had a lot of "goofy" times together in California, in spite of our busy schedules.

The "glamorous" Ryan family having pancakes at Grandma's in Alvin.

After the Mets won the 1969 World Series, Nolan and I posed for a magazine picture at a friend's home in Alvin. We didn't have a house to pose in!

The kids loved to visit Dad in the dugout.

I was proud to carry the Olympic torch in Alvin in 1984, especially since I couldn't even run 100 yards just a few years earlier.

September 26, 1981. Though it was Nolan's fifth no-hitter, it was only the second I had seen. My mother and I celebrated after the game.

I feel very fortunate to still have my mom and dad with us today.

The Home Team suits up for Halloween, 1988.

I'm the proud mom in the middle! My good-looking bunch and I enjoyed the rodeo in Fort Worth.

Can you find the Ryans in this picture? We were posing in camouflage for a sporting goods company promotion.

I never lost that "butterflies in the stomach" feeling watching my husband in a game.

The only thing that's changed about watching Nolan for 26 years was the glasses. Here I was watching him win his 300th game.

Watching the game with Wendy, who's turned out to be everything I'd ever dreamed a daughter would be.

Hanging out with other baseball wives in Aspen. From left to right: Mia Smith, Vicki Scott, Hilda Darwin, Lori Doran.

Nolan and I with Jim Reese.

Nolan and I celebrated his 40th birthday in Las Vegas.

ABOVE: *A bittersweet day for the Ryan family—the day Nolan officially retired from baseball.*

Wendy snapped this photo of us clowning around at home during Nolan's busy first summer of "retirement."

Disabled

There is no way to describe the feelings that swept over me when I opened my eyes and saw him silently standing there beside Reid's bedside. I was so relieved to have him there with us, but at the same time it broke my heart to see him looking down at his son with such pain in his eyes. His lips were squeezed together in a tight line, and he swallowed hard as he looked at Reid's swollen leg and stomach and watched the little face contort with pain. Then Nolan looked at me and asked, "What do the doctors say?"

"They don't know," I answered. "They're going to operate."

I don't mean to make our experience seem overly dramatic. After all, our son survived, and many do not. But there is nothing that makes a parent feel more helpless than the pain of his or her child. And in that moment we felt very helpless indeed.

Today, long after Reid's accident, our whole family is living proof that God gives us strength in adversity that not only makes us strong enough to face what must be endured, but also enough to share with others.

Twice during Nolan's career, he underwent surgery, and I nervously kissed him good-bye as they wheeled him off to the OR. But somehow kissing Reid good-bye before they pushed his gurney through those swinging doors seemed a million times harder, I guess because Nolan at least always knew what was going on, and Reid, already sleeping as they took him away, looked so young and small and innocent. I squeezed Nolan's hand and bit my lip as the doors closed behind our son.

The surgery confirmed the doctors' suspicion. Reid's spleen was irreparably damaged. I felt tremendous relief that they had found that problem. They also discovered that one of Reid's kidneys and a ureter were damaged. It had been leaking urine into the abdominal cavity, and that had been the cause of much of the pain. The doctors repaired the kidney, and when they brought him back to us they told us they had done all they could for now.

Reid continued to have problems, and his broken leg still hadn't been set. The doctors said they couldn't put his leg in a cast until they had solved the internal damage. What I didn't understand was that they were waiting to see if the repaired kidney and ureter would regain their function again.

They didn't.

"We're going to have to remove the kidney," one of the doctors told us gently two weeks later. "But it's completely possible to survive with one kidney and no spleen," he quickly added. "The fact is, we have no choice right now; the kidney's got to come out."

Reid was in intensive care for several days, then he was moved into a room with three other beds. He was in traction for quite awhile longer, and he didn't leave the hospital for another two months. We hid nothing from him; we told him everything the doctors told us, and we were with him every possible minute.

Nolan and I took turns spelling each other at the hospital and spending time with the two younger kids at home. Gene Autry and the Angels could not have been kinder or more considerate. They told Nolan to do whatever he needed—skip a road trip, miss a turn in the rotation, whatever. But for Nolan to pitch at all, he had to maintain something close to his regular routine. He adjusted by not going on road trips until the day before he was due to pitch. On the days he was home, he either went to the hospital or stayed with three-year-old Reese and two-year-old Wendy. When he wasn't in a baseball stadium or on an airplane that summer, he was with his kids either at home or at the hospital.

The hospital wouldn't allow parents to spend the night unless there was an especially critical situation. So on the days before home games, I would get up early and head for the hospital around 6 A.M., then Nolan would relieve me about 11 A.M. or until he left to go to the park at 4 P.M. Then I would come back and stay until Reid fell asleep at night. Marilyn Carew and a lot of other friends and neighbors were invaluable in helping us cope with all the challenges we had to handle that summer.

Although we were overjoyed when Reid finally got to come home, in many ways having him at home was the most tiring part of the whole experience for me. He was in a body cast from the chest down, so I had to carry him everywhere. I hadn't realized all the lifting the nurses and aides at the hospital had been doing every day. Reid was completely immobile; I had to do everything for him as well as tend

Disabled

to the two younger children. Bathing Reid and taking him to the bathroom became enormous undertakings.

Nolan was out of town the day Reid came home, but my niece, Tracy Klansek, had come out from Texas to help, and after that first day at home with Reid, she and I collapsed in the kitchen and sat there staring glassy-eyed at each other over the table. "I just can't do this!" I told her. "I can't handle it."

"We'll get through this," she said. "Somehow you'll do it, Aunt Ruth. And someday we'll look back on all this and maybe we'll laugh—or at least smile a little."

She was right. We *did* get through it, and sometimes we do smile a little, thinking about those awkward body-cast bathroom scenes. But the things we experienced that summer still affect our lives today in much more somber ways too.

Reid, for instance, remembers everything about the accident. He remembers believing with all his heart that he was going to die. As a result, he lives every day to the fullest—full-tilt-boogie, I heard someone describe it once. He seems to wake up each morning with a smile on his face, glad to be alive, and he packs so many things into every day, it's as if he can never get enough of whatever life has to offer.

He still bears the physical effects of the accident too. Without his spleen, Reid has been more susceptible to infections. I worried about overprotecting him, and I worried about what might happen if I didn't. Despite all my precautions, Reid developed osteomyelitis when he was fourteen, after a cut on his elbow became infected and the bacteria settled in his hip. He came home from basketball practice one afternoon appearing perfectly normal, and the next morning he had a 104-degree fever and couldn't put any weight on his leg. He looked so ill, I felt all the old fears resurfacing.

He had to be hospitalized for three weeks, and then we had to keep him on an IV at home for six more weeks. I learned to hook it up and keep it going myself so that he could leave the hospital.

The doctors told Reid he could not play any contact sports, and I knew there would be battles over that edict. I ruled out soccer and said no when he wanted to play football in junior high. Reid argued that

he could just be a kicker, but I pointed out that kickers sometimes get tackled. I just wanted to limit his risks, and Nolan backed me up.

Reid ended up playing basketball and baseball. Last summer he was drafted by the Texas Rangers and spent the season with the club's minor-league team in New York.

Reid isn't the only one who was changed by what happened that summer. Our lives were touched not only by what we went through with him, but also by what we shared with the other patients and families we came to know.

Reid was in the ICU with other children who had all sorts of *horrible* problems: birth defects, cystic fibrosis, cancer. Every time we left that room we would go home so thankful for our healthy kids and for the fact that Reid's problem was "fixable." We knew he was going to be okay. I never went through any great change in spirituality because of what we went through with Reid; I went into it believing that God was watching over us and that He would give us strength to handle whatever happened. And He did. That's the only way we all came through that experience with our family and our sanity intact.

We both knew that serious problems like Reid's accident could threaten any marriage, and there were plenty of times when, in our fear and worry and exhaustion, we could easily have said things we would regret or have done things that would have been disastrous. But we pulled together and managed to keep our priorities straight, and in the end we came out stronger and closer because of what had happened.

Our lives were also touched by the people we encountered during those months in the hospital. We'll never forget the heartbreaking time we spent with the parents of a child who had just died, and we cherish the memory of what happened when we became friends with a single mom whose boy had cancer. She asked Nolan if he would be the one to talk to her son about what would happen to him when he went through chemotherapy—the nausea, hair loss, and other side effects.

Doing something like that was awfully hard for Nolan. In fact, just being there with his own son was hard for him because he had always had a fear of hospitals. I didn't know why, but I knew his fear was real.

So when she asked Nolan to do this, I was sure he wouldn't *want* to do it—no one would—but I wasn't sure how he would answer her. I should never have doubted him. Nolan didn't even hesitate. He just said, "Sure, if you think that would help."

Kids are funny. They accept the truth really well if you don't get coy or put too much sugarcoating on it, and of course that's just the way Nolan would naturally talk to anyone. He took the boy outside and talked to him like he would have spoken to his own son. I don't know what he said—he never wanted to talk about it—but whatever it was, the mother thought it was wonderful; she assured Nolan his words had helped her son—and her too.

One of the lessons we learned from that mother was that you have to stay on top of everything that is being done to your child when he or she is in the hospital. You have to ask questions, check out things yourself. The doctors and nurses are skilled and caring, but they really don't know all the answers.

I admired that mother so much; she must have had a lot of faith and courage and strength to go through all that. Her son handled it well too. Thinking about them makes me teary-eyed, even today. And I'm happy to report that that boy is still alive today, a bright young man living in California. The mother even came to Houston once, and we got to see her again. There is not a doubt in my mind that that woman saved her son's life with the things she did for him—little things like having a sports celebrity talk to him about the side effects of chemo. She did everything she could think of to give him courage and build his strength. I watched her fight for him, urging his spirit on when he was too weak to fight for himself. She's just one of the heroes we were blessed to know because of Reid's accident.

Other parents in the hospital also asked Nolan to say hello to their sons or daughters. Sometimes they would say, "This may be her last birthday. Could you just come by and say hello? It would mean a lot to us."

I would go home after an encounter like that and think I was the luckiest woman in the world to have been spared such a blow, and I vowed to never take good health for granted. Now I stress healthy food and a healthy lifestyle to my family every day, and I try to live out that example. I also try to remember that no matter what challenges come my way, someone somewhere has faced something even worse—and come through it. I met many of those people in the ward at Children's Hospital.

Each time after a mother had asked Nolan to talk to her child, Nolan would look at me and draw in a deep breath. "I don't know what to say to these kids, Ruth," he would admit. But I guess God gave him the right words, because he always went. And afterward, many of those parents wrote us to say, "Your visit meant so much to him."

Nolan didn't just talk to the kids in the hospital; he brought them souvenirs from the ball club and joked with them and made them laugh. He wasn't the type back then to do these things naturally; it was never easy for him. He was just as afraid of the suffering he saw as the rest of us were. But he did them; he learned what to say, how to help. We both learned.

And we learned the good that could come from Nolan's simply *being there*. Even now, so many years later, it still amazes me what a difference it can make to a person or a group or a good cause if a celebrity merely shows up to sign autographs or shake hands or share a meal. We are very careful in what we choose to support, but when we are certain that the cause is a good one and we feel comfortable in lending our support, we're glad to go.

We learned a lot that year, 1979. We hurt a lot, too, and we worried and struggled and tried to focus on what really mattered. And when it was over, we felt we had been rewarded for our labors. Our family was intact, our spirits were much stronger, and, at the end of the baseball season, we moved back home to Texas.

Permanently.

Part Four

. . . .

The Astros

13

Heading for Home

$\mathcal{A}$s I followed another baseball wife down the steps in the Astrodome in Houston and we made our way to our seats before the game began, I overheard a man near the aisle say, "Who's that? She's good-looking."

His friend answered, "Oh, that's so-and-so's wife."

Then, as I walked by, he said, "And who's that?"

"Nolan Ryan's wife."

"She's kind of cute."

"Yeah," the friend replied, "but anyone could look good with a million dollars."

Of all the things that were said about the Astros' offering Nolan a million dollars a year to move to Houston, I don't know why this is the one that sticks in my mind. The 1980 contract made Nolan the first athlete to break the million-dollar-salary mark; overnight, he became the highest-paid player on any team sport.

I was thrilled that we were moving back to Texas. The Astrodome was just a thirty-minute drive from our house in Alvin, and I looked forward to settling into our home there at the end of the '79 baseball season and finally having a sense of permanency. But the money made this move back home different in many ways.

We had always come home to Alvin at the end of each season and simply "taken up where we left off," just like any hometown folks coming back to "roost." But when Nolan's million-dollar salary made all the news, we suddenly felt conspicuous in our little hometown, and in some ways we almost felt we were disappointing some of the people, especially those who didn't know us well.

As strange as it seems, some people—none of our friends and family in Alvin, but outsiders who were aware that we lived here—seemed surprised when they found out Nolan drove a pickup truck instead of some kind of fancy sports car. They were also surprised when we enrolled Reid in first grade at Stevenson Primary School in Alvin instead of having a chauffeur haul him into some prestigious day school in Houston every morning. They seemed surprised, too, that we still shopped for groceries and put gasoline in the station wagon, and ordered chicken-fried steak at the local lunch spots, and bought socks and T-shirts on sale.

On the other hand, most folks in Alvin treated us the same way they always had. It hadn't mattered to them when Nolan moved from high school baseball to the major leagues, and it wouldn't matter to them whether we were millionaires or blue-collar workers.

We still joke about the winter a Mets teammate, another pitcher, came to Alvin to go hunting with Nolan and to play a few games of basketball at the prison gymnasium in Angleton. (I don't know why they played *there*, but they did.)

This was right after the Mets had won the World Series, and the guy quietly suggested to Nolan that he didn't want any fuss or fanfare made during his visit. Nolan said he didn't think it would be a problem.

By the end of the week, the friend had the anonymity of a fence-post. "Nolan," said the future Hall of Famer, Tom Seaver, "I appreciate what you're doing for me. But I've been here a week and no one has even asked my name!"

That's Alvin, Texas.

The truth is, we continue to live the way we were raised, and we were raised to cherish true friends and to value hard work and the money it earns. This lifelong frugality was demonstrated one winter day when Nolan went hunting near Alvin with another teammate, Phil Garner. They stopped at a convenience store to buy some supplies, and Nolan picked up a can of gun oil. When he saw that the price was double what he normally paid for it, Nolan promptly put it right back on the shelf and muttered that he would buy it somewhere else.

Phil thought that was really funny. He said, "Nolan, you're such a tightwad! You just signed a million-dollar contract, and you can't spend five dollars on a can of gun oil." But somehow the frugality of Nolan's upbringing would not allow him that extravagance.

My dad says such situations show what a fine line Nolan has walked these last several years: The people from Alvin don't seem to resent his celebrity because he never gave in to it. Still, among outsiders he has to be careful. If he spends too much money on things, he appears to be flaunting his wealth; if he spends too little he looks miserly.

I've heard my own share of comments. Besides the remark I overheard in the Astrodome, another memorable situation occurred in one of the stores in Alvin. In Wal-Mart one day, I came across the kind of bicycle Wendy had been wanting; we'd been unable to find this special kind and suddenly here it was. I had run into the store to pick up something real quickly, and I'd come without my wallet. All I had was a twenty-dollar bill in my pocket. So I decided to put the bike on layaway. There was a line at the layaway desk, and when it was my turn at the counter, I told them my name and what I wanted to do, and the woman behind me said, "Ruth Ryan—*Nolan Ryan's wife?* You *can't* be Ruth Ryan! I've seen her on television, and you don't look anything like her!"

I was probably wearing a jogging suit or some other casual clothes that any other person might have worn to Wal-Mart, and I probably didn't have any makeup on. I looked at her with my mouth hanging open and no idea of what to say. She had drawn so much attention by her loud proclamations that I felt like everyone in that part of the store was now staring at me, thinking, *Good grief! Could that really be Nolan Ryan's wife?* and *What on earth is she doing in the layaway department?*

It was embarrassing, to say the least. I quickly turned back to the counter, signed the papers, and hurried out of the store. It was just one example of how we didn't seem to live up to outsiders' expectations. But while such experiences were embarrassing, they didn't really affect us that much. By then we knew that a lot worse things could happen to us than being embarrassed. Still, such reactions made us all the more thankful for the friends and relatives who continued to accept us as nothing more than we'd ever been—their pals, Nolan and Ruth.

A few times people asked us why we didn't move into Houston or live somewhere a little more trendy, but we never seriously considered living anywhere else. One or two times when Nolan played with the Angels I thought maybe we should settle permanently somewhere nearer the team, but I didn't want to give up my kids' seeing their grandparents. And besides, Alvin is home. Our families, our histories are here. Nolan can hunt here; in fact, as much as I resented Nolan's hunting when we were first married and when the kids were babies, I have to admit that now we all enjoy those annual hunting trips in South Texas.

We feel safe in Alvin, and we can live like normal people here. Alvin isn't the greatest spot on earth. It has twenty-two thousand people now, almost all of them friendly (up from a population of seven thousand when Nolan and I were growing up here). The spreading live oaks are beautiful, but the rest of the scenery isn't much, and the humidity is high.

"It's no great attraction," says Nolan, "but it's home. We never found a place we'd rather live."

I remember when the sportswriters covering the New York Mets teased Nolan about coming from a town named after a chipmunk. I guess Alvin could be a joke to a lot of city dwellers, but it's also the place that defines Nolan and me and the kind of people we are. There's a sense of community here that we haven't found anywhere else.

Our church is here, and many of the families in it are the same ones who were there when we were growing up. And although we haven't been regular churchgoers—after all, in baseball, Sunday is a workday—we keep the connection alive. I know the church is there for us, and it would take care of us should we ever turn to its members for help.

That's one of the things I do regret, that we didn't attend church as much as we wanted to. Nolan would like for all of us to get dressed up every Sunday morning and go to church, but we're so rarely home on the weekends that that's just not been a possibility for us.

I remember one Sunday when the kids were little and Nolan was traveling with the team, I decided to take the kids to Sunday school and church. It took me nearly an hour and a half to get all three of them bathed and dressed, but I finally did it. Then I had allowed fifteen minutes to take a shower and get myself ready.

When I got out of the shower, the first thing I noticed was that Wendy's bedroom door was closed. When I opened it, my heart jumped into my throat; I thought the room was full of smoke. Then I realized it was baby powder. All three kids looked like someone had dipped them in flour; they were covered from head to toe. They'd had a great time creating a regular blizzard right there in Wendy's bedroom, and they were giggling merrily when I walked in. I was frustrated and furious—not the best attitude to have when you show up at church—but I was also determined. I thought, *I've worked so hard to get to this point, I can't stop now.* So I brushed them off as best I could, and we went anyway. I'm sure everyone knew when the Ryans arrived that Sunday.

I remember another Sunday story that Nolan's mom liked to tell. Wendy, the proverbial tomboy, had spent the night there, and the plan was that she was going to go to church with Grandma. Everything went smoothly until Wendy found out she was going to have to wear a dress.

She said, "No way, Grandma!"

I guess there was quite a little scene, complete with plenty of cajoling, crying, and bribes. All I know for sure is how things ended up: Wendy wore shorts to church.

All these little family memories made our move back home to

The Astros

Alvin seemed like part of a natural progression. After all, our goal when Nolan began playing major-league ball was that he would play four or five years. That was what we hoped for. Then he would have a pension, and he could go to Texas A&M and get his veterinary degree. I would have my teaching degree by then, we assumed, and we would move back home to Alvin and be a veterinarian and a teacher and live happily ever after.

I've already described how difficult it was for me to attend college and be a baseball player's wife. It was even harder for Nolan when he enrolled in Alvin Junior College to take a few classes. He would arrive back in Alvin in mid or late October and try to catch up on the three weeks of work he'd missed while working full time at the gas station or appliance store or unloading freight. It was just more than he could manage at the time. He tried correspondence courses, too, but without any success. I suppose he's got fifteen or twenty credit hours right now, and I've probably got about sixty.

This was worrisome for us at first, that we didn't get our degrees, because we never equated baseball with making money. We thought of it as a temporary thing, an adventure, a peek into a different world. And when it was over, we always pictured ourselves ending up back in Alvin and leading a normal life.

So it seemed perfectly natural when we sold our home in California, moved back to Alvin, and did our best to be an ordinary family living in an ordinary town. Nolan was thirty-three years old and had been in professional baseball nearly fifteen years when the Astros signed him for a three-year, three-million-dollar contract. So we came back to Alvin thinking Nolan's career was nearing an end and our days of living a split life between two homes were over for good.

But we were wrong.

14

Changeup

*N*olan holds a lot of baseball records. But I think one of his proudest moments came in a play that didn't have anything to do with records.

On April 12, 1980, during his very first start for the Astros, Nolan stepped up to home plate in the Astrodome and drove a pitch from L.A.'s Don Sutton into the left-field stands with two runners on base. I don't think any other moment in any other game ever tickled Nolan more. After all, he hadn't swung a bat in a game in eight years while he had played for the Angels under the American League's designated-hitter rule.

What a thrill! As I watched that ball sail out of sight, I yelled and cheered as Nolan rounded the bases until my voice was almost gone. It seemed like some kind of omen that we really had made the right decision in moving back to Texas. It was something we laughed about and celebrated for a long time to come.

Something we didn't celebrate so much was an incident that happened at a game against San Diego in August 1980. Playing in the Astrodome, Dave Winfield, San Diego's six-foot-six outfielder, was apparently offended by an inside fastball that knocked him down. He jumped up from the dirt and headed for the pitcher's mound, focused on Nolan like a charging bull. Luis Pujols, the Houston catcher, tried to stop him, but Winfield gave him a football stiff-arm, and Luis went down. Then the umpire got in his way, and Winfield pushed him aside.

Sitting in the stands behind home plate, I couldn't believe what I was seeing. It all seemed to happen in slow motion. As Winfield neared the mound, Nolan just seemed to freeze, as if he couldn't believe what he was seeing either. Suddenly Winfield reached out with his long left arm and grabbed Nolan's head, as if he were lining him up, then he swung wildly with his right.

Nolan didn't try to defend himself. He had been trained to believe that the most prudent reaction for a pitcher to take, especially when he was charged by someone maybe four inches taller and fifty pounds heavier, was to avoid injury at any cost. That's why when Winfield fired that wild swing at him, Nolan ducked and collapsed on the ground, curled up in a fetal position with his arms over his head.

Out of the corner of my eye I saw a photographer—I recognized him as someone who worked for the *Alvin Sun*—running onto the field to help Nolan, his hometown hero. The security guards kicked the poor guy out of the stadium. I always felt bad about that; after all, he was just doing what I wanted to do too!

Nolan had reacted the way he'd been trained—but he didn't like the feeling he took home with him that night. He didn't say anything in the pickup as we rode home, and he didn't sleep well.

I kept telling him, "Nolan, what good would it have done to start swinging back at Winfield and get yourself injured and maybe miss the rest of the season? You did the right thing." But my words had little effect, and Nolan vowed he would never back off again.

"I'll never give anybody else that opportunity," he said with a scowl, hating the memory of being curled up in the dirt as Winfield, thrown off balance by his swing, had sprawled on top of him and started flailing at Nolan with punches. "From now on, if anyone comes out to the mound looking for a fight, he'll get one."

It would be thirteen years in coming, but when it happened, Nolan's next fight on the pitcher's mound would make front pages all over the country.

Winfield left San Diego and wound up with the Yankees, and he faced Nolan again at the All-Star game in 1985 in Minneapolis. The first time Dave came to bat, Nolan's first pitch sent him sprawling. Now, the All-Star game isn't exactly a blood rivalry, but it isn't a re-union either. The pitch was a reminder of old times not forgotten. They didn't speak to each other socially until 1989, when Winfield congratulated Nolan on getting his five-thousandth strikeout.

When a reporter asked him about the 1980 encounter, Winfield answered, "We're both competitors. You never talk about that stuff. It's just part of the game; when a pitcher knocks you down, you get up and get a hit."

Nolan didn't dwell on it either; he was on to bigger and better things. A little more than a year after the incident with Winfield, on September 26, 1981, he pitched another electrifying no-hitter. In the history of baseball, there had been four thousand pitchers, and none of them had ever pitched *five* no-hitters.

Until now.

I was in the Astrodome that day with my parents, sister, brother, and Nolan's mother. (The kids couldn't be there because their soccer teams were playing.) As we settled into our seats, we were expecting a good game, and we obviously weren't alone in our expectations because the game was being televised nationally. Several friends from Alvin had come to the game that day, too, and there was a party atmosphere, a high feeling of anticipation in the stands.

The game began normally enough. But as the innings passed without a Dodger hit, I found myself wringing my hands as I watched Nolan hurl the baseball through the strike zone again and again while batters seemed to come and go without a hope of getting on base. The magic was back—and so were the butterflies in my stomach.

When it was all over Nolan had walked three, struck out eleven, and racked up another unbelievable entry in the record books. The Astros beat the Dodgers, 5-0.

The Astros

Nolan was thirty-four years old. It had been six years since his last no-hitter, which had tied him for the record with Dodger pitcher Sandy Koufax. The only other pitchers ever to have held more than two teams hitless were Bob Feller, Cy Young, and Larry Corcoran, with three each.

The fifth no-hitter couldn't have come at a better time. Nolan had been on the disabled list from May 18 through June 6 that year due to a stress fracture in his lower back. Not only did the no-hitter rejuvenate his career, which everyone had been assuming was nearing its end, but it also came during a game against an excellent ball club in the midst of a five-game playoff for the Western Division title. The circumstances just couldn't have been better. And from my personal point of view, it was absolutely perfect because for the second time I was there to see it in person.

Unfortunately, the Astros lost the playoff series, but even that didn't dim our delight in enjoying Nolan's fifth no-hitter. Nor did we let it bother us that Nolan had unintentionally helped someone else set a record earlier that year. In a game against the Phillies on June 11, he had given up a first-inning single to Pete Rose, letting Rose tie Stan Musial's National League record for career hits.

As if to punish Rose for getting the hit, Nolan struck him out his next three times at bat that day, every pitch but one a fastball. Rose tossed his bat in disgust after the third whiff, but he turned as he reached the dugout, then grinned and tipped his cap to Nolan in a silent salute.

These memories help blot out the downside of the 1981 season, a players' strike that began on June 12, the day after Nolan's encounter with Pete Rose. They were out for nearly two months over the issue of compensation for free agents.

Several factors were at work to build a feeling of discontent that year. I heard Nolan say occasionally that he wondered whether the fans would ever support the teams again after the strike the way they had before the players had walked out. He also thought that Astros owner John McMullen didn't promote the team the way he should have. Nolan never believed the fans really felt welcome when they came to the Astrodome.

Those feelings continued into 1982, and by the end of that season, Nolan, who had then been with the Astros three years, was doing well as a pitcher, but he was growing increasingly dissatisfied with the way the team was run. So many times, he felt that the organization's attitude toward the players made them feel that they were nothing more than impersonal beings, robotic workhorses who were paid a lot of money to perform on cue. What no one in management seemed to realize was that little things, little signs of appreciation here and there, can really mean a lot to people, no matter how much they're paid.

Whatever the reason, the Astros at that point began what seemed like an unstoppable slide. They fell in the standings, and attendance plummeted. Sometimes I would sit in that giant Astrodome and feel literally ill, looking around and seeing so many empty seats and knowing Nolan and the rest of the team were just as aware of the poor attendance as I was. I knew it had to be demoralizing for them.

Between April 17 and July 13, 1983, Nolan set a major-league pitching record for the longest winning streak (eight games), and on August 3 he pitched a one-hit game against San Diego. Other players were doing well, too, but still the fans stayed away. Some Astros games drew fewer than four thousand people.

The apathy continued into 1985, when Nolan was nearing his four-thousandth career strikeout, something no other pitcher had done. We were surprised—and I'll admit it—a little hurt that the Astros ownership seemed to have little interest in promoting this feat. In fact, when Nolan did achieve the mark that year on July 11, striking out Danny Heep of the Mets (a former Astros teammate), the Astros didn't even have a team photographer there to record the event.

Team morale dropped along with the attendance. Some of the players described it as almost like playing in a vacuum. Occasionally they would sit in the dugout, look up at the empty seats flanking the outfield, and wonder, *Does anybody care what we're doing here?*

As the 1986 season began, some sportswriters predicted the Astros would lose one hundred games . . .

❖   ❖   ❖

The Astros

With a sinking feeling, I watched the Astros' morale decline and Nolan's dissatisfaction increase. I knew things couldn't go on this way, and I wouldn't blame Nolan if he decided he was ready to move on—either to another team or to leave baseball altogether. But I hoped and prayed that somehow things would work out so we could stay where we were. It had been wonderful, after all those years of moving every spring and fall, to finally get to live through all four seasons of the year in one place.

When the kids were young and we could all be together during spring training, that became my favorite part of the baseball season. Nolan would leave around 8:30 in the morning and be finished up around 2 P.M. unless he was pitching in an exhibition game. We had the afternoons off to be with the kids, take them fishing or whatever, and have a nice dinner in the evening as a family. That sounds like a simple pleasure, but a ballplayer's hours are so different than most families' schedules, just being together becomes a special gift.

For instance, later, when the regular season started and the kids were in school, Nolan rarely got to see the kids. When he was in town, the kids and I were up early so they could get to school on time. Since he had probably gotten home from the ballpark about midnight the night before, Nolan slept in. The kids would get home from school around 3 P.M., just about the time Nolan was leaving for the ballpark. When he got home around midnight again, they had gone to bed. So even when he was in town, Nolan didn't see the kids much during the baseball season except on weekends. And it was very tiring for me to keep those hours, going to bed late with Nolan and getting up early with the kids. That's why summers and spring breaks were very important times for us to be together. When the kids got older and more involved in their own summer activities, it was really hard for me; it seemed I always needed to be in two or three places at once.

The kids and I still made at least an appearance at spring training after they started school in Alvin, but we didn't go along for the whole time as we'd done before. Sometimes, though, we would make arrangements to take along the assignments and go for a week or so. Other times, I went alone for two or three days at a time. I didn't like being away from the kids, but I realized I couldn't be with them every minute of the day. I also felt that my marriage wouldn't survive if I didn't spend time with Nolan. So I'd make arrangements to travel with him—but for two or three days instead of two or three weeks. By that time I'd found a fine, caring friend I trusted to stay with the kids.

All in all, things were going fairly well for us during those years, but of course, life is never perfect. We worried about what would happen with the Astros, and sometimes we were concerned about the kids.

I even worried about kidnapping and ransom possibilities. So before they started driving themselves, I took the kids to school every morning and picked them up every afternoon, even though the school bus came right by our house. I guess I was a little overprotective, but I thought it was a small enough thing to do to give me a little peace of mind. I was also a willing chauffeur whenever the kids needed a ride to lessons or practices, and if I couldn't be there, one of the grandparents would pick them up or take them wherever they needed to go. It was just something we did; I accepted it as my responsibility.

There were other concerns too. Once there was a bomb threat at one of the kid's schools. Another time the school got an anonymous call from someone who asked, "Does Nolan Ryan's kid go to this school?"

Such incidents have been so rare, though, that we all feel very safe here in Alvin. We have had reservations at times about putting our kids in public schools, but we believe there's a lot that's good for them there, and we want them to be exposed to all kinds of people—of different incomes and different races. Still, I've told my kids all their lives that the whole world is not like Alvin, and I've tried to prepare them for what they'll face when they're on their own.

This is not to say that the kids' school years have passed without a few waves of contention here and there. Both our boys had learning disabilities.

We now know that Nolan had similar problems as a child too. He was the youngest of six kids, and his older brother and four older sisters are all supersmart, but he had trouble with reading and spelling.

And of course when you have trouble with reading, you have trouble with everything else because it all hinges on that crucial skill. When he was in grade school in Alvin, Nolan's teachers would say, "I had your brother and sisters in my class, and I know everyone else in your family is smart. What happened to you?"

In the second or third grade, Nolan's teacher told his mother she was going to fail him. She said, "He will have to repeat."

I think Nolan's mother knew that Nolan was smart and that he had a problem, but back then no one knew what it was. She said, "No, you're not going to fail him. No child of mine will repeat a grade."

He went on to the next grade.

When Reid started school, I could see that he was struggling. And like Nolan's mother, I knew he was a very smart kid, so I couldn't understand why he was having so much trouble. By then the schools were more sophisticated about recognizing learning disabilities, but they weren't always quick to respond. We seemed to live in limbo a long time, trying to figure out what Reid's problem was and finding a way to help him.

When the same thing happened to Reese when he started second grade a few years later, I recognized that he had the same problem as his brother. I told the school, "I've been through this before with Reid. I know he's got a learning disability, and he needs some special help." The school said Reese would be put on a list for testing, and it would probably happen within six months to a year. But I wasn't willing to waste a year and put Reese through the embarrassment of falling further and further behind.

My brother-in-law is a school psychologist, and he helped me find facilities where Reese could be tested privately. Even though I had help in sorting through all the things that had to be done, it was still an ordeal, and the testing cost about five hundred dollars. I wondered at the time what parents—and children—go through if they can't afford this private help. It must be agonizing to be put on a long waiting list, knowing your child needs help and the help is there, but you just can't get it.

After Reese's testing was completed, I showed the results to the school, and they said, "Oh! He does need to be in a resource class. He does have a learning disability."

I felt such relief to know Reese would finally get the help he needed. Little did I know my battle had just begun!

The school had a wonderful resource teacher for the primary grades. But Reese didn't want to be put in that class; he said he didn't want to "go to school with dummies." He would hide his work under his jacket so no one could see it. But I knew that teacher was good for Reese; I could see him improving every day. He had that teacher for several years and he thrived under her guidance, but everything changed when he moved on up to the next school for grades four through six. After one day at the new school, Reese was ready to run away from home.

I can't tell you how I knew that one school's resource program was right for Reese and the other one was all wrong, especially when he fought against going to both of them. It might have been instinct; I just don't know what else it could have been. But I listened to Reese that day, and I knew something had to be done.

So I went to the principal and said, "I need to take Reese out of this program, put him back in an average class, and work with him at home. I'll get a tutor."

The principal said, "You can't do that."

I said, "Yes, I can—and I am." I told her I had to go on mother's intuition, that my child was refusing to go to school. "I've evaluated my options," I said, "and this is what we've decided to do."

When I argued with the principal, I did have second thoughts. But I told her I would take the responsibility for my decision. If I was wrong, I said, I would be the first one to admit it and Reese could go back into the resource program. And as always, Nolan backed me up. He wasn't there for many of these struggles as the school year began, but we talked every day by phone, and he always supported me and gave me encouragement and good advice.

I wish I could say that what happened next was a wonderful, rewarding time of mother-and-son togetherness, when we put our heads together over his little workbooks and laughed and worked together and everything was rosy. But that's not the way it was.

I did work with Reese at home, and we did have times of laughing and enjoying the work. But there were lots of pouting and tears and book-slamming too.

I made arrangements with a good, understanding person—a woman I had gone to school with—to tutor Reese, and I took him to a speech therapist two days a week after school. That was hard, too, because Reese didn't want to go and neither did the other two kids who were forced to ride along. They all begged and whined and cried; it was a battle just to get all three of them in the car every time we had to go.

At night I would go through Reese's homework with him, step by step. By nine o'clock, we were both physically exhausted. Nolan was often gone or he would come in at midnight from a road trip and need me to be there to listen to him and spend time with him—and I wanted to be with him. But I was so tired . . . so very tired. When the team was in town I would rush home from the tutoring session, change clothes, and head for the ballpark. If the kids didn't have school the next day, they would go too. Otherwise, a sitter would come over.

One of the best things that happened was that we found a doctor who specialized in visual therapy, and she was a godsend to all of us. She worked wonders with Reese, doing things such as showing him a paper with shapes on it and asking him to try to duplicate the shapes. At first Reese would draw incomplete designs, but she worked with him on his fine motor skills, and he loved doing the exercises with her. She made them seem like a game.

So three days a week after school I was doing a lot of driving and listening to a lot of complaining and arguing in the car. Any mother can tell you how stressful that is, especially when you are always in a mad rush to get to whatever is next on the list: some kind of practice or lesson, dinner, homework, etc. Sometimes we ate snacks—or even dinner—in the car. Nolan could never understand why I couldn't keep the car clean or why there were French fries and empty Coke cups on the floor.

None of this was easy, and it certainly wasn't cheap, but it paid off. Today I'm so proud of the progress Reese and Reid have made. Both boys have very high IQs, and they are obviously using them. Reese now does math in his head faster than I can do it on paper. So when I look back on all the hassles we went through, I can say to myself, yes, they were hard, but they were worth it.

If I had not been able to afford eye, speech, and psychological testing for Reese, I don't know where he would be today. When I thought about that and wondered what parents do if they can't afford to find these services privately, I looked around for a way to help. Now I serve on the board of the Behavioral Health Institute to help learning-disabled kids who can't afford the private facilities and tutoring they need.

The institute, based in Waco, Texas, does research into learning disabilities, and it brings kids in from all over the region for testing, then it helps them find the assistance they need. Professionals and students from nearby Baylor University assist with the institute's work, and they compile information to help parents understand and support their children.

I know firsthand how valuable this information can be because I had to learn on my own what I could do to help my boys. For instance, I was able to work with the teachers to modify the boys' assignments. It would take hours for Reese to copy something off the board, but if you handed him the same information on a sheet of paper, he could learn it quickly and know it thoroughly. I asked his teachers to try giving him tests orally instead of written tests; I said, "He knows the material, but sometimes he can't read the questions." I was fortunate that most of his teachers were willing to help in any way they could.

There are booklets and other resources now that tell parents about ideas like this. I recommend that if parents suspect their child has a learning disability, they start asking for help right away—and they keep asking until they start seeing improvements in their child. If you aren't satisfied with the counseling, resource, or psychological facilities at your child's school, contact the state department of education to ask for information and referrals to government-sponsored programs.

The Astros

The education system is a lot wiser now than it used to be about the ways children learn; it's obvious now that not everyone learns in the same way. Unfortunately, that wasn't common knowledge when Nolan was growing up. He's had to overcome a lot of his problems on his own. In addition to some learning disabilities and his exposure to teachers who constantly compared him with his older siblings, he also had a lisp when he was a boy, and one year he had a mean teacher who was not understanding of his problems and his painful shyness.

Nolan is a very private person today, although over the years he has become much more outgoing since he's been forced to live in the spotlight. When I think of how reticent and quiet he used to be, though, I can't help but wonder if it might have something to do with those early days in school and how he was made to feel inferior.

Despite these difficulties with the boys' schooling, the kids' elementary-school years were some of my favorites. I coached Reese and Wendy's T-ball teams, and I coached Reid's Little League team for a while. I enjoyed the coaching, and I loved being with all the kids. I taught them how to stretch and then warm up by running around the field. Sometimes they would whine and say, "We don't want to run," so I would run with them. I would play little games with them to get them to work on fundamentals and reward them with sticks of gum or pieces of candy when they did something well—or when they just tried really hard. I enjoyed coaching, but when the kids got to be on different teams that had practices and games at different times on different fields, I had to give it up. It was all I could do just to get them where they were supposed to be and pick them up again. Lots of times I had to rely on my parents or my mother-in-law to help me out.

When I moved from the teams' benches to the grandstands, I sometimes had to bite my lip when the kids had coaches I didn't agree with. I know that this kind of coaching is a voluntary job, and I'm always grateful for parents who will spend their free time working with my kids and everyone else's too. But I also get frustrated when someone seems to lack the proper training. There are so many books, tapes, and other training materials out there now that I see no excuse for any coach teaching poor fundamentals and mechanics.

I also get upset about coaches who tell a kid, "You're no good; get off the field," or "If you don't catch this ball you can run ten laps," or "If you screw up you'll give me ten push-ups." I hate to see coaches using any kind of beneficial exercise—running or push-ups or whatever—as punishment. It creates a mind-set that this kind of activity is bad when, in fact, it's very beneficial. Running hard and training hard are important aspects of sports. I believe a coach's job is to teach kids to learn from their mistakes instead of putting so much pressure on them they are afraid to try for fear they will fail.

I also resented those guys who wanted seven- and eight-year-olds to pitch. If kids pitch at this age, the whole game slows down for everyone. Fewer balls are hit, and that means less activity for everyone else in the game. Batters become afraid of the ball because many of the pitchers are wild. I have even seen coaches tell their hitters not to swing the bat at all—just to stand there and try to draw a walk or get hit by a pitch. To me, that is not why kids play baseball at that age. You defeat the whole purpose of these early teaching years. Adults need to pitch during these early years. It's the only way to keep a seven-year-old center-fielder tuned into the game instead of chasing butterflies in the outfield.

And while I'm on my soapbox, I want to say a couple of words to parents and coaches who think they have to win: Back off. Winning is fine, but it's not the purpose of T-ball and Little League. That comes soon enough in junior high and high school. I also can't stand coaches who are constantly negative or who berate the kids in front of others. Usually, the kids know their weaknesses better than anyone else. They should be told what they are doing wrong and then told how to correct themselves. Positive reinforcement is the only way to get results, in my opinion. If a child doesn't listen or if he or she pouts while being corrected, it's fine to have him or her sit on the bench for a while, but it should be done in a calm, reassuring manner.

All those years of sitting in the stands and watching Nolan play baseball gave me a good taste for what was to come when our kids got involved in sports—I've put in thousands of hours on every kind of bleachers imaginable watching Reid play basketball and baseball, Reese play football and baseball, and Wendy play volleyball, softball, and basketball and also compete in swimming, diving, and gymnastics. Sometimes I consider myself a professional grandstander.

Too often it seemed I sat in the stands by myself while Nolan was out of town. I kept looking forward to the day when he would be with me and we could watch the kids' competitions *together*.

I had no way of knowing it then, in the mid-eighties, but that day was still a long way away.

Part Five

. . . .

Miracle Man

15

Leaving Houston, Bound for Glory

When Nolan and I get angry, we react in similar ways. He clams up and won't talk. I go to my room, slam the door, and pout. Although I was raised to believe that losing my temper was about the stupidest thing I could do, I'm still capable of ranting and raving a couple of times a year when frustration builds up inside me until it finally explodes in one big tirade.

Fortunately, I'm usually able to keep my rare temper tantrums private. About the only time I've lost my temper in public was in the airport in Houston when we were supposed to be leaving on a romantic getaway—the first (and last) "vacation" we ever had alone after the kids came along.

We were going to the Virgin Islands for a three-day weekend, and although I was nervous about leaving the three kids, I had found an Alvin woman we trusted to stay with them. She was an older woman, kind and gentle, who had raised five or six kids of her own. It was the first time I had left Wendy, who was only about two months old, and I was nervous about that, but I knew she would take good care of Wendy and the boys, who were one and five.

It was exhausting to make all the arrangements—change the sheets; plan the meals; write out all the schedules, doctors' phone numbers, and emergency backup plans; make sure there were enough diapers, formula, and groceries in the house; and then pack for both Nolan and me. If you're a mother of small children and you have ever tried to go on a trip without your kids, you know what I'm talking about. By the time you get everything arranged so you can leave, you're so worn out the only place you want to go is to sleep! You're too tired to even think about going to some exotic destination—but off you go anyway.

As we left the house that morning, all three kids were crying—and so was I. Reid tried to run after us, but the baby-sitter held him back. It was not the way I had pictured our departure for this romantic getaway, but I was determined to see it through.

Finally, we got to the airport, parked the car in long-term parking, and carried our bags to the gate. We thought we were there well ahead of time, but when we stepped up to the ticket desk to check in, the agent said, "Your plane just left!"

We had made the arrangements months ahead, and the airline had changed the schedule without notifying us. I looked at Nolan in shock and asked, "What are we going to do?"

"We'll go back home," he said with a shrug. "We'll start over tomorrow."

"Oh no we're not!" I answered hotly. "I am not going through that again. I've nearly killed myself getting us to this point, and I'm not going back and starting all over. I'm not going to say good-bye to the kids again. I'm not! No!"

I told Nolan we should fly on to Miami and spend the night there, then catch a flight to the Virgin Islands the next day.

"Ruth, I'm not going to spend the night in Miami when I could just as well sleep in my own bed. We're going home. We'll leave tomorrow."

Nolan picked up our bags and started walking up the corridor.

I followed after him, trying to get him to put down the bags. We were yelling at each other right there in the middle of the terminal, our arms waving, our faces turning red. I'm sure it was quite a spectacle. I told Nolan, "I *can't* go back home! I just can't do it!"

He said, "Yes you can. We're going to spend the night in our own bed and start over tomorrow. It'll be all right. Now come on; let's go."

Even now, fifteen years later, I still can't believe he talked me into going back home. I didn't speak to him all the way to Alvin.

The next morning, we did it all over again—complete with all three kids crying as we made our break. But as we drove to the airport, I got a bad feeling. It was terribly foggy in Houston, and sure enough, the flight was delayed.

Nolan said, "If we're delayed and miss the connecting flight again, we're just not going. It probably wasn't meant to be."

"Oh yes we are!" I told him. "We are going to the Virgin Islands and we are going to have a good time and we are *not* going back home until we've done it!"

I kept thinking that I had wanted to fly on to Miami the day before. If we'd done that, we would already be there for our connecting flight; it wouldn't matter that Houston was fogged in.

Finally, we were able to take off, but by the time we landed in Miami we had just five or six minutes to get to the next plane. We ran all the way, carrying our bags and dripping with sweat. I remember finally collapsing in the seat on the plane, hot, trembling, and exhausted. But by golly, we were on our way!

When we finally got to Saint John we had a wonderful time, even though all Nolan could think of was calling home and checking on the kids. Since we had missed a day of our trip we only had two days there, so it was really a short vacation. But it let us remember what it was like to be alone with each other again, just the two of us. The trip was long enough to let us know we liked it—but we wouldn't want to try it again for a while!

I remembered how mad I'd been about that almost-missed vacation when I saw Nolan's reaction in 1987 when he came home from the clubhouse under an obvious black cloud. He was as close to being livid as I'd ever seen him.

"You're not gonna believe this!" he told me, shaking his head and grimacing in a resigned sort of smile. "They've put me under a pitching limit: 115 pitches in a game, then I come out, no questions asked."

"Why?" I was as surprised as he was. I couldn't imagine why the Astros would limit how many pitches Nolan could throw in a game.

"Dick Wagner says he's trying to save my arm," Nolan replied, still shaking his head. He and Wagner, who had become the Astros' general manager in 1986, had not hit it off. Their first disagreement had come when Wagner put Nolan on the disabled list that year without even consulting him. By putting a pitch limit on Nolan in 1987, he was once again doing what he thought was best for his forty-year-old pitcher. But Nolan disagreed.

The team's 1986 season, the one in which some writers had expected them to lose a hundred games, had been instead a victory of sorts. The Astros' Mike Scott won the Cy Young award, first baseman Glenn Davis hit thirty-one home runs, and Nolan won twelve games and lost eight, striking out 194 batters in 178 innings. They won the division but lost a heartbreaking championship series to the hated Mets. Nolan had reached 253 career wins by the end of the 1986 season, but it seemed unlikely he could improve that mark when he was pitching under a 115-pitch limit, and he knew another no-hitter was probably out of the question.

He had started the 1987 season in good shape, pitching an average of 135 pitches per game without pain, and he fussed and fumed so much about the pitch limit that the Astros expanded it to 125 late in the season. Despite that restriction, Nolan still led the league in strikeouts for the first time in eight years and broke a big-league record by averaging 11.48 strikeouts per nine innings.

I watched all this and similar unsettling incidents happen month by month, and even though Wagner was fired after the 1987 season, little changed in 1988 except that after the pitch limit was lifted, Nolan led the National League in strikeouts for a career total of 4,775. Still, Nolan's relationship with the Astros management seemed to grow increasingly strained. As Nolan put it, he still wasn't jumping when Astros owner John McMullen said "jump." I knew something had to give, but I didn't like thinking about what that might mean.

Leaving Houston, Bound for Glory

Nolan had played for the Astros since the 1980 season, and he was still making big money—a million dollars a year. But several players had passed that mark soon after Nolan broke the million-dollar ceiling while Nolan's salary had stayed the same. He hadn't asked for an increase because he felt the benefits of living in Alvin and seeing his kids grow up there were worth the trade-off of working without a raise for nine seasons. Although he was growing increasingly dissatisfied, he was thinking that when his million-dollar-a-year contract expired at the end of the 1988 season, the Astros would be happy to extend it for one more year. Then maybe he would retire.

As it turned out, the Astros had other ideas. They offered to renew his contract for another year—if he would take a 20 percent cut in pay.

16

Dallas

$\mathcal{N}$olan was the starting pitcher in seventeen season-opening games, but none had a stranger countdown than his first appearance in a Texas Rangers uniform.

The parting with the Astros had been bitter. If they had just said they wanted Nolan to stay another year at the same salary, he probably would have signed on the spot. He had just about made up his mind that 1989 would be his last season anyway. Instead, faced with the Astros' offer of a 20 percent pay cut, Nolan decided to test the free-agent market, and the Astros encouraged him to do so, figuring not many teams would be interested in a forty-two-year-old pitcher who had won twelve and lost eleven in the 1988 season. But the Astros' scheme backfired on them.

The Angels, Yankees, Giants, Brewers, and Rangers all contacted Nolan's agent, Dick Moss. Our old friend Gene Autry was ready to fill up a saddlebag with money to bring him back to California. But it was hard for me to think about leaving Texas with the kids in school and all the activities they had going on.

I suppose I was the one who narrowed down the choices. I wanted him to go where he would really be wanted, not where they would just pay him a lot of money. That was why we ruled out New York—been there, done that, and neither of us wanted to go back. I knew that the California Angels wanted Nolan, and the fans and ownership there were terrific. But I just couldn't imagine commuting between California and Texas every week. My choice was the Texas Rangers.

The team had accomplished very little since it had moved in 1972 from Washington to Arlington, outside Dallas. The Rangers had finished sixth in their division in the 1988 season and lost ninety-one games. But that winter, under a new ownership group headed by George W. Bush, the Rangers had made a commitment to winning. They had traded for Julio Franco and Rafael Palmeiro, and they were delighted to think Nolan might be willing to become part of the team.

A few months later, in early 1989, Nolan signed with the Rangers for $1.6 million, double the salary he would have made had he accepted the cut the Astros offered. He had an option for $1.4 million in 1990.

All of that was behind us as the Rangers flew home from spring training, and we were expectant and excited about beginning a new season with a new team. The Rangers had a day off after the team returned from Florida, and a luncheon was planned for them then; the season opener was set for the afternoon of the following day. We spent that night—our first—in a house we had rented in Arlington.

The next morning, Nolan couldn't get out of bed.

I was still sleeping when I heard him cry out, "Ruth, something's wrong!"

I jumped out of bed, scared silly. Nolan couldn't stand up straight; he was dizzy, weaving, and seeing double. We were both terrified, thinking at first he was having a stroke or a heart attack. Nothing like this had ever happened before.

Eventually, we realized his problems had nothing to do with his heart or his brain, so we managed to move back from panic to mere anxiety. As we calmed down a little, the same unspoken thought flashed through both our minds: The Rangers had spent all this money, most of North Texas seemed excited about seeing Nolan pitch, in a few hours we were due at a team luncheon . . . and Nolan couldn't even stand up!

I helped him back into bed, then ran to the phone and called Bobby Valentine, Nolan's former Angels teammate and now the Rangers' manager. I didn't know what else to do. His wife Mary answered the phone, and she could tell from my voice that I was on the brink of hysteria. Bobby, in contrast, thought I was joking. After all, he had seen Nolan just the night before, and he'd been fine. How could anything so drastic happen the day before the opener?

I took a breath and repeated myself, slower this time: "Bobby, something is wrong. He can't walk. He can't stand. He has double vision."

Now there was dead silence on the phone. He realized I was serious. He also realized the press would have a field day with this story about the team's new acquisition.

"Don't tell anybody," he said. "Don't call *anybody*. Get him right to the doctor, and I'll have somebody meet you there."

I helped Nolan dress and get into the car, then I drove him to the doctor's office. I nervously paced around as the doctor began the tests. I couldn't imagine what could have caused such a mysterious illness so quickly, and all sorts of worst-case scenarios passed like an endless newsreel through my mind.

Finally, just after noon, the doctor determined that Nolan's condition was caused by an inner-ear problem, but it was unclear whether the problem was caused by a virus or an allergic reaction. It might have been a reaction to something he had eaten or to the fresh paint in the bedroom. We had no idea, but we were tremendously relieved that it didn't seem to be something permanent.

The doctors put Nolan on medication and said if he didn't improve overnight they would admit him to the hospital and run another battery of tests. But he did get better. He got dressed and we went to the luncheon, arriving an hour late, making an unintended grand entrance and trying to seem nonchalant about our tardiness because we were under orders from the club not to explain what had detained us.

I thought Nolan looked pale and strained, but nobody else seemed to notice. Everyone at the luncheon was caught up with opening-day fever. At the head table, Bobby Valentine kept giving me a quizzical look, asking with his eyebrows if Nolan was going to be okay, if he was going to be able to pitch.

Luckily the mysterious ailment lasted only twenty-four hours, and the next day Nolan walked out to the mound in Arlington Stadium feeling fit and confident. His first start for the Rangers was a no-decision. In the first part of the season the team had seventeen wins and only five losses. On April 23 in Toronto, Nolan went into the ninth inning without allowing a hit, then Nelson Liriano broke up the no-hitter with a triple. It was the ninth time in his career that Nolan had taken a no-hitter into the ninth inning and the fifteenth time he'd pitched a game allowing fewer than two hits.

When I couldn't go to the out-of-town games, I was usually home in Alvin, watching the game on television. If it wasn't being televised on one of the regular channels, I often watched it with neighbors who had a satellite dish. If they weren't home or weren't watching the game, I could only pick up the game on the radio, and sometimes in Alvin, depending on the weather conditions, the interference would drown out the broadcast. When that happened, I often jumped in my car and drove madly around town, adjusting the radio, trying to find a spot where I could bring in the signal more clearly.

One night I wound up in the parking lot of a supermarket three miles from my house a half-hour after it had closed. It was the only place I could hear the game without static. I was sitting there, alone, at the wheel of our station wagon parked in the empty parking lot, when one of Wendy's classmates happened to be coming out of the church across the street.

He recognized the car, saw that it was me in the front seat, alone, and immediately went to a pay phone and called our house. I would hate to guess what was going through his mind. When she answered the phone, he almost yelled, "Wendy, what's your mom doing by herself in the parking lot at the HEB store? The place is closed."

"Oh," said Wendy casually, "she's listening to the Rangers' game on the radio."

"Yeah, that's right," he said. "I forgot your dad is pitching tonight."

Dallas

In 1989, just about the first thing you saw when you drove up to Arlington Stadium was a huge (twenty-by-twenty-five-foot) picture of Nolan on the wall above the ticket offices. He was in mid-windup, preparing to deliver a pitch. The Rangers drew more than two million fans that season, an all-time record for the club, and Nolan won sixteen games and lost ten, proving he was more than a gate attraction. He showed he could still pitch.

He threw two one-hit games, took a no-hitter into the eighth inning twice, and had 301 strikeouts to lead the American League in strikeouts, just as he had led the National League the two previous seasons. Before a sellout crowd on August 22, with the temperature around one hundred degrees, Nolan went over the five-thousand-strikeout mark for his career when he struck out Oakland's Rickey Henderson.

It was a marvelous day. Nolan started the game with 4,994 strikeouts, so everyone knew it was possible that he would go over the top before the last inning. The tension rose and fell with every pitch, and I think we all enjoyed the roller-coaster ride. It wasn't one of those butterfly experiences I'd endured so often where the tension mounts and mounts and mounts—and then disappointment sets in. In this case, everyone knew it was going to happen, but no one knew exactly when that would be. On the way to the stadium that day, Nolan was so distracted that he drove right past the exit.

The first batter to strike out was José Canseco; then Dave Henderson was followed by Tony Phillips, Rickey Henderson, and Ron Hassey. Each time, the packed stands went wild with applause and madcap cheering. Ironically, Nolan struck out all five of these batters not once, but *twice* in this record-breaking game (plus a humiliating third time for Ron Hassey). It was Rickey's second at-bat that put him forever in Nolan's record book.

That night really stands out in my mind because you could feel the electricity in the air. People were buzzing around before the game, purchasing souvenir programs and T-shirts, but when the game started, no one left his seat, and there were flashbulbs popping everywhere when number five thousand was recorded. It reminded me of being in the World Series in 1969.

When it was all over that day, Nolan's career strikeout record stood at 5,007. That night we invited our family and friends back to the house for a merry celebration, and believe it or not *I cooked:* ham, corn on the cob, and hot rolls. It wasn't fancy, but it was fun.

We settled into a hectic but pleasant routine that summer, dividing our time between Alvin and Arlington. It wasn't as easy as it had been when we just had one household to maintain, but it wasn't bad; Nolan's success made up for any inconveniences we had to endure.

The hardest part was trying to remember what was where. I'd be in Alvin and reach for the bag of potato chips I knew I had just bought and then remember, *Oh yeah. That was in Arlington.* I'd buy coffee cream in Alvin, then we'd spend a week in Arlington, and the cream would be sour by the time I got back. All the traveling and the food-stocking problems made it much easier just to eat out—but even that wasn't simple.

People in Dallas were starting to recognize Nolan so we had to work at finding ways to be able to go out in public without drawing a crowd. We did best by going late and avoiding weekend nights whenever we could. Sometimes I made reservations in my name, hoping we could slip in unnoticed, but these surprise appearances sometimes caused such a commotion we were besieged for autographs throughout our meal. Other times, I used Nolan's name and asked the restaurant if we could have a table in the back or somewhere we wouldn't be so visible. But that sometimes backfired too because, as often as not, the restaurant staff would then have a pile of stuff to be autographed when we arrived.

It was a rare evening when we ate out and our meal was not interrupted. One time a man even pulled a chair up to our table, uninvited, and made himself comfortable. I always wished Nolan would say, "I'm eating right now, but if you'll just give me a little time to finish I'll be glad to sign something for you later." Sometimes he did say that, but not nearly enough to suit me. Whenever we came out of a restaurant and found people waiting there for Nolan, hoping for an autograph, I always thanked them for waiting and letting us eat our meal without being interrupted.

I know it can be said that Nolan "asked" for this problem when he stayed in a high-visibility career for so long and when he chose to do commercial endorsements that made his face familiar all across the country. I understand that point of view. On the other hand, I think all people owe each other a few common courtesies, and being able to eat a meal in public with your family is one of them.

Nolan's increasing popularity was also due, in part, to the fact that he was finally with a ball club that knew the value of promoting its star players. It was something the Astros had never quite recognized, and it created one of those Catch-22s that make life so interesting. Nolan's talents were finally being recognized and promoted the way I'd always thought they could be. The result was a lot more fame and celebrity—and a lot less privacy.

But the worst—and best—were still to come.

17

Field of Dreams

I don't remember when the idea came to me—but it didn't come in time for much planning. It was June 1990, and school had just let out for the summer. Nolan was in Oakland, facing the World Series champions in his second start after coming off the disabled list. I don't know why the urge came over me as it did, but suddenly I just felt I needed to be in Oakland, and I wanted the kids to come with me.

So, on June 11, Reese, Wendy, and I hurried to catch a plane at the last minute; I was sorry Reid couldn't come, too, but he was pitching in a summer league before going to Alaska to play with the Anchorage Bucs. He took us to the airport and said he'd be watching the game on television with some of his teammates.

It was chilly in the Oakland Coliseum that evening, and I knew that wouldn't be good for Nolan's back, which was still sore from the stress fracture that had put him on the disabled list for three weeks. Just as everyone seemed to be thinking he was out for good, his back had loosened up and he was put back in the rotation. Still, I couldn't help worry a little that he wasn't in top shape, and I knew that Rangers catchers Gene Petralli and Mike Stanley were out with injuries, so

161

Nolan would be pitching to a new catcher, John Russell, who had been cut from the Braves and had been called out of a high school coaching job to join the Rangers only a month before. He had never caught for Nolan before that night.

Wendy and I hurried to find our seats in the stands, and Reese, then fourteen, headed for the clubhouse to suit up as a bat boy. I knew how excited he was about the new job the Rangers had given him, and I was hoping he wouldn't say the wrong thing or bother anyone. But I really didn't need to worry; he had been around ballplayers all his life and knew how to behave.

As I watched Nolan warm up before the game began, I couldn't help but wonder about the strong feeling that had made me hurry to the airport earlier that day. *Was it God's way of telling me Nolan would need me here for comfort and support? Was he going to injure himself tonight? Why had I felt so compelled to come?*

But by the third inning, my mood was changing. The Rangers had scored three runs, and Oakland had only managed to get one man on base—Walt Weiss, on a walk. By the fifth inning the score was 5-0 Rangers, the A's still hadn't gotten any more base runners, and I finally realized it wasn't worry that was making my stomach feel queasy.

It was those old familiar butterflies.

I wasn't the only one who had begun to recognize the magic that danced invisibly around the coliseum that night. Sitting beside me, Wendy looked at me often, flashing a wide, nervous smile, and Nolan said later he realized early in the game he had "good stuff" that night.

Reese also sensed the potential that seem to flicker over the mound. What people could see on television that I missed from the stands was the sight of Reese rubbing his dad's back in the dugout between innings. He had been watching the first part of the game on the big television screen in the clubhouse, and when Nolan hadn't allowed a hit after four innings, Reese discreetly eased himself down to the bench and began massaging his dad's back. It made him feel he was contributing, and I know it was comforting to Nolan to have him there. The network cameras returned to the scene again and again, and Rangers manager

Bobby Valentine said later that that father-and-son image was the thing he would remember most about this night.

I didn't know what was going on until we saw some of the highlights later. Then I could also see how uncomfortable Nolan looked early in the game, until the no-hitter started to loom in front of him. Then everything changed.

They clocked his fastball in the high eighties at the start of the game. By the sixth inning, it was in the mid-nineties. This time his curveball wasn't working, so he rarely threw it; instead he relied on his fastball and changeup.

With one out in the ninth inning, Rickey Henderson stepped to the plate. He was batting .342, and he surely was hoping for a chance to repay Nolan for making Rickey his five-thousandth strikeout victim the previous season.

The count went to 2-2.

Rickey hit a slow grounder to shortstop Jeff Huson, who scooped up the roller and fired it to first for the out.

The butterflies had turned into dive bombers. *One more out to go.*

Willie Randolph obliged with a fly to Ruben Sierra . . . and Nolan became the oldest pitcher in history to throw a no-hitter, an unbelievable sixth for his career.

He had struck out fourteen batters, all of them swinging, and walked two. It was his first no-hitter since September 26, 1981, a record for the longest time between no-hitters. It had been seventeen years since his first no-hitter in 1973, which created another record: Nolan had pitched no-hitters in three different decades, something no other pitcher had done.

It was an incredible night. The only things that could have made it better would have been if Reid could have been with us and if we could have been in Arlington, where the fans had become such loyal supporters.

When we finally got back to the hotel, we hustled up to the room and ordered lots of food, the kids enthusiastically reliving the game play by play as we all stuffed ourselves with a veritable feast. Ironically, the only one who didn't get into the celebration was Nolan. He just wanted to rest his aching back, but he encouraged us to celebrate for him. And we did.

You might think when he had set all these records, Nolan would be content to just ease off a little and ride into the sunset with a feeling of contentment and peace. But it always seemed there was one more milepost to be reached, one more record to be broken.

On July 20, Nolan had the 299th win of his career; it was his tenth win that season in fifteen starts, and he was pitching in pain. Only nineteen pitchers in the history of baseball had won 300 games during their professional careers. Now it seemed obvious (at least to me) that Nolan would be number twenty.

Many fans and some reporters were actually debating whether Nolan had suddenly improved with age. It was true that he had added a pitch, called the circle change. Joe Nuxhall, a longtime broadcaster for the Cincinnati Reds, taught him the pitch that Mario Soto had used so successfully. Nuxhall was a former big-league pitcher himself; at age fifteen during the war years, he had been the youngest ever to start a game in the major leagues.

Nolan had learned the pitch in 1981 and had worked on it, typically, for nearly four years before he began using it in a game. By the time he moved to the Rangers, it gave him an effective third pitch to go with his fastball and slider. But we both knew that the circle change was not the reason for his headlines and his ever-growing fame and wave of endorsements. No, he had been around for nearly a quarter of a century, and the records coming to him now were the result of his longevity. Nolan didn't kid himself about that sort of thing.

The big one was going to be the three-hundredth win, partly because that accomplishment was, in itself, a Hall of Fame number. It would also be a personal pleasure because a lot of his critics had doubted that he could reach that goal even if he pitched forever. Also, unlike no-hitters or strikeouts, the three-hundredth win made for an easy countdown. Once he reached number 299, the goal was in his sights.

Nearly five hundred members of the national media descended

on Arlington for Nolan's next start. He faced the Yankees before a sold-out stadium that hummed with the sounds of anticipation and excitement.

Several of our friends and family members from Alvin were there that night, along with Nolan's sister, Lynda, who lived nearby and who tried to attend all his games. Afterward, we planned to meet at a local Mexican restaurant in Arlington to (we hoped) celebrate. The restaurant had even decorated a huge cake for Nolan.

But the game started off badly for the Rangers when the Yankees' Deion Sanders led off with a triple—and things went downhill from there. Nolan couldn't find any consistency. He was wild in the strike zone and kept getting worse and worse. The Yankees scored seven runs, and the game wound up as one of Nolan's worst appearances of the year, a no-decision. Nolan felt terrible, not that he hadn't broken three hundred but that he had disappointed the fans, who had become like a huge, extended family to him.

Even though the game was a huge disappointment for Nolan, he dutifully joined the rest of us at the restaurant and tried to eat while visiting with his friends, shifting his focus from the game he'd just come from to the one ahead of him. Nolan was always great about burying a game once it was over, but that was much harder for the family and me.

Now that Nolan is retired and is more of a fan himself, he sees how emotionally draining such things can be on a family, and he's much more sympathetic. Recently, after one of Wendy's volleyball losses, he was in a foul mood all night and the next day. He just had to tell himself not to let it bother him so much, but most competitive, driven people have similar feelings I'm sure.

Nolan's next start in pursuit of the three-hundredth win was in Milwaukee, where more than 250 press credentials were issued for the July 31 game and the stadium was packed with a standing-room-only crowd of 55,097 fans. I was delighted that several friends were coming north for the game. Among them was Don Sanders, a Houston investment broker and former Astros' shareholder who chartered a private plane to bring several of our pals; Mickey Herskowitz, a book author and writer for the *Houston Post;* and Jim Stinson, who invited my sister, brother, and father to accompany him in his plane.

What we all wanted Nolan to be able to avoid was having the chase for the three-hundredth win drag out. We knew that all the attention focused on the magic number—and the stress that accompanied it—could wear him out. And the truth was, while it seemed like a milepost the press and the fans expected, Nolan was trying hard to treat it just like he would any other game. When reporters repeatedly asked him how meaningful the number would be to him, Nolan tried to explain that he hadn't thought about it.

Nolan's dreams have always been modest. "When I broke in with the New York Mets," he told them, "my goal was to play four years because that was what it took to qualify for the pension plan. And there were many times when I thought that was in doubt. For example, when I went to Houston as a free agent in 1980, I asked for a three-year contract, and I felt I'd be out of the game by the end of it."

Nolan said he could recall hearing only one pitcher ever say that his goal in life was to win 300 games—Don Sutton, still needing 50 when he joined the Astros in 1981 and ending his career several years later with 324. "But that was never my goal," Nolan insisted.

I really think that was Nolan's way of keeping things in perspective and on an even keel. One of the most difficult things about being a baseball player is keeping yourself emotionally balanced. If you put too much importance on one particular game, you risk being extremely disappointed if you lose. On the other hand, the adrenaline rush and elation you feel after a victory is thrilling. For Nolan, trying to keep his focus the same for every game was the best way for him to keep his highs and lows on a more moderate level. For me, keeping things stable at home during this time was like managing a circus. Everyone wanted an interview or a comment or a new angle, and lots of people tried to use me as their contact with Nolan.

But even if he was trying to stay cool about nearing three hundred wins, the rest of us were clearly excited for him. And finally, he admitted that it was a milestone to be appreciated.

"It's not just another game," he conceded, looking around the room at the Stadium Club at newspeople from across the country. "I'd like to win it tomorrow with one of my best starts of the year, if not my best. But I have to keep it in perspective and not try to do more than I can."

This was Nolan's way of saying he takes nothing for granted. Those piercing eyes of his seldom gazed beyond the next inning, the next batter, or the next pitch. Yet I was well aware of how sweet it would be for him to reach coveted number three hundred. The way he looked at it, three teams had given up on him. In 1971, the Mets figured he would never harness all that power. Then, in a decision that caused him so much bitterness it still haunted Nolan for years, Buzzie Bavasi, the Angels' general manager, had explained how the team would replace Nolan: "We'll go out and get two eight-and-seven pitchers." He had been thirty-three then. The Houston Astros thought there was still life in the old workhorse at forty-two, but not a million dollars' worth of life, and they had let him leave.

He went over the top this last day of July 1990, throwing mostly fastballs to beat the Brewers, 11-3. He left the game to a standing ovation in the eighth inning with the Rangers ahead by only 5-3. Then, in the ninth inning, his teammates came through to seal the victory when Julio Franco hit a grand-slam homer. The Brewers could console themselves over their loss by counting their largest gate of the season.

Most of the fans had wanted one of Nolan's masterpiece games. At the least, they had wanted him to finish what he started. Instead, he gave them what he always does: an honest night's labor. He threw 146 pitches, struck out eight, and allowed six hits. In the end, everyone in County Stadium seemed to be a Ryan fan; the ballpark echoed with "NO-lan! NO-lan!"

I thought it was sort of poetic that the Rangers won by eight runs and Nolan had to sweat for it. He had learned years ago not to expect any handouts; he would just keep picking up his lunch bucket and going to work until the job was done.

And while I'm bragging on him—and at the risk of sounding way too biased—I think his number of career wins should have been closer to four hundred. He was, as others pointed out, a no-hit pitcher who spent most of his career with no-hit teams. He prided himself not just on winning, but on pitching into the late innings and keeping his team in the game. There were many times in earlier years and with the designated-hitter rule when Nolan threw two hundred pitches or more in a game—or stayed for ten or eleven innings, hoping to finish what he had started, always showing his dogged determination. He was always a real "gamer" who pitched many times when he was not physically 100 percent. Nowadays, when I see players who want to sit out a game with a "headache" (possibly on the day they have to face a Roger Clemens) or who don't feel like playing (maybe they stayed out all night), I don't have a lot of sympathy.

The achievements of that magical 1990 season helped ease some of the pain that had scarred the year's beginning. In January, Nolan had gone to Dallas to work on some business related to the ranch when his sister, a counselor at Alvin High School, called and asked to speak to him. When I told her he'd gone to Dallas, she drew in a long breath. "Oh, Ruth," she said, "it's Mama."

Nolan had called his mother that morning on his way to Dallas, as he did every morning during the winter. He had gotten no answer but assumed she was outside in the yard or running errands.

His sister Jean had gotten no answer either, when she made her daily call, so she had gone over to check on her mother. After Nolan's dad had died in 1970 his mother had continued to live alone in the house where Nolan had grown up. She had done well, despite a serious accident a few years before, and she was devoted to her family.

That morning Jean found the car still in the garage; the coffee had been made, but no one answered her call. She finally found her mother lying on the bed, fully dressed. She had apparently gotten up for the day and done her chores but returned to lie down when she didn't feel well. That's where she died.

My sister, Lynn, and I each took one of my kids and went door to door through the neighborhood, breaking the news to each friend and neighbor. She was such a good friend to so many, we wanted to tell each one individually. I wanted to shield my children from the pain of their grandmother's death, but they wanted to go to her house with me, and I let them. Wendy helped us tell the neighbors, and Reese helped the people from the funeral home; I realize now this was a good way for them to deal with the pain of losing this dear woman we all loved so much. Their concern and love were a great comfort to me.

That night, I met Nolan at the airport with the bad news. "I'm sorry," I told him. "Your mother passed away this morning."

It was such a shock for him—for all of us—because it was so sudden and so unexpected—and because it was such a devastating loss. She was the family's most loyal supporter, the most enthusiastic cheerleader, the source of undying love. As Reid put it, "Wherever we went, Grandma Ryan was our home base. She was our anchor."

Even in death she gave us a gift—a reminder of how quickly life passes, how much our loved ones mean to us, how important it is to cherish them and take time to be with them, even if it requires a special effort to make it happen.

There is a story people in Alvin love to tell, and it explains the town and Nolan's family and why people feel the way they do about them. It involves one of our neighbors, Lucinda Ackley, who grew up three houses down from the Ryans.

Lucinda was a freshman in high school in 1976 when Nolan was getting his first touch of stardom with the Angels. One day after school she took a plastic Angels batting helmet to Nolan's mom and asked if she would ask Nolan to autograph it for her. Martha Ryan said she would. A year passed, then two. Lucinda was too embarrassed to go back for the helmet. Eventually she graduated from high school, got married, and started a family.

One Halloween night, as Lucinda was taking her four-year-old son and her three-year-old daughter around the old neighborhood for trick-or-treating, they knocked on the door of the Ryan house.

Mrs. Ryan answered, saw who it was, and said, "Oh, Lucinda, wait right here. I've got something for you." Lucinda, now a secretary at the high school, waited patiently, having no idea what was to come. But as Mrs. Ryan hurried back to the front door, Lucinda's eyes grew as big as saucers. "She brought back the helmet, signed, still in the plastic wrap," Lucinda told us with a merry laugh. "She said, 'I'm sorry I didn't get this to you sooner.'"

It had taken awhile, but she hadn't forgotten.

With both of their parents gone, the six Ryan siblings faced one of the most difficult duties any adult children can ever know—cleaning out their parents' house and preparing it for sale. I know the four sisters did most of that heartbreaking work, but Nolan and Robert were involved, too, and it was a poignant, memory-filled time of sadness and loss.

Nolan took the death of his mother hard, but he kept much of what he felt inside. That was his way. We have grown very close during more than two decades of marriage, but there are some times when Nolan doesn't want to talk, when he withdraws into himself and holds in his feelings. That was one of those times.

I've learned how to "read" Nolan pretty well after all these years, and he's fairly good at discerning my feelings most of the time too. I know, for instance, that he usually doesn't like to talk much after a game; that was probably something that took a while for me to understand, and a long time ago I probably talked more than he'd like after games. I would be eager to go through it all again with him and discuss what had happened, what it looked like from the stands, and what it was like out on the field. But so often Nolan is bombarded by reporters with questions about his pitching, about the game, about his records, about the team's standings and prospects, that when he gets in the pickup to go home, all he usually wants to do is drive in silence. Usually it's just the two of us on the way home. Sometimes I would turn on the radio real low and listen to the postgame wrapup—maybe they would replay an interview with Nolan or one of the other players, and I'd enjoy hearing what they had to say.

With most jobs, if a person has a bad day at the office, he or she can come home and tell a spouse and maybe enjoy a sympathetic ear. But if Nolan had a bad day at the "office," the whole world knew about it, wanted to talk about it, criticize it, and offer opinions about how to fix it.

Once, Nolan had left a game early after getting shelled for eight runs or so, and when we climbed into the car after the game there was a thick, awkward silence. Finally, I said, "That sure was a nice pickoff move you made to first base early in the game."

Nolan started the engine, cocked his head, and gave me a big, lop-sided grin, so pathetic had been my attempt at cheering him up. Yet, in a clumsy way, I guess I had.

It was always hard for me to keep from asking the questions that were most important to me, especially during those last three years when he was hurting almost all the time. I wanted to ask, "Are you all right, Nolan? Does your arm hurt? Is your back okay? Are your ribs sore?" But I tried not to ask.

Even at home I could tell sometimes that Nolan was in pain, but I learned not to fuss over him or treat him like an invalid. On the other hand, when he couldn't sleep at night, when he got out of bed in the morning and couldn't straighten up, or when I'd see a grimace of pain flash over his face, I had the feeling that even though he didn't want to talk about it, he wanted me there with him. So if he was at home and he was hurting, I tried to be there; I let the grocery shopping go awhile and canceled appointments I had made.

Sometimes those days got very long and frustrating, especially during the winter of 1989–90, when we were buried under a blizzard of *stuff*. Suddenly our house was full of all sorts of paraphernalia: balls, hats, photographs, and assorted other memorabilia to be autographed, fan letters everywhere, products to be considered for endorsement, and assorted odds and ends everywhere—on the kitchen table, the dining room table, the kitchen counter, the dressers. And while all the *stuff* was accumulating, the phone was ringing off the hook.

There were days when Nolan was hurting and didn't want to talk to anyone and I did nothing but answer the phone and the mail. I got tired of it. *Real* tired. I guess that winter when the "stuff blizzard" hit was also the winter of my discontent. Sometimes I literally dreamed of running away from home.

That was also Reid's senior year of high school, and I was very involved in his basketball and baseball games, his Project Graduation party, and his other activities. All this involvement took a lot of time and effort, even though it was a labor of love. I also had emotional moments thinking about my firstborn growing up and leaving the nest, wondering how I would handle the quiet, the void that would result from his leaving home. It was, overall, a very unsettled time, to say the least. I worried that Reese and Wendy were not getting enough attention, but they were going through the crazy junior high years, so I didn't know if it was my reduced attention toward them or those unpredictable adolescent hormones that were causing the craziness.

The phone was a constant irritant. Sometimes I would answer and it would be someone Nolan didn't want to talk to, but I wouldn't know that and I would hand him the phone. After a few confrontations about that, I got so I would automatically say, "He's not here, but I will have him call you." I told him, "I can't read your mind. I don't know who you do and don't want to talk to, and I don't care."

One day I was working around the house, wearing an old shirt, stained shorts, no makeup, and my hair uncombed, when a large van pulled into our property carrying a load of kids. Nolan saw the van and told me to tell them he wasn't home. A few of the kids climbed off the bus with a couple of grownups, who explained that they were with a church group on a scavenger hunt. "We just need Nolan to come to the door and let us take a picture of him," one of the men said, "so we can prove we saw him."

I apologized and started explaining that Nolan was not there. Out of the corner of my eye I was aware that a corner of one curtain had been pulled back from the window behind me; I assumed Nolan, who had just told me he wasn't there, would stay hidden long enough for the bus to drive out of sight. But just as I was finishing my cover story and inviting them to drop by another time, the door swung open and there was Big Tex.

"Aw, yeah, I'll be glad to do that," he said as I stormed past him into the kitchen. I gave him a look that would exterminate head lice as he suddenly put on his Mr. Wonderful smile as the Wicked Witch of the West, after telling these innocent children he wasn't home, disappeared in a puff of rage.

Finally, I told Nolan something had to change. I told him that all the little white lies and the answering-service duties and my being responsible for the fan mail were making me feel very unimportant, like a servant-secretary. One day I said, "Nolan, I cannot answer that phone one more time. I can't take care of the dogs, kids, houses, and everything else and be your secretary. I don't *want* to be your secretary. I want to be your wife, the one you share your time with, the person you love. I don't want to be the office manager who organizes your phone messages and answers all your fan mail."

I threatened to throw everything away if he didn't get an office and a secretary. That was when we hired someone to be Nolan's personal assistant, a capable woman who keeps his office and his schedule running smoothly and his fan mail under control. Things have changed for the better since we hired someone whose full-time job is taking care of all the things I used to try to handle in addition to being a wife and a mother. I'm still constantly battling a deluge of *stuff,* but I no longer feel like someone who's being taken advantage of.

Looking back, I can see how fortuitous it was that we got these issues resolved when we did. As we rearranged priorities and drew new lines of responsibility, it was as if we were hurrying to respond to some unheard but deeply perceived voice that was whispering, "You ain't seen nuthin' yet!"

18

Bush League

*W*hen the call came to our office from the White House, our secretary, Kim Spilman, was visibly excited. She transferred the call to Nolan, who spoke directly to President George Bush, whom he has known since the late sixties when Nolan was in New York and George Bush was ambassador to the United Nations. Bush's uncle, Herbert Walker, was a minority owner of the Mets, and his son, George W. Bush, is one of the owners of the Rangers (as well as being the newly elected governor of Texas).

The president was calling to invite us to a state dinner at the White House for Queen Margrethe II and Prince Henrik of Denmark! I am very grateful to President and Mrs. Bush for our memories of that night, February 20, 1991. What a great honor and privilege Nolan and I felt to be included in such a memorable evening.

Our invitation included not only attending the dinner, but also staying overnight in the White House. Previously we had turned down a couple of similar invitations due to Nolan's baseball schedule, but this time Nolan felt that, due to the personal nature of the invitation at such a busy time in the president's life (this was during the Persian

Gulf War), we should attend if at all possible. Of course, I agreed wholeheartedly!

As any woman would do, my first thought was, *What am I going to wear?* After all, I didn't exactly have any "meet-the-queen" gowns hanging in my closet! I did have some short evening dresses, but the attire was to be black tie/formal with the women wearing long gowns.

Since I did not want to look like a prom queen, mother of the bride, or Miss America glitzy, I began my search for the perfect dress: elegant yet comfortable, appropriate and lovely yet non-revealing. Somehow these prerequisites tended to eliminate practically everything in the stores! Another problem was that this was just after New Year's, so the stores were already filled with spring fashions and bathing suits rather than the winter dress I needed. Even though I searched hard at some very nice stores, I couldn't find anything. I was getting desperate when a friend told me about Loehmann's, a discount store that carries eveningwear with the labels cut out. It's *not* a fancy place—it doesn't even have dressing rooms!

But that's where I spotted a long, black dress with beading along the neckline and a peplum ruffle. I took it off the rack, paid the cashier $125, and took it straight to my mom's house to ask her to shorten the sleeves. When the alterations were finished, I felt like Cinderella getting ready for the ball. As for my prince, all Nolan needed was to get his tux cleaned and buy a new dress shirt and some cuff links, then we were in business.

When we arrived at the airport in Washington, we were met at the gate by our White House driver. Due to the Persian Gulf War, there was added security everywhere, and we were checked out thoroughly before even our official White House car was allowed to drive through the gates.

Except for the scaffolding on parts of the building that were undergoing a face-lift, the White House looked beautiful that day as we rode up the drive to the entrance framed by two huge, old magnolia trees. As we stepped out of the car, I was overwhelmed by feelings of patriotic pride and thoughts of our troops overseas. We both felt extremely lucky to be there.

As we were being led upstairs to our sleeping quarters in the Lincoln Bedroom, I tried to take in all my surroundings at once. Every painting, portrait, bronze, and other work of art seemed to come to life as we passed by, and the scent of freshly cut floral arrangements permeated the air and added extra beauty to every room. I was in awe of everything.

The Lincoln Bedroom is actually a suite that includes a huge bedroom, a bathroom, and a living room with high ceilings, beautiful floral rugs in soft greens and yellows, and priceless antiques everywhere. Green moiré drapes gave the tall windows a soft, elegant look. Antique sitting chairs, small tables, and beautiful old lamps made me feel as if I had gone back in time. An old Bible on the table was dated 1799, and most of the books were so fragile-looking I was almost afraid to touch them. The headboard on our bed, made of rosewood with ornately carved birds and flowers, was the most impressive thing in the room, so large it nearly reached the ceiling. Mrs. Bush later told us that Mary Todd Lincoln had purchased it and the matching dresser because she liked to shop and it was the most expensive one she could find.

Above the antique mantle clock was a bronze plaque that had been placed there during the administration of President Theodore Roosevelt to remind visitors the room had been the scene of the signing of the Emancipation Proclamation. There were portraits of Mary Todd Lincoln, Abraham Lincoln, and Andrew Jackson on the walls, and in the corner of the bedroom was a glass case that contained the speech President Lincoln had delivered at the national cemetery in Gettysburg on November 19, 1863. In March 1864 he had prepared this fifth and final copy, the only one to be titled, signed, and dated, for reproduction for a war charity.

As we read it over on February 20, 1991, in the midst of the Persian Gulf War, the Gettysburg Address had new meaning. I became misty-eyed as I read over the familiar, handwritten words.

We were just beginning to unpack our bags when we heard footsteps coming down the hall and a voice calling loudly, "Yoo-hoo! Yoo-hoo!" As we turned our heads toward the door, we were pleasantly surprised to see Barbara Bush standing in the doorway in her blue jogging suit with her dog, Millie, at her side.

Friendly and down to earth, Mrs. Bush immediately made us feel comfortable. She told us if we didn't like our bed she would have another one made up next door. Of course we told her the Lincoln bed was just fine!

A few minutes later, another couple, Armando and Margurite Codina, arrived and moved into the bedroom across the hall. Mrs. Bush introduced us to these friends of their son Jeb, and we had a friendly chat in the hall. We laughed as she told us about the time the Codinas had been invited to an informal dinner at the White House but mistakenly arrived there resplendent in formal, black-tie attire. This time, Mrs. Codina said, she had made her husband call three times just to make sure about the dress for this event.

Standing there chatting in the hallway of the White House, I thought how refreshing it was to have a first lady who was so warm and candid, self-assured and able to laugh at herself, and very adept at making others feel at ease. I have great admiration and respect for Barbara Bush.

Millie, who had just been out for a walk, was soon met by Ranger, the president's rambunctious dog, who bounded down the hall to join the fun, with the president himself not far behind. He cordially greeted us and asked us if we would like to tour the grounds while they let the dogs get some more exercise. I don't know who was more excited, Ranger or me! As we rode the elevator to the ground level, the dogs were barking excitedly and President Bush was reprimanding them, telling them to "settle down and behave." Sounded like home to me.

Security was very tight; Secret Service people seemed to be everywhere, but we certainly enjoyed our personal tour of the White House grounds. As Mrs. Bush, Maggie Codina, and I made small talk, President Bush showed us the tennis court, swimming pool, workout room, and, of course, his horseshoe pit. We also visited a little garden area where children of former presidents had made handprints in the sidewalk. We saw the East Lawn of the White House, where various ceremonies are held, and we walked by the rose garden.

Back inside, I tried again to absorb everything I saw and embed it in my memory. I didn't want to forget a single thing. I was fascinated by the beauty of the White House, the essence of grandeur, but I especially loved the many little personal touches that gave it a feel of "hominess." Family pictures dotted the walls in many of the family living areas, and pictures of children and grandchildren filled the president's personal office and private retreat. I noticed an oil painting of bluebonnets on the wall (his own touch of Texas) and a watercolor of the Bushes' Kennebunkport home in Maine.

As our tour continued, I savored every moment. There were many people bustling about in preparation for the reception and dinner scheduled for later that evening. The large dining area was being set up, and musicians were preparing for the evening's entertainment. Beautiful floral arrangements graced every table and every room. The Green Room, the Red Room, and the Blue Room were filled with *objets d'art* and reminders of past presidents, including portraits of Presidents Johnson, Carter, Ford, and Kennedy.

The official portrait of Nancy Reagan in a long, flowing red gown made her look so fragile and thin. I asked Mrs. Bush if she had already had her portrait done, and she said, "Not yet," but added that she had decided on the artist, a young American woman. She said she had thought about having Millie in the portrait with her but worried that since Millie was ill with lupus it might not be a good idea. Then Mrs. Bush mused that she had better "hurry up and have it done, because I'm getting older by the minute!" Such comments made her seem "real"; I found myself liking her a lot.

President Bush asked if we would like to see the upstairs areas where his grandchildren usually stayed when they visited. That was such a treat! In one room was a pool table, and in another, larger playroom there were dozens of games and stuffed animals as well as a television and Nintendo. A small kitchen with large windows held a small refrigerator and had enough room to make snacks—truly a child's dream play area. Several small bedrooms opened off the hallway, and I noticed little pillows on the beds monogrammed with the grandchildren's names. At the end of the hall was a little ramp (probably used by the kids for running up and sliding down). We also saw the White House viewing room where family members and friends could spend time watching movies and (undoubtedly) munching popcorn.

After the tour, Nolan and I went back to the Lincoln Bedroom to lay out our clothes and prepare for dinner. Just before she left us, Mrs. Bush showed me the guestlist for the state dinner, an impressive collection of prominent officials and well-known celebrities. She gently informed me that Nolan and I would be sitting at different tables. *There goes my security blanket,* I thought. I couldn't help but grow nervous, just thinking that Ruth Elsie Holdorff from Alvin, Texas, would be seated next to Walter Cronkite and Secretary of State James Baker!

Mrs. Bush tried to ease my mind. "Don't worry, Ruth," she told me. "Both of those men are fellow Texans, and you'll probably have a lot in common."

I kept hearing my mom's soothing voice whispering in the back of my head, *Ruthie, just be yourself, and you'll be fine.*

Mrs. Bush also told me I would go through the receiving line behind my husband (or the "principal," as they say) and that I should address the queen as "Your Majesty" and the prince as "Your Royal Highness." I felt like an actress preparing for opening night! Even Nolan was a little nervous as he heard his dinner assignment. He was to be seated at the queen's table next to President Bush and *Today Show* newcomer, Katie Couric.

As we went downstairs and entered the large reception room, our names were announced: "Honorable guests Mr. and Mrs. Nolan Ryan."

I felt momentarily important as we made small talk with General Colin Powell and his wife, CNN president Tom Johnson, and Katie Couric and her husband. Katie was pregnant with her first child, and she, too, made me feel at ease when she told us about her "rented" maternity evening dress.

At one point during the cocktail party a woman reporter stopped me and asked who had designed my gown. I certainly didn't want to tell her that I didn't know because the label was cut out and that I had bought it at a discount store! I thought, *Of all the people here, why did* *she pick me to ask that question! Why didn't she ask that other guest, the woman who had told me her daughter had picked out her dress—an $8,000 designer gown?*

Luckily I didn't have to answer because about that time all heads seemed to turn at once toward the door as a suntanned and very handsome Don Johnson and stunningly beautiful Melanie Griffith made their entrance. Melanie's dress was truly a Hollywood show-stopper (judging by the looks on the faces of most of the men in the room). Try to picture it: a low-cut, off-the-shoulder gold lamé sheath that was the shortest, tightest "formal" evening gown I'd ever seen. It was extremely difficult not to stare. I don't want to sound catty (even if I did feel like a Sunday school teacher next to her), Melanie Griffith would look beautiful in a feed sack, but I wondered if she shouldn't have worn something a little more appropriate.

This was the quote that appeared in the *Washington Post* the next day: "The celebrity attraction of last night's guestlist had to be Melanie Griffith, who was poured into a low-cut gold dress guaranteed to upstage any number of luminaries."

As one appreciative soul quipped, "That was a great dress she was almost wearing."

The second most dazzling sight that night was the jewelry worn by Queen Margrethe, a tall, stunning, and truly regal woman dressed in an elegant red velvet dress and wearing a necklace, earrings, brooch, and matching tiara made of the biggest diamonds and pearls I had ever seen.

When dinner started I was apprehensive about doing the right thing and using the proper silverware. Luckily James Baker, seated on my right, was served first, and I just watched him and did what he did! The menu included lobster medallions, Gruyère bow ties, crown roast of lamb, and raspberry soufflé with vanilla sauce and fresh raspberries.

At the end of dinner we were treated to a beautiful violin serenade by the Washington National Symphony. Then we were ushered to an adjoining room for coffee and after-dinner drinks. Finally, we were entertained by Frederica Von Stade's incredible operatic voice, including an unforgettable rendition of "Ave Maria." Champagne was served after the entertainment, and although a few persons were dancing, we decided to call it a night.

When we went upstairs into the parlor next-door to our room, President and Mrs. Bush invited us to sit and visit with their son Marvin, and his wife, Margaret, their daughter Dorothy Le Blond (now Dorothy Koch), the Codinas, and Don Johnson and Melanie Griffith. I sat next to Melanie, and we chatted about her children, their new home in Aspen, and her new movie. She seemed embarrassed when her husband mentioned the tattoo on her ankle. She claimed she had it done in a moment of weakness.

Around midnight, the president, looking weary by then, suggested that we all take a brisk walk outside around the driveway (with the dogs) and then call it a night. He pulled some Texas Rangers, Houston Astros, and Denver Broncos jackets out of a closet for us ladies to wear over our gowns, and off we went for the finale to one of the most memorable evenings of my life.

When we returned to the Lincoln Bedroom a short while later, it took us a while to go to sleep as we incredulously relived all the events of the day. It truly seemed as if we'd spent a day living in a fairy tale.

But I knew that tomorrow my carriage would, most likely, turn back into a pumpkin.

19

The Fame

$\mathcal{A}$s March 1991 became April, Nolan was about the most nervous I had ever seen him.

He was preparing for an exhibition game, nothing that would matter in the record books, but something that would, for one short span of time, completely consume our family. The event was an April 2 match-up between the Rangers and the University of Texas at the university's Disch-Falk Field in Austin.

The starting lineup would include Nolan, pitching for the Rangers, and our son Reid, a freshman at UT, as the starting pitcher for the Longhorns.

Nolan didn't say much, but I knew he was concerned about two things. He didn't want the game to turn into a farce, and he didn't want Reid, then eighteen, to be embarrassed. In the meantime, Reid was concerned that his dad might injure himself or pull a muscle playing on a college diamond with aluminum bats in a game the Rangers had scheduled as a courtesy to the university.

I was concerned about both of them, and I was upset because it seemed obvious to me that the school was using Reid. Otherwise why would the coaches make a big deal about starting Reid, a freshman who had only pitched three or four innings all season, in a game against a major-league team in front of a sellout crowd?

When Nolan had first mentioned the game to me, I'd said, "Oh, that's nice." But I hadn't realized how much the game would be promoted. As the hype reached unreal proportions, I began to feel that Reid was being thrown to the wolves. After all, he was far down on the roster of a team that had several good, more-experienced players, and the coaches hadn't even put Reid in any practice games to let him prepare himself.

I wasn't happy, but the game was scheduled, and both Nolan and Reid seemed to accept the idea. Still, none of us was all that comfortable with it. A week before the game, Reid telephoned Nolan to warn him that the mound at the university field was in rough shape. Nolan mentioned it to the people in the Rangers' front office, and they sent a couple of groundskeepers to Austin to rebuild it. Reid was looking out for his dad, and we were all grateful for that. The Longhorns netted a good day at the gate and a new mound out of the game, along with a slew of national publicity.

As the game date neared, I could tell Nolan was uptight about it— and justifiably so, in my opinion. But I knew better than to ask questions or try to find out if he had anything specific planned for the game. I just bit my tongue and bided my time. The Rangers' pitching coach, Tom House, commented on Nolan's temperament the night before the game. He said he had never seen Nolan so distracted. I knew Tom was right. Nolan was antsy and couldn't concentrate—and I couldn't either. For one thing, this was the first time I had ever rooted for the opposing pitcher!

Reid, as usual, handled the situation with great aplomb and his indomitable sense of humor. As the game began, he chatted easily with the fans and joked with the other players while his poor parents struggled mightily with a bad case of nerves. Nolan was a wreck, and my stomach was tied in one big knot. Reese was asked to do some interviews for a television station, so he was excited about that, and Wendy seemed anxious that all this attention was focused on her family. I was asked to throw out the first pitch before the game, which I thought was a nice gesture by the UT people.

I thought it was going to be a totally draining time for me, but once the game got going, everything changed. Suddenly I had the proudest feeling I had ever known. It was hard to believe I was old enough to be watching my husband and son on the same field. I thought of a fan letter Nolan had received from a man in California who said his dad had taken him to see Nolan pitch when he was a kid. Now he had done the same with his son, the letter had said. That was part of the feeling I had, this warm and poignant realization that the time had come to make way for the next generation.

The Rangers scored four runs off Reid in the two innings he worked that night, but he did all right and I was proud of him. Nolan worked three innings, gave up a couple of hits and a run, and seemed more uptight than anyone else in the stadium. After the game, Reid happily told us good-bye and hurried off with some of his teammates to have dinner and hang out. I was glad it was over, and I was happy to admit that the night I had dreaded had turned out to be a fun time. But all in all, Reid's freshman season at the University of Texas wasn't a happy one, and the next fall he transferred to Texas Christian University in Fort Worth.

I had worried about him attending a school the size of UT in the first place, especially coming from such a protected environment as Alvin. But Reid has a good sense of who he is, and he had always handled well the predictable references to his dad. In high school, he had pitched and played third base, and the opposing players and their fans would often try to rattle him with remarks about Nolan. Once when Reid was warming up, the ball slipped out of his hands, and the other team really let him have it. But he started laughing himself as he retrieved the ball, and that just deflated the other team's condescension. Another time Reid was playing third base when the opposing players began making cracks about how long his "old man" had been around. Finally Reid walked over to their dugout and said, "Yeah, Nolan Ryan's my dad. He's been in the big leagues twenty-seven years. Is that the worst thing you can say about him? And by the way, what do your dads do?"

Of course, you have to know when people are teasing and when they are being cruel, but if he was hurt by anything he heard, Reid was able to cover it up with humor. His easygoing nature helped him make a smooth adjustment when he transferred to TCU, where his coach was Lance Brown, who had been a coach at Rice University in Houston and pitched batting practice for the Astros during Nolan's years there. Lance had known Reid since he was a Little Leaguer, and he and Reid worked well together. Best of all, with Reid in Fort Worth, he was much nearer to our home in Arlington, and we could see him a lot more often.

I have always been superproud that both my sons had the guts to even play baseball with all the comments and comparisons they hear. I know how difficult it must be to keep up your self-confidence when you have someone yelling that you're only there because of your dad. How insensitive some people are! But in baseball you have to have enough focus to block out distractions and keep going. Easy to say . . . hard to do; I know from experience. I tried through the years to keep up my tennis, and I play in a Houston-area league. During one match, a woman didn't like my line call and insinuated that I was cheating. That, in itself, distracted me to the point of losing my concentration and ultimately, the match.

The Rangers' exhibition game with UT had aroused tremendous attention, and the pressure of the spotlight on Nolan had never felt heavier as the regular season began. Nolan was forty-four years old, and he'd been playing major-league ball more than two and a half decades. We knew this real-life fantasy couldn't go on forever. But we didn't know when it would end. We also couldn't know that this season would include one of the best surprises of Nolan's career.

It happened on May 1, 1991, in Arlington in front of 33,439 enthusiastic Rangers fans—and I almost missed it. Nolan was to pitch against the Toronto Blue Jays on this Wednesday-night game, and I was at home in Alvin with Reese and Wendy, who were still in school. I had missed so few of his home games over the years, usually only when there was a conflict with what the kids were doing. But by Tuesday I had resigned myself to staying at home. The game wasn't going to be televised in the Houston area, so on Wednesday afternoon I called a neighbor, Jim Stinson, and asked if I could come over and watch the Rangers on his satellite dish.

He said, "Nolan's not pitching, is he?"

When I said he was, Jim said, "If I'd known, I'd have flown to the game. In fact, there's still time, Ruth. Do you want to go?"

I hurriedly made arrangements with the kids, and soon I was on my way to Arlington in Jim's private plane. A rancher and oilman, Jim was a partner with Nolan in a ranch called China Grove, near Alvin. We flew into the Dallas-Fort Worth airport and arrived at Arlington Stadium about a quarter of seven. I wish I could say I had a sixth sense about what was going to happen, but I was there on a fluke, a lucky phone call. The truth was, I had talked to Nolan that afternoon by phone, and he'd said he had a sore Achilles tendon and a sore back, and he was taking painkillers. After the doctor in California had warned us about the partial tear in Nolan's arm, I seemed to do more fretting before every start—especially these days, when it seemed as if there was always something hurting.

Even worse, as he was warming up, he opened up an old wound on the finger of his pitching hand. It all added up to a pessimistic beginning for this game against Toronto. He told pitching coach Tom House, "I feel old today, Tom. Everything hurts." He suggested that the Rangers keep the bull pen active because he might need to be relieved.

As it turned out, no one else would be needed.

Because he thought he didn't have his good stuff that night, Nolan threw mostly breaking pitches the first two innings. He figured he could always go to his fastball, but if the curve wasn't there he knew this would be a short night. I didn't know what strategy he was using to get through the night; all I could see from my seat was that the Blue Jays were making little or no contact with the ball. Batter after batter flailed away at it, then trotted back to the dugout with his bat in his hand.

Five innings passed, then six, and still there were no hits.

Miracle Man

I thought it was all over when Manuel Lee hit a blooper into short center in the sixth inning, but Gary Pettis made a running, shoe-top catch for the out. "I've made better plays," Gary said later, "but I don't know if I ever made one that was more important."

In the seventh inning I tried to be logical, thinking of all the things that could go wrong, all the other times Nolan had come close to a no-hitter only to see it slip away in a late inning. I tried to tell myself how unlikely it would be for a forty-four-year-old pitcher to throw a no-hitter when his back and foot and pitching hand were hurting. As a pitcher's wife, you always think in terms of best-case scenario versus worst-case scenario. For instance, if the bases are loaded with two outs, I would think to myself, *What is the absolute worst thing that can happen now? Grand slam and four runs scored. OK, what's the best? Strike this guy out, and the inning's over: no runs or hits or walks.* It's silly, I know, but it seemed to prepare my mind for whatever might happen—and in baseball, you never know what will happen! Things can be going great, but you can still lose a game in a minute on a fluke.

But my eyes were telling me a story my logical mind couldn't refute. Nolan was getting stronger as the game continued and the strikeouts piled up. Later I'd find out that his pitches were averaging ninety-three miles per hour. And I would also learn that he was pulling people from all over the country into his herculean effort that night. On cable, ESPN cut away from the Detroit-Kansas City game to show Nolan going for his no-hitter. And even as the game was being played on the field in Kansas City, the Rangers' game was shown on the Diamond Vision screen in center field. I thought about how odd that must have been, the fans in Kansas City ignoring a game taking place on the field in front of them to watch the telecast of a game being played a thousand miles away.

Reid, then at UT, put down a book report he was writing on a Louis L'Amour novel to watch his father pitch the last two innings. Harry Spilman, Nolan's former Astros teammate and then our neighbor, heard the game on his car radio and called Wendy and Reese. They could not get the game on television, so Reese was anxiously listening for the sports news to come on.

At Shea Stadium, where the Padres and the Mets had just finished their game, players from both teams left the buffet table to crowd around television sets in the clubhouses.

And in Arlington, fans were frantically trying to get to the ballpark for the last inning or two. From high in the stands, you could see the headlights of the cars backed up for miles.

The Rangers had scored three runs in the third inning, two of them on a homer by Ruben Sierra, to give Nolan all the support he would need. When the ninth inning began, only two Blue Jays had reached base, Kelly Gruber in the first and Joe Carter in the seventh, both on walks.

There were two outs in the ninth inning when Roberto Alomar came to the plate. I felt a real twinge when he took his stance, remembering that his father, Sandy, had played second base behind Nolan the night Nolan had pitched his first no-hitter for the Angels in 1973. When Roberto was a little boy, Nolan had given him pitching tips, and Roberto had gotten his first big-league hit off Nolan as a rookie second baseman with San Diego three years earlier.

But this was no time to get sentimental. Nolan struck out the young Alomar for his sixteenth strikeout to end the game 3-0 and nail down his seventh no-hitter.

Arlington Stadium went berserk. On the field, Nolan punched the air with his right arm in a gesture as familiar to me as the smile on his face, and his teammates swarmed to the mound, lifted him to their shoulders, and carried him off the field. The cheering and applause were deafening, and the atmosphere was charged with the excitement of knowing history had just been made.

I worked my way out of the stands and down to the spot where I always waited for Nolan outside the clubhouse. A couple of reporters spotted me there and asked me to compare this no-hitter to the others. I told them I couldn't do it—it would be like picking my favorite child. "They're all the same to me," I said. "I never get tired of watching him pitch."

There was just one distinction Nolan might have preferred not to have as he considered the records he broke that night: At forty-four, he was the oldest pitcher ever to get a no-hitter—and of course, in my opinion, he was also the best. After the game, we joined our friends at a restaurant to eat and celebrate, but I had to fly back home that night to get back to the kids. I was on cloud nine about the game, but I also felt that I was trying to lead two lives—one in Alvin as a "single" mother and the other in Arlington as the wife of a celebrity. I had to fly home that night so I could get the kids up for school the next morning. But it was hard for me to leave Nolan . . .

There's a lot to be said for all the fame and celebrity that came Nolan's way after the records started falling. In baseball, fame brings big money and adoring fans and a lifestyle filled with excitement and adventure.

But it comes with a price.

After Nolan's seventh no-hitter, the spotlight that had already seemed to overwhelm us at times with its brightness became even hotter, and our lives were split by a strange dichotomy. Without Nolan, the kids and I had almost complete freedom. We could go to the mall, eat out at restaurants, take in a movie, and do all the things most Americans take for granted. But we wanted to do those things with Nolan, and whenever he came along, everything changed. As soon as someone would spot him and come up to ask him for an autograph, others would notice, and soon he was surrounded.

I remember the first time Wendy played on the varsity volleyball team. Nolan and I walked into the gym, and someone spotted Nolan. Within seconds, we were surrounded. Wendy looked over there and saw what was going on, and she just dropped her shoulders and shook her head sadly; that kind of commotion always embarrassed her. When we talked about it later, she said, "Gee, Dad, I wish people wouldn't do that when you come in."

He asked her, "Well, Wendy, do you not want me to come?"

She said, "Of course not, Dad. I want you there."

Usually it's easier to watch the kids' games in Alvin, where everyone knows us and realizes we're just the same familiar Nolan and Ruth many of them have known since childhood; the local people leave us alone to let us watch our kids compete. But sometimes when fans of the opposing team spot Nolan in the stands, there's a steady stream of people who climb up to sit or stand beside us, listening to our conversation until Nolan turns their way and holds out his hand for the ball or program or T-shirt they're asking him to sign.

At many of the boys' baseball games he's had to retreat to the car, parked close to the fence, so he can watch Reid or Reese play. Or sometimes he goes to the press box—but when he does that, he knows that some people will start thinking that he considers himself better than they are. He likes to be just another person—even though he's different.

When people come up to him at one of these events, I wish Nolan would say, "I would be happy to sign when the game is over." Then what could they say? In a few rare instances, he's done that, but as often as not, he smiles and signs. And even if they do wait until the game ends, it can be a hassle.

Last year at one of Reese's out-of-town baseball games Nolan stood at the gate as we waited for Reese and signed autographs for twenty minutes after everyone else had left the stands. One person even went home to get something she wanted Nolan to sign and asked him to wait until she could get back. Sometimes, of course, we enjoy seeing what people ask him to sign. We're still laughing about the Nolan Ryan doll one woman brought him to be autographed. Nolan always refuses to sign "body parts."

Others get in the autograph line and ask for favors, encouraging Nolan to donate to a cause or provide a loan or endorse a certain movement or group. I can't count how many times we've been the last ones to leave a stadium or gymnasium because Nolan's been cornered by someone wanting something from him. Usually he stands there listening politely, his head hanging down as his boot scuffs the dirt while I smile gently at the inquisitioner and tug sharply on Nolan's elbow.

Of course, the autograph seekers were more plentiful after Nolan's own games. I've waited in the shadows of a hundred ballparks while Nolan scribbled his name, sometimes after a loss, sometimes when he was hurt. He only had a few rules: First, things had to be orderly. If the fans couldn't police themselves, if the line turned into a mob scene, he would leave. And second, to a very minor degree, he tried to monitor what was going on. If he sensed that there were repeaters trying to stock up on autographs to sell, he would cut the session short.

"I try to give everybody an equal chance and accommodate as many as I can," he said, "and I try not to let those kind of people dominate my time, but I know it happens and I guess I just have to live with it."

After ball games at Arlington Stadium he would very seldom stay to sign autographs, simply because there were too many people. It would take hours to sign autographs for all of them, and he did not like to sign a few and then leave, disappointing the others who were waiting. He knew if he signed one and left, he'd be considered a heel to those left out. Also, many (not all) of those people were simply there to get and sell autographs. And by midnight after a game, Nolan had been at the stadium since 3:30 in the afternoon. He would be tired, hungry, and ready to see his family. Besides that, he usually spent at least an hour in the clubhouse every day signing balls and various other things for people connected with the teams. In other words, by the time the game was over, he was sick and tired of signing and being pulled in different directions, and he was physically tired from the workouts and games. Enough!

The baseball memorabilia industry seemed to explode right about the time Nolan left the Astros to sign with the Rangers. That became apparent when all sorts of things started appearing before Nolan with requests for autographs. But he was so methodical, so deliberate, that he reduced the process to a science and learned to sign almost anything without even blinking. Watching Nolan sign his name was like watching one of those corn-shucking machines. He signed bats, balls, photos, posters, baseball cards, T-shirts, ball gloves—anything you could imagine, but only one to a customer.

Sometimes during spring training he would sit on a chair just inside the stadium fence and two clubhouse kids would open the gate just wide enough for one fan at a time to hand the attendant his or her souvenir of choice for Nolan to sign.

The Sporting News wrote that Nolan "holds the record for most free autographs signed by a professional athlete in any sport." Writer Michael Knisley added, "Because Ryan signs so often and because he carries with him so robust a responsibility to his fans, he has undercut the value of a Nolan Ryan autograph. The market is flooded."

It wasn't just signing autographs and being mobbed at sports events that became a problem for us as Nolan's popularity rose. Any kind of travel became a real challenge. We tested several methods and still couldn't decide whether it was less disruptive to everyone if we tried to board the plane before everyone else, after everyone else, or mingled in with the other passengers. Any one of these methods could cause a commotion. It was embarrassing for Nolan and annoying, I'm sure, for the airline and the other passengers. But the only way we could have avoided it would have been not to go, and most of the time that just wasn't an option for us.

However, there were (and still are) some things Nolan tries to avoid whenever possible. One of them is shopping; he breaks out into a sweat just thinking about having to go to the mall. So we were very fortunate when I met a woman whose husband hates shopping trips as much as Nolan does. She told me about a tailor who came to their home in Dallas and measured her husband for custom-made suits and shirts. I called the man, and he's been a godsend for us. It's one luxury I'm glad we can indulge in because it saves us both an enormous amount of time and frustration.

Despite our discovering ways to get around all the attention, I couldn't imagine living with it indefinitely; on the other hand, I saw no indication that the attention would ever ease up. Nolan was on the disabled list twice in the 1991 season and made only twenty-three starts to pitch 173 innings—his fewest in twenty years. But after pitching the seventh no-hitter and finishing the season at 12-6 with an ERA of 2.91, his popularity was still strong as the 1992 season began.

In fact, Nolan's celebrity status may have even grown between seasons because, knowing his career was nearing its end, he had started taking on obligations he would never have considered in the past. At first, he had shied away from getting involved in the commercial side of sports. But in 1989, as he began to reach more and more magic numbers, he accepted several offers as selectively as he could. He knew those opportunities might not be there very long, and Nolan saw it simply as a chance to squirrel away a few acorns for the winter. By 1992, he probably had more local and national endorsements and television spots than any athlete in America, except for maybe Michael Jordan.

I'll never forget our first shock as we were whizzing down the highway and the kids looked up and saw their father's face on a billboard for an office-supply company. The sign was probably thirty feet wide, and Nolan's picture took up half of that space. Wendy shrieked from the backseat, "What is *that*?"

Nolan laughed and said, "Why, that's ol' handsome Dad."

Thousands of others were recognizing Nolan's face from the commercial endorsements too. One woman who rushed up to him in an airport just as we were catching a flight asked for his autograph and then blamed him because she wanted it. "Look at it this way," she said. "If you didn't make all those commercials and weren't so famous you wouldn't have to go through this."

He just asked if she had a pen and then signed his name.

I've sometimes wondered if Nolan has ever been jealous of me occasionally because I'm still able to have a pretty normal life when I'm on my own. Most of the time I can travel and shop and go to sporting events without ever being interrupted by a stranger or asked for an endorsement or being besieged by Nolan Ryan fans. After all, *my* face hasn't appeared on thirty-foot billboards or on television screens across the country.

On the other hand, when Nolan was breaking records right and left and someone would recognize me in a crowd, it wasn't unusual to be greeted with, "How's Nolan's arm?" or "Is Nolan here with you?" or "Can you get me Nolan's autograph?" or "What does Nolan think about so-and-so?" instead of, "Hello, Ruth, nice to see you."

Although I did—and still do—have control over my life, in some settings I've felt as if I were nothing more than an appendage of "Nolan Ryan the Legend." This was especially true during those wild, record-breaking days with the Rangers, and it reemphasized what Mets scout Red Murff had told me on my wedding day, that I would have to share Nolan with the world. I *have* had to share him, but I've learned to accept that, and in many ways I've felt that I was a part of his accomplishments. If it were included in the bonus round on *Jeopardy!* it might go something like this:

The answer: "She recently retired from baseball after twenty-seven seasons, 324 victories, seven no-hitters, and more than fifty-seven hundred strikeouts, even though she never played in a game."

The question: "Who is Ruth Ryan?"

No, the numbers aren't really mine. But I was a part of them, and most of the time, my life in baseball has been wonderful, even with all the hassles that come with my husband's fame and celebrity.

But more than once I have wondered if I could have an identity of my own or if, in fact, I even needed one! While the question usually came in times of mental anguish, it never took me long to sort out an answer: *Yes.* I *am* a separate person, and I've worked hard to keep a part of my life separate from baseball. I am still an independent person with my own thoughts and feelings and needs—and my own friends.

I'm sure there are people who will read this and think that I only live vicariously through my husband's accomplishments. But the truth is, I *chose* to be a helpmate, especially in the world of professional sports, which is hard for an athlete to do alone. And I also believe that doing a good job as a mother is the most important job in the world; likewise, the pride I feel as a mother is the most important reward I could ever wish for. I will never regret the time I've spent with my family. On the other hand, I know I might have regretted not being there for my children had I chosen to have my own career.

This kind of independent attitude came naturally for Nolan, but it hasn't always been easy for me, living in his shadow. I've been lucky that Nolan is a very understanding man who works as hard as I do to keep our lives in balance. When I'm with him, no matter what is happening around us, I never feel anonymous. He always lets me know I'm important to him and to our family. And sometimes just knowing that has been the thing that has helped me most.

20

The Fans

I was in the stands at Wrigley Field, waiting for the game to begin, when I felt a tap on my shoulder.

"Mrs. Ryan?" a tall, thin teenage boy was nervously looking into my face. "Would you please tell Nolan I said thank you for the letter he sent me? And the picture and the other stuff . . . I really liked it. It helped a lot. Tell him I'm okay now, and I sure thank him for what he did."

I rose slowly out of my seat and reached to shake the young man's hand. When I realized who it was, a chill crept up my spine.

A few months earlier one of the sportswriters had told Nolan he had a friend who'd been in a car crash. The boy had been badly burned and disfigured; he'd lost his hearing and couldn't speak very well. The prognosis was bleak. The writer had asked Nolan if he would sign a baseball for the boy, and Nolan had sent the ball the writer requested, along with a copy of his book, some other memorabilia, and a note urging the boy to hang in there and fight hard to get well.

The sportswriter told Nolan later the gifts had seemed to work miracles in the boy's life. "It made such a change in him," he said. "I know it sounds corny, but it really seemed to give him a reason to live."

Now here was that young man, standing in front of me, saying thanks. I had to wipe away tears as I thought of all he'd been through.

It never ceases to amaze Nolan and me what wonderful rewards can come from the smallest effort. It's probably the best part of his being a celebrity, seeing what can happen when a sports figure steps in to offer a word of encouragement or just to listen to someone's story for a moment.

Sometimes fans write to me, asking me to intercede for them. One letter came from a mother who wrote to ask if I would send Nolan's autograph to her son. I sent the autograph and some stuff I picked up at the ballpark, and I was surprised but pleased to get a thank you note a few days later from the little boy. It said, "Thank you for the autograph and the Rangers things. I lost my daddy. He's in heaven now, and I'm sick too. I'll see my daddy soon."

Sometimes I think of the lives that have touched mine because of Nolan's career in baseball, and I'm so grateful for everything that has happened. I'm thankful for the good things Nolan has been able to do, and I'm thankful to those people who shared themselves with us. Their stories have given our lives a richness, a depth that otherwise we could never have known.

Of course, there have been some ugly encounters too. Some people call themselves fans—but they are actually fanatics. I can talk about this now that he has retired, but before I didn't feel I could. While Nolan was playing, some frightening things happened, and we tried to keep them secret because we didn't want to do or say anything that might encourage someone with a sick mind to snap.

In about 1977, when we were living in California, Nolan picked up the phone one day and the caller asked, "Is Ruth there?"

Nolan handed me the phone and walked out to the patio. As I answered, a man's voice said, "Leave five hundred dollars in a paper bag at such-and-such a store by 5 P.M., or you die."

I said, "Is this a joke?"

He simply repeated the threat, word for word.

I dropped the phone and raced outside, hyperventilating. I shouted,

"Nolan, there's a man who is going to try and kill me if we don't give him five hundred dollars! Quick, call the police!"

In his calm, logical way (which can be so infuriating), Nolan said, "Aw, I wouldn't take it too seriously. A real kidnapper would ask for more than five hundred dollars."

"But he knew my name!" I insisted. Our phone was listed under the name of the couple who had leased us the house. We immediately called them and got their permission to change the number. Nothing happened; I don't think we even called the police. Nolan took it right in stride, but I didn't sleep well for a few nights.

Twice that I'm aware of, Nolan was the target of death threats. The first was when he pitched for the Angels; the caller left the message with the stadium switchboard. When the team informed Nolan, he brushed it off just as he'd done when the call was for me. "I'll just wear someone else's uniform," he joked.

The second threat also came in Anaheim in September 1993, when Nolan was there to pitch for the Rangers in one of the last games of his career. When a friend picked me up at our house in Arlington, she mentioned reading about the threat on Nolan's life in the newspaper. I almost fell out of the car. I said, "What! Nolan didn't even mention it when he called me!"

Once again, Nolan didn't take the threat seriously, but the Angels were troubled enough to add extra security. Nolan had a police escort to and from the bull pen when he warmed up before the game, and two armed guards stood in front of the Rangers' dugout after every half-inning.

When I talked to Nolan that night on the phone I was still angry with him for not telling me. I know his intentions were good—he didn't want to worry me—but I couldn't help but fuss at him, "I'm your wife!" I reminded him. "Not that I could have done anything, but you should have told me. You'd have a fit if someone called us and threatened me or one of the kids and I didn't let you know."

He said, "Ruth, I know you're right, but I have to tell you: Of all my worries right now, getting popped off by a sniper in the middle of a baseball stadium is pretty far down the list."

Actually, there really wasn't much anyone could do to protect a player from such a threat except maybe keep him out of the game. The truth is, if someone could smuggle a gun or a rifle into a stadium, it wouldn't be hard to pick off a player. Nolan couldn't help but chuckle grimly as he told me the police had made him move around on the bench that day, and they had told him where *not* to stand. "A lot of good that did," he said. "Half the time, the shooter would know exactly where I'd be—right there on the pitcher's mound."

These are not worries we take lightly, but Nolan is a realist, and his daily problems occupy most of his thoughts. Warnings like this surface every so often, but fortunately no incident has ever taken place. I just pray no one ever gets crazy enough or angry enough to carry out one of these disturbing threats. What a tragedy that would be.

Other spooky things have happened from time to time. I've received letters that frightened me or made me worry about Nolan. We've also had letters from angry fans.

And fans *do* get angry; we're well aware of that. Nolan has upset them sometimes when he had set out with deliberate intentions to do something that would please them. For example, he swears he'll never do another baseball-card show after the first one he did turned into a disaster.

He was supposed to be there two hours to sign autographs, and the fans were lined up and waiting when he arrived. When the two hours were up, the line was still just as long as it had been when he started, so he stayed another two hours. Eventually, he had to leave because he had to catch his plane, but as he got up from the table, the people left standing in line shouted at him, angry that he was "walking out" on them.

Sometimes fans use children to get Nolan's autograph when they think he might not sign otherwise. One morning in Florida when he stepped outside to get the newspaper about 7:30, he found a tiny little girl sitting on our doorstep holding a baseball and a felt-tip pen. Nolan knew that tiny child wasn't interested in his autograph. He asked her, "Who sent you?" She just shrugged and smiled and pointed across the parking lot. He signed the baseball and handed it back.

The Fans

The worst public relations fiasco probably occurred after Nolan's book, *Miracle Man,* was published in 1992. Hundreds of people sent copies of the book for Nolan to autograph and mail back to them. Sometimes they included return postage; sometimes they didn't. Nolan's secretary and I spent days opening the envelopes, getting the books ready to sign, and then stacking them in front of Nolan so he could sign them one by one. But the stacks continued to grow; no matter how many books Nolan signed, we just didn't seem to be making any headway. At one point, it was almost impossible to get into Nolan's office because the envelopes of books were stacked five and six feet high all over the floor. There was just a little walkway from the door to the desk.

It was another one of those Catch-22s of being a celebrity. Nolan was gratified and flattered that so many fans had bought his book and wanted his signature on it, but after spending a couple of days out of each week doing nothing but signing books, we realized something had to be done. The books were still pouring into the office, and Nolan was running out of time. He was still playing baseball for the Rangers, running two banks and two ranches, and traveling almost every week. For one of the first times in his life, he looked at those stacks of books waiting to be autographed and felt the sinking feeling of defeat.

We decided to call a halt to the book signing. Neither of us liked the idea, but we didn't see any other way out. We started returning the books, unsigned, with a photograph of Nolan and a note that thanked the fans for buying the book, apologized for being unable to sign, and asking them to understand that the demand had simply overwhelmed us.

Shortly after that, we received a copy of the book with a note from a woman who said, "Here's your book back. I bought it as a gift for my husband and sent it to you to sign, but you wouldn't do it. Well, my husband died, and I don't need your book anymore. Here it is."

I read that note and wanted to cry. I felt so bad that we had disappointed this couple, and I was so frustrated that we had been unable to fulfill her simple wish. As we read her note, we both realized there were many others whose requests had been just as special as hers was, and we agonized over our inability to comply with the favors they asked. Yet at the time, we honestly did not see any other way around the problem.

Miracle Man

We've learned to accept the fact that now and then we may make one person mad because he or she feels slighted, but with the same actions we make a thousand people feel good. We try to focus on those good feelings and get over the bad ones as quickly as we can.

Some of the requests we get don't ask for autographs or memorabilia. Sometimes they just ask for advice. Occasionally, these letters come from young baseball wives. One letter came from a young woman who described herself as "very independent, the same as you." She said she was trying to finish college despite her baseball-playing boyfriend's preference that she move with him wherever he is.

The problem, she said, was that "both of our lifelong dreams seem to be coming true at exactly the same time, causing a difference in priorities for each of us. . . . Frustration has set in for both of us, due to our responsibilities in different worlds and our not being able to be together."

She asked for my advice on how to deal with her situation. "How do we make it work, and still remain happy as a couple?" she asked. "Do I chase him all around the country or try to create a life of my own, excluding him? But, mostly, how do I deal with the loneliness?"

Tough questions! I thought a long time about my answer to her. Here's part of what I wrote to her:

> I must say that I don't have all the answers to make things work, but your love for each other and your maturity will carry you a long way.
>
> At age eighteen, I did not think clearly about my future, only about being with Nolan. He was already playing minor league baseball, and the only way we could be together was to get married. Afterward, I tried to stay in college and pursue my own career, but after one year, in which we spent maybe two months together, I decided our marriage would end in divorce if I did not quit school and go with him. I have never regretted that decision for the sake of our marriage, but I have had many periods of self-doubt and loneliness as well as identity crises or times when I felt I was totally wasting myself "just being a wife." After we had children, though, my life (my job, actually) became

raising them. In the very unstable lifestyle of baseball, I needed to stay home and be a stabilizing force for them.

Although there were times when I felt frustrated, left out, or lonely, I knew in my heart that Nolan needed my love and support to keep doing what he did. Today, when I see my three children as happy, productive, well-adjusted young adults, I am very thankful I was able to stay home and raise them myself. And I am very proud of the "job" I did and also very proud of them.

It takes a very strong person to share a husband with the world of baseball, so I think it is very important for you to develop your own interests and a career, if possible. Some of the ways I helped myself were going back to college in later years, becoming trained in teaching aerobics and exercise classes, coaching my children's baseball teams, etc. Playing tennis with my friends (completely separate from baseball) also helped.

Because of the nature of the game (which involves a lot of travel, trades, and an unstable lifestyle), many baseball wives do not work. But I have known some who are nurses, teachers, flight attendants, and designers, who seem to be able to balance their careers with their husbands'. But I have also seen that conflict cause divorces in some baseball marriages.

If your relationship is a strong one, then you and your boyfriend will survive the pressures, the separations, and the emotional ups and downs. If it is not strong, then it really wouldn't matter what job he has. The money nowadays makes it easier to live, but making a lot of money does not necessarily make a marriage happy. You two will have to decide first what your priorities are . . . then, just trust your own instincts!

You are probably the most important person in your boyfriend's life and the one who will support him through good or bad, but don't lose sight of your own roots or your own importance. Good luck! May your relationship and/or marriage be as blessed with happiness as mine has been.

21

The Farewell

February 9, 1993, the day I both dreaded and looked forward to for more than four years.

As we drove to Arlington for the annual Baseball Writers' Dinner, a strange sense of excitement and foreboding seem to surround us. Our lives were about to change; before the dinner Nolan would announce that 1993 would be his last season to play baseball. The decision we had considered so many times over the years had finally been made only the day before.

Nolan had talked it over with all of us—Reid, Reese, Wendy, and me—just as he had discussed all his major career moves during the last few years. At the beginning of each season, he had said he'd like to play one more year, and no one had objected. He had even reconsidered his decision in 1992 and thought about retiring in the middle of the season when problems with injuries had seemed insurmountable, but then things took a turn for the better. The injuries healed, and Nolan had a strong finish. Now, as the 1993 season got under way, he thought one more summer was enough; the timing was right for the family and right in a baseball sense too. It was time to go.

"I'll miss seeing you pitch," Reid had said when Nolan told us what he wanted to do and asked for our opinions, "but I'll enjoy having more time with you." That was how we all felt.

The thing that had finally caused Nolan to make the decision was the constant questioning about when he planned to pitch his last game. It seemed to be the primary topic on the mind of every sportswriter he encountered. He wanted to make a public announcement, something he did not do often or lightly, so he wouldn't have to deal with that question every time he went into a different city.

Both of us felt the same way. There were other things we wanted to do, and we looked forward to having more time to devote to our family, especially now that Reid would be attending TCU in Fort Worth and playing baseball there, and the two younger kids, Reese and Wendy, were actively involved in several sports in Alvin. There would still be plenty of sports in our lives. *Finally,* I thought, *I won't have to attend so many of the kids' games alone.* I fantasized about how nice it would be to have Nolan there beside me on the bleachers.

We had always known Nolan would never have to be released or forced out. He loved the competition as long as he felt physically able to pitch and was contributing to the team. But now he was mentally tired, and he saw the distance widening between himself and his younger teammates. He liked them but he was excluded from some of the playfulness and mischief in the clubhouse. The generation gap was part of it, I suppose. Nolan himself was quite a practical joker, but things had changed a lot over the years. In the later years he might mention a name, Johnny Cash or Winston Churchill, and be met with blank looks.

The dinner seemed an ideal time for the announcement because most of the media outlets would be represented there. Nolan could do one news conference instead of twenty interviews. Of course, it didn't work out quite that way. He made his announcement at noon, and then he was besieged by writers wanting to interview him privately so they could put their own "exclusive" slant on the story.

The next day I was listening to the car radio and I heard one of the taped interviews. The writer asked Nolan if he wasn't being a little presumptuous by making the announcement now. "Won't you want to come back if you have a good season this year?" he asked.

Nolan replied, "It would be great to have a good season. But there is nothing that will change my mind. Good season, bad season, this is it."

Even though Nolan's words were no surprise to me—he'd told the kids and me the same thing when we discussed his retirement—the old ambiguous feelings swept over me as I heard Nolan state them publicly. *It's really going to end; we're really leaving baseball*, I thought, feeling sad and maybe even a little fearful. After all, our whole marriage had revolved around Nolan's baseball career. What would we do to replace this ever-present dynamic? Nolan was giving up a career that had dominated our lives and made possible everything we have, including three ranches and two banks. How would he fill his time? How would he invest his energy? What would he do with the nine months he used to hang around the ballpark every day? Sometimes I worried that he was giving up his security blanket, his real identity, this knowledge that his real job started in February.

The surge of emotions—sad nostalgia mingled with happy anticipation—continued as we flew to Florida a few weeks later for Nolan's last spring training. There we felt a finality darkening everything we did as we realized, with each familiar step through the season, that this was our last time through.

Nolan was leaning back in a chair near the spring-training clubhouse one day, watching the team in a practice game, when it all began to sink in. He told me later that he sat there and thought, *This is really it, the last time.*

On that same sunny spring afternoon, I sat on a picnic table outside the clubhouse door. An exhibition game was being played on the big field while players' kids were running around the grassy play area, some swinging plastic bats and throwing tennis balls. It reminded me of the hours I used to spend entertaining the kids while we all waited for "Daddy to get off work."

And that memory triggered another: Once when Reid was in kindergarten his teacher asked him to tell the class what his father's job was. Reid answered, "He doesn't have a job. He just plays baseball all day."

As the memories continued to flow through my mind, I also thought of Wendy's birthdays, most of which had been spent in Florida. *At least she won't miss that,* I thought.

We hadn't really known what to expect from the fans when Nolan announced his plans to retire. Would they dismiss him as a waste of time, a forty-six-year-old has-been? Would they figure a retiring pitcher in his mid-forties was hardly worth watching? We just didn't know . . . but we soon found out.

Beginning in spring training, the interest in Nolan and the demands on him escalated to the point of craziness. The Rangers had to fence off a parking spot just so he could get from his car to the clubhouse and back. A battalion of fans would wait all day for his autograph.

Maybe those fans had started to think, as many writers were speculating, that it would be a long time before anyone would play the game of baseball as long as Nolan had—twenty-seven seasons. Today the travel makes it impossible, and the money makes it unnecessary. Nolan was a throwback, a carryover from another era, the kind of pitcher who threw as hard as he could, for as long as he could—and usually burned out early.

Nolan said it, too, telling one writer, "My style of pitching seems to have been lost somewhere in baseball. It's antiquated now. It's just another reason why I feel like it's time for me to get out, because I'm not going to change. I have to do what I think is right."

Of course, I saw the irony in Nolan setting the record for the most years played. Had he signed again with the Astros in 1989, I think it was likely he would have retired in two years or less. By doing so, he would have missed the amazing rebirth he had with the Rangers. But at the time, all the Astros had to do was not demand that he take a two-hundred-thousand-dollar cut. Nolan respected Dr. John McMullen, but once he feels someone is trying to take advantage of him, that person has lost him.

All that was behind us as spring training rolled along. It was a hectic and sentimental time, with clusters of reporters and autograph collectors swarming him every chance they had. They would follow us to restaurants after practice or to our condominium. One day they went to the mall with our family, and it was very difficult for Nolan not to show his annoyance with these people. He doesn't like to be rude, but after all, they were the ones who were being rude and intrusive.

Nolan had worked as hard as he had ever worked over the winter, hoping to reduce the risk of injury during his final season. As part of his routine that spring, he stayed in Port Charlotte, the Rangers' spring-training headquarters in Florida, working out on his own whenever the Rangers were on the road. He lifted weights, stretched, rode the bike, threw to an extra catcher—and signed autographs everywhere he went.

While the enthusiastic fans at spring training should have given us fair warning, we had our first real taste of how wonderfully hard and tearful and joyful Nolan's last season was going to be when the Rangers and the Astros met in the Astrodome on the second day of April. The game was billed as the Lone Star Classic, a title that may seem a little pretentious for a preseason game, but this one drew 53,657 fans, the largest crowd ever to see a baseball game in the state of Texas, including the 1980 and 1986 playoffs, when Nolan had pitched for the Astros against the Phillies and the Mets in the National League championship series.

The long wait before the classic had been almost intolerable for him. The Rangers president, Tom Schieffer, had approached Nolan when they were drawing up the spring schedule and said the Astros would like to have him pitch there the week before the season opener. Nolan was fairly casual about it. He said, sure, if the rotation worked out, that would be fine.

But as the game drew near, the meaning of it sank in. "I don't think any of the other games during the season will compare unless it's my last home game in Arlington Stadium," Nolan mused.

The game took on even more significance because it was promoted weeks in advance. The Alvin Chamber of Commerce had been publicizing the game since the middle of January, and local people often told Nolan proudly, "Hey, I bought tickets to see you pitch against the Astros."

He tried to tell them, "Well, you know, that's a long way off, and a lot could happen between now and then." We couldn't help but remember the minor-league game in 1967 when Nolan had been scheduled to pitch and the Mets' farm team had promoted him heavily. That was the night Nolan had thrown out his arm warming up for the game, and the owner had been forced to offer fans their money back when Nolan was dropped from the lineup.

Luckily, Nolan had enjoyed a stronger, healthier spring training than he had had in any recent years. He had avoided the muscle strains and pulls that had nagged him so often in the past, and he looked as powerful as ever. In his final start in Florida, he had gone seven innings against the Orioles and allowed only one hit.

Now he was back in Houston to say hello again . . . and good-bye. The Houston fans had always been wonderful to us, and I was overwhelmed that they came out to the Astrodome for a farewell tribute to Nolan. The last reserved seat had been sold a month before the game date, and I was hosting a party before the game in the Astrohall, next door to the dome. I wanted a chance to thank our friends who had supported Nolan during his nine seasons in Houston.

Drayton McLane, the owner of the Astros, and Rangers president Tom Schieffer were nice enough to allow me to have this reception before the game. It was great to get a chance to visit with people who had had an influence on Nolan's career. More than three thousand relatives and friends, including Nolan's high school baseball coach, Jim Watson, and my high school tennis coach (who was also Nolan's basketball coach), Aubrey Horner, were there. Red Murff, the scout who had signed Nolan, was there, too, as well as Mickey Herskowitz, the legendary *Houston Post* sportswriter who had covered Nolan since he was in high school. On a sad note, Anita Martini, the first female sportscaster in Houston, attended in a wheelchair; she died from cancer a few months later. Anita had interviewed our sons when they were youngsters hanging out in the Astros clubhouse, and she always talked about how nice they were and how they loved the microphone.

The only problem was that the party would cause me to miss the start of the game, but I felt I needed to be with the last of our guests. Many of our relatives, friends, and neighbors from Alvin came to the game in a convoy of buses and cars led by a police escort. Nolan, the kids, and I had talked about it. I knew if I was to be on the field with Nolan for the pregame ceremony, I would have to leave the reception early. But I also knew there were going to be a lot of people at the party I hadn't seen for a long time, so I decided to stay. Wendy stayed with me.

I had resolved not to think too much about how we were going to get through this season, but my resolve was pitching my mind against my heart. Those same battling emotions swept over me many times that night, especially as I considered how symbolic the Astrodome was of Nolan's career. He had started (and lost) his first big-league game there for the Mets in 1966, after being called up from the minors for the team's last road trip of the season. That night his parents, his sisters, and a whole cheering section from Alvin, including his coach, Jim Watson, and I had headed to Houston to see Nolan's debut. Ironically, some of Nolan's fans got caught in traffic getting to the game and missed seeing him in action—he was gone by the second inning.

He had recorded his first big-league victory in the Astrodome on April 14, 1968, pitching six and two-thirds innings and beating Larry Dierker, 4-0, in a duel of young right-handers. He had allowed only three hits, struck out eight, and walked two.

On April 12, 1980, he had hit his first major-league home run in the Astrodome in his first start in a Houston uniform, and it was here, in 1981, that he had pitched his fifth no-hitter, beating the Dodgers, 5-0, and breaking Sandy Koufax's no-hitter record. It was in the Astrodome in 1985 that he had struck out his four-thousandth batter.

Before the Astrodome was even built, while we were dating in high school, Nolan and his father and I went to the old Colt Stadium to see Sandy Koufax pitch for the Dodgers. It was my first professional baseball game, and I couldn't understand why Nolan was so mesmerized by this left-hander who threw the ball so hard. Nolan didn't even talk to me the entire night.

So the Astrodome had been a special place in our lives, and Nolan wasn't entirely comfortable before the Lone Star Classic, knowing there would be a lot of fanfare. He wanted to concentrate on his pitching and on the season itself. At that point, he was still hoping he could slip quietly into retirement without every game turning into a spectacle.

Fat chance!

No matter how emotional I thought the night might be, I wasn't prepared for the love fest it turned out to be. Even though we were both nervous before the day began, we were very grateful to the Rangers and the Astros for making it happen and for allowing us to have our pregame party.

Right from the beginning, the fans made it clear why they were there. Nolan was pitching in the Astrodome for the first time in five years and for the last time in a career that was not quite as old as the Dead Sea Scrolls. This was indeed a big night for Houston fans, Ryan fans, and nostalgia fans.

While he was warming up in the bull pen along the left-field stands, Nolan glanced up and spotted a familiar face among the throng of fans at the railing. It was his fifth-grade teacher, Melba L. Passmore, now eighty-one years old, who had recently been honored when the Alvin School Board voted to name a new elementary school after her. Nolan stopped his warmup, headed straight for Mrs. Passmore, and handed her the baseball he had been using. The people who saw it said she brushed away tears as she climbed back up the steps to her seat.

I knew Mrs. Passmore too; she had been my Sunday school teacher. When she was interviewed during the game, she said she remembered Nolan as "a sweet little boy," and added that he was the teacher's pet. She noted that Nolan's signature had been on the petition to get the new school named in her honor. She said she would ask the board to let her put the baseball he gave her in a display case in the entrance to the school.

In the pregame ceremonies, Astros manager Art Howe, who had been a key player on the 1980 and 1986 playoff teams, presented Nolan with an embroidered saddle, a gift from the team. Someone quipped that they should have given him a horse, too, so he could ride off into the sunset at the end of the season.

Nolan responded by thanking the crowd and saying, "I've always been an Astros fan, and I always will be."

The Farewell

That was true. He had followed the team since its first year as an expansion franchise, and he had been a little hurt, I think, that they didn't show more interest in him before he was drafted by the Mets. But Red Murff, the Mets' scout, said the Astros weren't interested in him early on because Paul Richards, the Houston general manager, thought Nolan was too skinny and had a sunken chest and would lack stamina!

The first ball was thrown out by the former president of the United States, George Bush. I slipped into my seat just as the Astros' Craig Biggio stepped up to the plate to lead off the bottom of the first inning. Biggio said later, "I never saw the first pitch. It was just about a thousand flashbulbs, going off in my face."

As I watched Nolan down there on the pitcher's mound, it dawned on me that I had been in the Astrodome only once since the night Nolan had pitched his last game for the Astros on September 19, 1988. He had pulled a hamstring muscle and been forced to leave the game that night. We couldn't know then that it would be his last game for Houston. His injury had kept him from pitching again that season.

The game in Houston wouldn't count in the standings, but Nolan wanted to do well for all the obvious reasons, and I knew he had worried about it. The account in the next day's *Houston Post* described the mixed results:

> There was less than a storybook touch to the evening because the Astros were the ones who wound up with the fatted calf. They collected 10 hits off Nolan, who wasn't able to give the crowd what it really craved. The King of Swing-and-Miss struck out only one batter and walked none.
>
> Houston scored twice in the second and sixth innings. . . . That was enough for a 4-3 win for the Domeboys, as if anything was actually hanging on the outcome.
>
> What really mattered was the chance to give several overdue and final ovations to the handsome rancher from Alvin, who enriched baseball in Houston for nine years, and baseball everywhere for going on 27. For a night, forgotten was the bitterness of his departure, the universal anger at John McMullen, the former

Astros' owner, for misjudging Nolan's value and his appeal and pushing him out the door with a low-ball offer.

To paraphrase Dr. McMullen, "If I knew then what I know now, I would never have let him go. But if I knew then what I know now, I would not have voted for Nixon."

It wasn't necessary for Ryan to blow everyone away this night. . . . In fact, how he finishes this season is almost incidental. His legend is secure. He was an artist on the mound and a normal, model human being away from it. We never had to worry about weird things happening with his hair, except for losing some of it, or ornaments dangling from his ear, a gold bangle or a carrot or whatever.

In truth, Houston fans were desperate for even a glimpse of him this night. They received six full innings and it was almost, if not quite, like old times.

The omens looked good, although the reminders of how the time had flown by were everywhere. In his final year, Nolan was playing under a new pitching coach, Claude Osteen, whom Nolan had beaten in 1975 when Osteen played for the Dodgers; it had been Nolan's ninety-third career victory. By the time the 1993 season ended, he would have 324. He would also have a new Rangers manager, Kevin Kennedy, who was eight years younger than Nolan. Bobby Valentine had been fired late the previous season, a situation that is always sad. Kevin was Nolan's fifteenth big-league manager.

Before we realized it, the calendar had fast-forwarded to April 9, 1993, and Nolan was pitching at the Rangers' home opener against the Boston Red Sox. He gave the crowd six solid innings, allowing four hits and striking out five in a 3-1 victory. We began to allow ourselves to dream a little. Maybe, just maybe, he would go out with a healthy and winning season. And just maybe, the Rangers might finally contend for their first division title . . .

The dream faded a little in Nolan's next start, when he pitched in some of the worst weather Arlington Stadium had ever seen: damp, dreary, and forty-eight degrees. He left after only four innings; he gave up six runs, three of them unearned. Nolan wanted to stay in the game so badly that, in the middle of the third inning, he had the team doctors drain fluid from his right knee. But the pain continued. The next day he underwent arthroscopic surgery on the knee and was placed on the disabled list. For all the talk about the injuries that nagged Nolan toward the end of his career, this was only the second time he had undergone surgery in twenty-six years. The only other time was in 1975, when he was playing for the California Angels and had the bone chips removed from his right elbow.

I wondered at the time why the club let him start on a night so threatening. But as Osteen, the pitching coach, put it, "It was unfortunate, but . . . when your turn comes to pitch, you've got to pitch."

Watching from the stands, I knew how frustrated Nolan was as he struggled to continue through the fourth inning of that season-opener. He said later he had to alter his delivery because he couldn't get his leg up due to the pain and stiffness in his knee. He couldn't balance on his right leg because of the knee, so he had to go to a modified windup, and he just wasn't successful with it.

He told a writer, "I didn't have command of my pitches. I couldn't throw where I wanted. I was wild and out of the strike zone, and I didn't have real good stuff. It was a bad combination."

I knew how much it meant to him to stay in the game, and I knew that draining the knee in the third inning was a desperate measure. This was the only time I could remember his having a knee drained during a game, ever.

"It's not something you want to have done if you can keep from it," he had told me once. "They have to stick a pretty big needle in there."

But he had agreed to have it done, and it hadn't helped. Surgery was scheduled, but just as he was recovering from the knee surgery, he pulled a hip muscle in May.

The weird part was that Nolan had played so many years with so few major injuries, and now things were happening to him that even the doctors hadn't seen. For instance, his hip injury, in which the muscle rim pulled away from the pelvic bone, is more common among teenaged runners. The Rangers' team physician said he had never seen it before in an adult.

"Nobody I knew had treated it before," said Dr. John Conway. "We just had to play it by ear. He would think he felt better so we'd let him try to throw, and that would make it worse. Then we'd back off again until he felt better. Then he'd throw again, and it would get worse again. Finally, we just said, 'No throwing,' and gave him some time off."

He wasn't a model patient when it came to rehabilitating himself by doing nothing. Then, in one of those odd twists where something bad turns into good, he sliced open the bottom of his foot while vacationing at the river near our ranch at Gonzales. It is easier to stay off your feet when one of them has seven stitches in it. By the time his stitches came out, the doctors could see a marked improvement in his hip.

But that meant for two months Nolan didn't throw. He didn't run. He didn't do anything outside the weight room. He had never had such a period of inactivity before. When he started throwing again in early July, he came home and said, "I was pathetic. It was the worst I've ever thrown in my life." Any wife of a professional athlete will tell you that no "slump" is as bad as nursing an injury and not being able to play. Pro athletes are terrible patients. Someone asked me once if I lived vicariously through my husband's achievements. I don't know about that, but I do know that I suffered vicariously through his injuries! Every day I saw what he went through, how he struggled. But despite all the pain, all the frustration, he could not abide the idea of saying, "I give up. It's over for me." He wanted to work his way back, but just trying to keep his workout schedule at the same level was very difficult.

He had made a commitment to pitch that season, so he was consumed with doing whatever it took—even pitching in pain—as long as he wasn't hurting the team.

Having fought back from three injuries—knee, hip, and foot—on July 19 in a game with the Milwaukee Brewers, Nolan made his fourth start of the 1993 season, his first in seventy-three days.

In twenty-seven seasons, this had been his longest stay on the disabled list. As I drove to Arlington Stadium for the game with the

Brewers, my heart was flooded with apprehension. I wasn't sure he could come back, and thinking only as a wife, I wasn't sure I wanted him to try. Yet I had to admire him. He didn't want to let the season get away. He wanted to help the team, and the Rangers needed him.

Sometimes people don't know what their limits are, but Nolan has exceeded his so often, I've learned not to prejudge him. Still, I felt tortured that evening, watching him warm up. Some nights it is harder to be a spectator than others, and when you know that someone you love—a husband or a child—is playing in pain . . . those are the hardest games to watch.

The long recovery from the three injuries had been almost intolerable for him, but I had enjoyed having him home in Alvin. We had gone together to watch our old high school's baseball team work its way up to the state finals as it had done thirty years earlier, in Nolan's senior year. The games had brought back many wonderful memories.

But they also brought frustration. Once Nolan had had to get up and leave the park because people had begun to block the view of the other spectators as they tried to crowd around him, asking for autographs and health reports. I can tell when he gets agitated, but he never shows it to a point where he might hurt someone's feelings. I knew he was annoyed, though, by the questions that made him seem like a bank for body parts. "How's the arm?" "How's the knee?" "How's the hip?" The same questions came over and over, and eventually he had to get away.

But in that start against the Brewers on July 19, something nice happened. He pitched well enough to win, leaving the game with two outs in the sixth after giving up three hits and two runs and striking out six. The Rangers won 5-3.

That night our hopes that his final season still could be salvaged did an instant uptick. His fastball was timed at between ninety-three and ninety-six miles an hour. He had his good curve. When he came out in the sixth, the crowd gave him a standing ovation. "Ryan's back!" I heard someone yell.

Only then, when it seemed he was going to make it through the season after all, did he admit that during his long stint on the disabled list he had struggled with the possibility that he might not pitch again.

But it wasn't over yet . . . not yet. The roller-coaster ride continued, and one of the peaks—and plunges—on that ride came on September 12.

What it amounted to was an all-day tribute that began sometime after breakfast and ended around suppertime. The game and the ceremony that followed were meant to climax a year of planning on the part of the Texas Rangers; the event would have everything but the right ending. When all those ambitious plans were made, no one knew that Nolan would be coming off the disabled list for the third time or that the dream season we had hoped for had taken all the wrong turns. The game began full of happy memories—and hope.

It was Nolan's last start for the Rangers in Arlington Stadium. The crowd of more than forty thousand included two Hall of Fame pitchers, Gaylord Perry and Nolan's hero, Sandy Koufax; six of his seven no-hit catchers; and several former teammates from his three previous teams who had come from all over the compass to be there.

Part of the plan that sultry Sunday afternoon was for Nolan to pitch six innings. When he was one pitch away from that goal, there were two outs, two on base with walks, and the score was tied at 1-1. It was just the way he would have loved to leave it. But that's when things went haywire.

He went to a full count on the next two hitters. Chip Hale drove in a run with a single off Nolan's glove, then Dave McCarty lashed a double near the left-field line to drive in two more, and Nolan was gone. His record fell to 5-4 in that star-crossed final season; his line for the game was four runs on four hits, five walks, and three strikeouts.

After the game, he made no excuses, in keeping with the habits of a lifetime. He said no, he wasn't bothered by his most recent plague (sore ribs) and no, he didn't feel tired in the ninety-four-degree heat and no, he wasn't distracted by all the commotion.

"It was just poor mechanics," he told his interviewers. "I went to the stretch and seemed to bounce back. I just wanted to get out of the sixth and keep us close. We're in a pennant race, and we needed to win. That's what I was thinking about, not personal things."

The Farewell

After watching Nolan lose an important game, I really didn't know whether to laugh or cry as I sat with him in an open convertible, waiting to take a final ride around the stadium. Video highlights of his career were playing on the giant screen on the scoreboard and the public address system was filling the air with the voice of Nat King Cole singing "Unforgettable." I had a lump in my throat that wouldn't go away!

Later, when the sportswriters asked him if he wished he had quit a year ago or if he would consider coming back next year and try to get this farewell thing down right, he answered, "My arm is fine. As long as I could stay healthy and give us a chance of winning, I wanted to pitch. But my body has been sending me messages all year. It's time to go."

Nolan and his body probably had some interesting conversations. He knows himself so well and monitors himself so closely that he feels what is wrong almost the instant it happens. And this season wasn't what he wanted, although in truth Nolan would have been the last person to buy into that dream-season stuff.

But the Rangers fans (and I) didn't want to give up hope that Nolan could heal and make a comeback. I couldn't keep from imagining that fairy-tale ending when Nolan would pitch the Rangers to the pennant and then strike out the last batter in the last of the ninth inning of the seventh game to win the World Series. But even if I had been able to seriously cling to that vision, Nolan doesn't think that way. His goal was just to get through one game at a time, to be healthy, to pitch well, and to give the Rangers a chance to win.

But I tried to push all those thoughts aside as the ceremonies began. More than anything else, I thought it showed how much his peers respected Nolan that even his "victims" were on hand for Nolan Ryan Day. Four of them represented his milestone strikeouts: Danny Heep, of the Mets, number 4,000; Brad Mills, of the Expos, number 3,509 (the one that broke Walter Johnson's career strikeout record); César Geronimo, of the Reds, number 3,000; and Ron LeFlore, of the Tigers, number 2,000.

Geronimo had the distinction of also being the three-thousandth strikeout victim for Bob Gibson, of the Cardinals. Asked how he felt about this coincidence, Cesar replied, "I guess I was just in the right place at the right time."

I knew all the praise and getting all the gifts would make Nolan squirm. He would have preferred to avoid any fanfare, but the Rangers had come to him with the idea, and, as he said, "I didn't really feel I could tell my home team, 'No, I'd rather not.'"

The trick would be to endure the praise, enjoy the gifts, and not make the game he just lost seem insignificant. One of Nolan's most attractive qualities is how well he does this. He may believe some of the praise, but never all of it.

Finally, it was Nolan's turn to speak, to put into his own words twenty-seven years of games and glory and occasional grief, and to give back some of the energy and affection the Arlington fans and others had lavished on him, even if he wasn't going to give them a storybook ending. He wouldn't use notes. To Nolan, that would be almost like cheating. Every word came from his heart, not from a script prepared by a friend or someone in the front office. This is what he said:

> First, I would like to thank everybody who stayed to be in atten-
> dance for this special day. And, believe me, this is a special day
> of mine, and I do appreciate it. I thought about what I should
> say and what I should discuss in my career. And I started look-
> ing back on all the things that have happened, all the people I have
> come in contact with. I think the thing that has made it the most
> special is the people.
>
> I used to think that I always wanted to play in one place from
> the time I started until the time I ended, to be in one organization
> and one team. But as my career went on and I went from New York
> to California to Houston, and now up here in Arlington, I realized
> I really was fortunate to get the opportunity not only to play on
> both coasts, but to spend fourteen years of my career in Texas.
>
> Today is special because of the people who are involved here—
> the people who took the time and all the effort to come over and
> spend the day with us here in Arlington. They traveled from all over

the United States. It makes you feel good to know that people think enough of you that they're willing to come out and spend the time with you. I sure appreciate it.

It's nice to see so many of my old teammates. Seeing them brings back a lot of fond memories—times that have gone by, things that have happened in my career, and what a role they played in my career. And they're here with my current teammates, and here we are in a pennant race, and we have a common goal of trying to bring a pennant to Dallas-Fort Worth, Texas.

As the season progressed, sportswriters have asked me, "What are you going to miss the most being out of baseball as an active player?" There are the obvious things. The actual competition. Pitching. Facing a lot of the great hitters. Winning. Losing. Trying to get outs. The satisfaction of getting the job done. The anxieties of not getting it done. Trying to go out and do better and help your ball club. Those are the things I'm going to miss that are obvious. I think the little things that you don't really think about and realize you're going to miss are the times with your teammates in the clubhouse laughing and joking, carrying on. Or maybe sitting on the bench at Anaheim Stadium with Gene Autry during batting practice, discussing careers, attitudes—those are very special moments. Special moments like being in the outfield taking ground balls with Dave Oliver or Jimmie Reese. Or just being with these guys during batting practice.

I'm going to look forward to my time away from baseball and the time I'll spend with my family. This is the only life we've known. It's going to be quite a transition for us. I think the whole family is going to go through an adjustment. But I feel like we will have fond memories, and we have a lot of things that we look forward to doing as a family.

I'd just like to cut it short and say thank you for coming out today. My career has certainly surpassed any expectations I ever had. Before I go I'd like to thank my family. They came in from all over. It's very special—probably the biggest gathering of the Ryan family, I guess, since we were small children. I appreciate all of you. It has been a thrill pitching here. It has been a thrill pitching for such good fans and I anticipate being a fan and supporter of this ball club for years to come.

Thank you.

Then came the gifts. Among them was a Nolan Ryan scholarship fund established at Alvin High School to provide a thousand-dollar annual grant to both a male and a female athlete/scholar. Contributors to the scholarship fund included the American and National League offices and individual clubs, Nolan's major-league sponsors, and the Texas Rangers.

Other gifts included a painting, "Return of the Longhorns," by western artist Melvin Warren, which we have proudly hung in the entry hall of our new ranch-style home in South Texas; a family vacation to Saint Thomas, Virgin Islands; a stunning "Farewell to a Legend" *assemblage* of photographs, mementos, and other paraphernalia highlighting Nolan's career by noted designer Ray Ward; and a beautiful bracelet made of gold- and diamond-encrusted baseballs with the dates of Nolan's seven no-hitters inscribed on the back. The benefactors even included a trip for me to the Grand Canyon Ranch Health and Fitness Spa in Tucson, Arizona!

Finally, Rangers infielder Jeff Huson presented Nolan with the team's gift to him: two longhorn steers for our ranch. Jeff told us one steer was named Robin and the other Ventura.

Nolan promptly changed the names of those steers!

22

The Fight

*O*f all the dips and turns of Nolan's career, the one that received the most *unwanted* attention came on August 4, 1993, during one of Nolan's last games.

The furor erupted when Chicago third baseman Robin Ventura charged the mound after one of Nolan's pitches nicked him on the elbow, and Robin, twenty-six, accused Nolan of throwing at him. He dropped his bat and went storming out of the batter's box, headed for Nolan. The next thing I knew, Nolan had Robin in a headlock and appeared to be giving his head a knuckle massage as both benches cleared. Later, the most popular line was that Nolan had thrown a six-hitter. As he pummeled Robin's head with a series of sharp noogies, the other players came streaming toward the mound to tangle in one enormous brouhaha.

Sitting in the second row behind home plate, I had a perfect view of everything that happened, and I didn't like what I saw. When Robin started for the mound, I felt a sharp, sick feeling deep inside me. That game and that night had meant so much to Nolan because the Rangers were still in the pennant race, and he had worked hard to rejoin the team after being on the disabled list much of the season.

Miracle Man

All around me the fans were going wild; I was probably the only person in the stands who was fearful. Everyone else was excited and rooting for Nolan, especially my kids and their friends. They were loving it, but all I could think about was what Nolan had already gone through—half a season of rehabilitation. I know how bruised and stiff anyone can get just from a fall, let alone having players from both teams pile on top of you. I worried about his spraining or breaking a finger or hurting his back or about reinjuring his sore ribs and being out for the rest of the season. After all, he wasn't twenty years old any longer.

All of that was on my mind as I watched the fracas going on in the middle of the diamond, with umpires and others frantically trying to pull irate players off the churning swarm of flailing arms and legs. Finally I saw Nolan squeeze out from under the pile, stand up, dust himself off, and tuck his shirt in. I anxiously studied his face, but he didn't look as if he was hurting. The crowd cheered, and gradually the melee ended. I relaxed a little, but I wondered what would happen next.

Fortunately, the umpires didn't agree with Robin that Nolan had deliberately thrown at him. They ejected Robin but allowed Nolan to stay in the game. I knew the episode had distracted him, though, and I wondered how it would affect the rest of the night. I shouldn't have worried, knowing how stubborn Nolan is. As soon as he starting throwing again I had no doubt he would put everything he had back into the game.

I don't believe the average fan can understand how hard it is to regain your focus when your adrenaline is pumping and your concentration has been broken. It's like coming out of a car wreck, dazed and staggering, and then trying to focus on something completely independent of the mayhem you've just experienced.

I was proud of Nolan for keeping his mental edge in spite of the fight; to me, that's the mark of a true athlete. We are always talking to Reid, Reese, and Wendy about staying focused when people are trying to distract them, yelling at them, trying to get them riled up. The best players are able to block out those things. Once an athlete makes it to the majors or to the top of any sport, everyone has talent. What separates the champions from the also-rans is mental—the ability to concentrate on the challenge at hand. That night Nolan showed he had the right stuff. He went on to earn the win, evening his season record at 3-3.

When the fight broke out, I never imagined it was going to be a national news story. Nolan pretty much downplays occasional eruptions, and after answering questions in the clubhouse he wasn't in a mood to talk about it. He told the media it was a split-second thing. "All you can do is react," he told them. "You don't have time to figure your options."

After we left the stadium, we took Reid and his friends out to eat. They kept rehashing the action play by play—or should I say blow by blow?—and finally Nolan had to laugh in spite of himself. But he was laughing at their excitement, not at the cause of it.

Reese had videotaped the game that night, and when we returned home some of us went into the game room to watch the highlights. Actually, of course, there was only one highlight anyone wanted to see. But having been at the game, I didn't yet understand all the fuss about the replays. I didn't realize the clip was being shown regularly on ESPN as well as on almost every newscast and on the late-night talk shows.

Nolan was at the kitchen table, sorting through his mail, as we were settling into the game room, and I said, "The kids are cuing up the tape. Do you want to see it?"

He didn't even look up. He just said, "No."

Wendy told us later she had stopped off with her friends at Bobby Valentine's restaurant, and she said the customers at the bar were cheering as if they were watching a real fight starring Muhammad Ali in his prime.

"Mom," she said, "people were just going crazy."

Nolan thought the excitement would have died down by the next morning, but he was wrong. It was plastered all over the newspapers, and the morning deejays had a ball discussing it on the radio. I can't remember ever hearing so much talk about an incident so unrelated to the outcome of a game.

I went to Dallas's Love Field to catch a plane home to Houston, and as I walked through the terminal I heard what amounted to an entire account of the fight, the travelers recounting it among themselves. All day long, I kept hearing Nolan's name.

Despite all the negative attention, I couldn't stay upset with Robin Ventura, who drew a two-day suspension from the American League office. I filed his actions under the label "That's Baseball," realizing that, if the truth were told, Ventura's bad luck was due in part to the fact that Nolan has such a sharp memory. He still hadn't forgotten the humiliation he'd felt thirteen years earlier when Dave Winfield attacked him after being hit by a pitch.

The painful memories of not defending himself against Winfield's assault had haunted Nolan for more than a decade. Thinking about how he had curled up in the dirt, as he'd been trained to do to protect his pitching arm, and allowed the irate batter to pummel him had been an unsettling image in his memory for all those years, and he'd vowed never to let it happen again. He had waited thirteen years, but that was the one thought he had time to recall before Robin Ventura reached him that night in August.

No, I couldn't stay upset with Robin for what had happened. What did upset me were some of the widely publicized comments made in the days following the game.

"The whole world stops when that guy pitches," the newspaper quoted Jack McDowell, the ace of the White Sox pitching staff. "It's like he's a god or something. He's been throwing at batters forever, and people are too gutless to do anything about it. I was glad when Robin went out. Someone had to do it. He's pulled that stuff wherever he goes."

That was nonsense.

Jack McDowell's comments sounded like sour grapes to me. For one thing, how could anyone say that Nolan was deliberately trying to hit Robin Ventura? Was McDowell a mind reader? Did he know exactly where every pitch would go when it was thrown? Could anyone, in fact, have 100 percent pinpoint control? No! Pitching inside, though, is part of pitching. Crowding the plate is part of hitting. Sometimes hitters don't react. Sometimes pitchers lose control. There are too many variables here and not enough definites. That's baseball. How could anyone else, besides the pitcher himself, know exactly where the pitcher is trying to throw a ball?

The headline on a column in the *Dallas Morning News* proclaimed, "Fight gives game a big black eye."

For the next three weeks, people actually carried on arguments in letters to the editor in newspapers across the country, either praising Nolan as a hero to the over-forty generation or faulting him for setting a poor example for the younger fans.

Of course, the fight was magnified because Nolan, the aging veteran and multi-record holder, was involved and because he was in his farewell season and had avoided controversy for much of his career. Now, some people speculated, he'd decided to go out with a bang. One commentator even suggested that the pitch that hit Ventura and the fight that followed were products of Nolan's frustrations over a final season gone sour, of too many weeks on the disabled list. But that was ridiculous; Nolan Ryan is a bigger person than that. He doesn't take out on others the frustrations caused by the passage of time. As in any sport, there is intimidation in baseball, and Nolan enjoyed that kind of mental gamesmanship. But he always knew where the lines were drawn.

I was also angry when I read letters from baseball fans who thought Nolan should have been tossed out of the game. I don't ever condone violence in sports, but I was proud of the way Nolan reacted. He didn't start it, and he didn't take any cheap shots. All he did was fight back. If Ventura had simply gone to first base after he got hit, nothing would have happened. Instead, he had streaked to the mound with vengeance on his mind.

The fight was one of the few times Nolan seemed to do something unpredictable. Maybe that was why he was able to laugh at one political columnist's suggestion that Nolan, at age forty-six, was the same age as President Bill Clinton and perhaps this was a good omen for the country. Many times the press put too much emphasis or meaning into an incident that really had no inner meaning. It just happened.

Nolan let most of the criticism pass without responding, but when he heard that Peter Gammons on ESPN had said that he hit Ventura on purpose, and Norm Hitzges, of Home Sports Entertainment, had described the pitch as a beanball, Nolan confronted them both. He pointed out that neither man had been at that game, then he asked them to repeat what they had said, and he responded by giving them his side of the story. I'm not sure either man was convinced, but at least Nolan felt he had been given a chance to offer his point of view.

He said, "If Robin had stopped before he got to the mound, I wouldn't have attacked him. But when he came out and grabbed me, I had to react to the situation. That's what I tried to tell people, but it looked like I used him for a punching bag when the TV people kept playing the film clip."

A lot of criticism came out of that tape, and it seemed unfair that it gave so many people a wrong impression of what Nolan is like. He doesn't lie, he doesn't boast, he doesn't ask for special treatment, and he doesn't start fights. But the commentators who showed the clip rarely pointed out those qualities. They didn't add that only one time in twenty-seven years had Nolan hit a batter on purpose, and he had admitted he did it. He later regretted it—because he acknowledged that he had hit the wrong guy.

The batter was Rick Miller, who played for the Red Sox in 1977, the year before Boston traded him to the Angels, where he became Nolan's teammate.

"I threw at him intentionally," Nolan admitted during an interview. "This was still early in my career, when I was having spells where I was very wild. They were riding me from the Boston dugout—yelling, 'Throw harder,' and things like that—taunting me and getting on me about my control. I looked over there and thought it was Rick doing most of the yelling, so I said to myself, 'That's fine; he's in the lineup.'

"When he came up, I missed him the first three times and then I finally hit him in the ribs on the fourth pitch. He just got up and went to first base and didn't say anything. I found out the next spring it wasn't Rick who had been getting on me that day. That was the first and last time I ever hit a guy on purpose."

I don't pretend to be an expert, but I couldn't be around Nolan all these years, sit through probably five thousand games, listen to the unending hours of pre- and postgame shoptalk, and not learn something about baseball. And the facts are these: Nolan threw a fastball that at least gave the illusion of rising. His curveball broke sharply. He needed to use the entire plate, and that meant pitching inside. And *that* meant sometimes batters got hit. It wasn't intentional. It was just a risk of the game.

There were pitchers who seemed to enjoy being "the enforcer"; they were the ones who retaliated if a teammate was hit or hurt or embarrassed. Don Drysdale might be considered one of those. He used to say, "If they knock down one of ours, I knock down two of theirs." He made it sound like the scene from *The Untouchables,* where the tough Irish cop tells Elliott Ness how to deal with the mob.

In Nolan's case, for most of his career his wildness and power were enough of a fear factor to work on a hitter's mind, and that, in itself, was an advantage.

And there's another thing fans should realize: Over the years, the strike zone has shrunk, the fences have been moved in, and many players agree that the quality of the umpiring has slipped. These are all advantages to the hitters.

I have the same mixed emotions of any fan who believes sports should be a test of skill and character and reveal the best in each of us. I understand that when you're giving everything you've got, tempers can flare, but I hate to see anyone try to disable an opponent. It is awful enough when unavoidable injury ends a season, or a career, without having vigilantes for opponents. For example, I hate to see defensive tackles try to knock quarterbacks out of a football game by intentionally injuring them. One of the great things about baseball, from a fan's perspective, is the one-on-one confrontation of hitter to pitcher. Unfortunately, in the heat of intense competition, injuries sometimes result from these confrontations. Dickie Thon suffered a career-threatening eye injury while with the Houston Astros when a pitch sailed inside and hit him in the head.

I once felt responsible for Nolan hurting himself, and then it really sank in how cautious a professional athlete needs to be. There is nothing delicate about Nolan—he has the hands of a farmer, but he always had to be concerned about spraining a wrist or a finger, just as a musician, artist, or surgeon has to do. I've even heard of some professionals who wouldn't shake hands with anyone because they didn't want to risk the slightest injury. They would walk through receiving lines with their hands clasped behind their backs, just nodding and smiling at the other guests or dignitaries.

Although I think this seems to be carrying things a little too far, I can understand their concern. The simplest things can cause damage, and when you make your living with your hands, you think twice about doing anything that could put you at risk. I learned that several years ago when some friends asked us to go bowling.

I said, "Fine, that'll be fun," but Nolan fretted. "Maybe I shouldn't," he said.

I finally pestered him into going. "Good grief, it's just bowling," I said. "What could go wrong if you're bowling?"

Well, I found out what could go wrong.

Nolan bowled one or two frames, and then I saw him wince. He didn't say anything; he just grinned and made a light remark and sat down, finished for the afternoon. Later, I said, "You didn't hurt yourself, did you?"

He had strained his elbow, and he didn't want to take a chance on making it worse. He was kind enough not to say, "I told you so." But still, all I could do was feel lower than a snail. It was another reminder of the trouble you can get into without thinking. Another time when I tried to talk him into joining a winter volleyball team with another couple, he just held up his hand and wiggled his fingers.

I dropped the idea without an argument.

Part Six

. . . .

Out to Pasture

23

The Family

*I*t ended in Seattle.

On September 22, 1993, in the Kingdome, after more than eighty thousand major-league pitches and just eleven days away from the end of his last season, Nolan's arm finally gave out for good.

Seattle Times reporter Bob Finnigan said in the next day's edition:

> Despite the brevity of his last appearance . . . the fans saw every-thing that made Ryan a legend of three decades.
>
> Those who came only to see him wound up with so much more, touched by Ryan's graciousness and greatness.
>
> Ryan knew his arm was injured before he came out to pitch, but he knew the people had come to see his final road start.
>
> "He went out anyway," said Seattle's Dave Fleming, who got the win that may become a trivia answer. "He didn't want to dis-appoint anyone. . . . In the end, he probably should not have pitched. But he wanted to give people something to remember him by."

Another reporter wrote, "He leaves behind 53 major-league records, a mountain of statistics, and 5,714 batters who fanned the wind."

After it was all over, we sat in a Seattle restaurant, reminiscing until late that night. For those few hours we seemed to be encased in a little bubble of peace and solitude, and we relished it, knowing it was only temporary. It felt weird. We had expected this change and anticipated its coming, but it happened so quickly we somehow weren't ready for it. With just a couple of pitches, our lives changed. It was as if we were on a train, slowing down to come into the station, and suddenly the train ran into a mountain that popped up in front of us.

When I called home to talk to the kids about what had happened, I tried to keep it simple. "Dad's hurt his arm, and he's going to come on home with me," I said. "He's all right; don't worry about him. We'll be home tomorrow afternoon."

We called them again from the airport the next morning. Reese, who was seventeen then, said, "Mom, reporters are calling all the time. They want to know when Dad's coming home."

I wanted to tell him to just stop answering the phone—but I needed to stay in touch with him and Wendy and make sure they were all right, so I couldn't do that.

The next time we called, Reese said reporters were at the house, waiting to talk to Nolan.

"Reese, tell them I'm just not up to it right now," Nolan said. "Try to explain to them that I need some downtime and then I'll make myself available to them."

We called again when we changed planes, and the situation was still the same. Nolan said, "Reese, just tell them no. Tell them I'm not going to talk to anyone today; I'm just not up to it."

After we had landed in Houston and were driving home, Reese called us in the car.

"I'm sorry, Dad," he said. "They just won't leave!"

"It's okay, Reese," Nolan answered wearily. "It's not your fault."

Then he blew out a long breath and said, "Tell them to set up their stuff on the tennis court, and I'll talk to them a couple of minutes."

The Family

As we drove up to our house, Nolan's face was grim; the yard and driveway were full of cars and satellite trucks. The reporters encircled our car as soon as we stopped.

Nolan smiled weakly at their familiar faces. "Just give me a minute," he said, then headed for the house. We had just lived through one of the most painful, frustrating, and disappointing nights of our lives, and now Nolan realized he was going to be questioned about that awful experience again and again—maybe forever.

Our mood changed when we got inside the house and saw the surprise Wendy and Reese had waiting for us: two stadium chairs that they had quickly personalized with Sharpie pens. Mine carried the complaint the kids say I yell most during their games, "Come on, ump!" and the back of Nolan's looked like the back window of the bride and groom's car after the wedding—with some modifications. It said "Just Retired." Beside the seats, they had set out a wonderful action photograph that Reese, a school photographer, had taken of Wendy, spiking the ball during a volleyball game. Wendy had inscribed the picture with "Have a happy retirement. I love you."

They stood there, smiling and watching us take it all in, hoping it would make us laugh, and I felt like my heart would burst with love and pride and thankfulness. They were just teenagers, but they had endured so much for so long with such patience and good humor. On this day when they had been hassled endlessly due to no fault of their own, they had found a way to think, not of themselves, but of us. Any parent would be proud of such kids.

Wendy just shrugged with a smile and said, "We thought we'd try to cheer you up, Dad."

He smiled and pulled her into a hug.

Reese had arranged the impromptu press conference on the tennis court, and in a few moments he went back outside with Nolan to face the reporters. I stayed inside with Wendy, watching through the window. It didn't last long. Then Nolan came inside and, one by one, the cars and satellite trucks left.

Gradually, the house grew quiet, and retirement began.

As I unpacked our bags, I couldn't help but think of some of the

235

things other baseball wives had told me about their lives after their husbands left the game. One had told me retirement was great; she said her husband had spent quality time with their kids and enjoyed every minute of all their family time together. Another had told me, "Retirement is awful!" And still others . . . well, I tried not to think about the ones who were divorced.

Suddenly I felt selfish. I had spent my whole adult life doing what I "should" do to make things work for Nolan and for our family. I thought, *Now, he'll be home all the time. Will I like it? Will I have any time to call my own, to do just what I want to do?*

I worried that the lifestyle we had enjoyed so much would somehow change. Sure, it had been hectic, but it had been full of excitement and adventure and fun. That made me remember the feature Jennifer Briggs-French had written about our family in 1990 for the *Fort Worth Star-Telegram*. After spending time with us in Alvin and Arlington, she wrote:

> A typical few weeks this summer meant Reid, 18, graduated on a Friday. Son Reese, 14, broke his wrist a few days later. Husband Nolan Ryan was pitching in Arlington so Reese decided he wanted to be there; he got his cast fitted in Arlington. Nolan pitched out of town. Ruth flew to Alvin. Reid ran over Buster the dog, slightly injuring him. Ruth flew into Love Field. Ruth drove daughter Wendy, 13, to tennis camp in Austin. Ruth went out of town with Nolan.
>
> In the middle of all this, it is Ruth who remembers to give Reid money to buy juice and snacks in Alvin and scoop up Buster at the vet's. It is Ruth who knows when Nolan's nephew is coming to mow the lawn, when Lone Star wants the gas bill paid and that someone needs to be called to fix the window in the master bedroom.
>
> And maybe some laundry needs a quick wash as well.
>
> This is the house that Ruth built, not of bricks and beams, but with equal parts patience and indulgence, devotion and discipline.
>
> This is a house in perpetual motion with family life and public demands, but one never too busy if Sue Horner wants to drop off

one of her homemade pecan pies Nolan likes so well, Reese and
Wendy need a ride to Sunday school, or Bea the [other] dog needs
a scratch behind the ears.

I smiled as I thought of all the busyness that had filled our lives
when they revolved around major-league baseball, and I couldn't help
but wonder how they would change.

And more importantly, would we like it when they did?

But even as I thought this, I knew some things would never change.
I knew, for instance, that Nolan, the kids, and I would continue to enjoy a wide range of sports, if not as participants, then as spectators.
The truth is, anyone who uses the word *contest* in our house has a
battle on his or her hands. I call it "family feud," the way instant competitions can arise.

We love to compete; that's always been a part of our lives. My dad
even tells the story of a long-ago family football match (in the days
before we became so cautious about Nolan not injuring himself and before Reid's accident). Dad still likes to brag about throwing a touchdown
pass to Nolan right over his brother's head.

Competitiveness has continued through every stage of our married
life. Even when I was pregnant with Reid, I remember the innovative
maternity tennis outfit my mother made me so I could compete in a
tournament long past the time when others would have retired to the
sidelines. My dad was always one of my favorite tennis opponents, and
neither of us ever gave the other a break. Now we stage impromptu
tennis tournaments whenever the family is together or when one of the
kids rounds up a bunch of friends.

Last winter Reid brought six friends home from college, and the
rest of the family tennis players came over for a wild tournament.
There were twelve of us altogether. Reid was my partner, and he was
so mouthy on the court I couldn't concentrate; I spent all my time
laughing, so we didn't win.

That reminds me of something else I hope will never change. I
hope my kids will always feel comfortable bringing their friends home

with them, and I know I'll always do my best to make their friends feel at ease here. That's important to me. I guess that's why I admired that trait so much in Barbara Bush. During our White House visit, she seemed to have an innate ability to make the people around her feel comfortable. I think if I had to name a role model it would be Mrs. Bush. Whenever I meet someone new, I try to remember how comfortable she made me feel the first time I met her, and I do my best to extend to that person the same cordial friendliness she shared with me.

Thinking of President and Mrs. Bush, I can't help but also remember the time Nolan and I were invited to San Clemente when the Nixons hosted a reception for the Angels. We were told exactly what time to get on the bus, exactly what kind of clothes (business attire) and shoes (daytime pumps) to wear. We were also told exactly what to do—get in this line, move forward, shake hands, say hello, move on. Mrs. Nixon stood beside President Nixon and shook hands with each of us, smiling demurely, but she didn't say anything.

If ever you see *me* standing in a receiving line somewhere, smiling demurely beside my husband, I hope you'll also hold this image of me in your mind: taking my stance at home plate, facing my grinning husband on the pitcher's mound, and taking at least one pitch clocked at eighty-plus miles per hour.

It happened in 1992, when Nolan finally accepted the kind of invitation he had received (and rejected) every winter for several years. He was invited to join a few of his teammates and coaches in hosting a fantasy baseball camp for seventy-two mostly middle-aged business types who were willing to shell out thirty-four hundred dollars apiece to play "let's pretend."

But this time, before Nolan could say no, I offered to go with him if the club would let me take part as one of the campers. I knew I would enjoy going, but I wondered if people would think I was crazy. (A few years earlier I had read an article about a woman who had attended one of those camps, and she said it was a great, fun experience for her.) I guess it was that old competitive nature coming out in me again. Actually, I saw it as a chance to spend four or five extra days with him away from the telephone.

The Family

The Rangers tailored a uniform for me, as they did for all the campers, and I requested the familiar number 34, the same as Nolan. The Rangers quickly agreed, not wanting to leave the public wondering if we were related. The idea lost a tiny edge, though, when it turned out that six other campers had requested the same number!

I had often been Nolan's catcher when he needed someone to pitch to in the winter, and although I could handle his throws in the seventy-mile-per-hour range I had never actually stood in the batter's box and tried to hit against him. I took it all very seriously.

I'll say this: I didn't get any special treatment. I played in double-headers on four days. One day I joined my fellow campers for eighteen holes of golf, then took on some of them in a few sets of tennis.

But, of course, the highlight came when I stepped into the batter's box and looked out at my tall, handsome husband, smiling mischievously at me from the mound. He did not see fit to go easy on me. He threw at least as hard as he did to any other batter, and I tried hard to concentrate and swing if the pitch looked good.

For the record, I took a fastball that was outside, fouled off two more, and then hit a grounder sharply up the middle. The ball hit the screen in front of the mound and bounced to the third baseman, who threw me out.

I might have done better if I hadn't been concealing an injury. Two days before we left Alvin, I had slipped on a sidewalk and sprained my wrist and one finger. I kept them iced to make sure I wouldn't miss the camp. But during my time at bat, Nolan jammed me with a pitch, and I bruised the finger again.

A friend of ours, a writer in Houston, could not believe his ears when he heard what had happened. "You *jammed* her?" he said to Nolan accusingly. "Your own wife?"

"I had to," Nolan explained matter-of-factly. "She was digging in on me." Then he bragged, "She did real well. I probably did throw a little harder to her because I knew she wouldn't want to do it any other way."

He was right. But I must admit that my heart was beating a little faster and my adrenaline was pumping when that eighty-five-mile-per-hour fastball whizzed by my nose.

Out to Pasture

It's times like this that remind me how much fun it's been to be married to Nolan Ryan for nearly twenty-nine years. Consider birthdays, for instance. Last year on my birthday, Nolan came in and said he wanted me to come outside and see my present. I could tell by the twinkle in his eye that he was pleased with himself, and since the gift was outside I certainly didn't expect something lacy or scented. On the other hand, I wasn't quite ready for what he had waiting for me.

I stepped outside and looked in the back of the pickup as he posed expectantly beside the tailgate. There stood a big metal bucket on wheels with two mops and a squeegee leaning up against it. I couldn't keep from laughing. "A mop bucket," I said with a smile, a challenge in my voice. "How romantic, dear."

He smiled his impish grin and said, "But it's for the ranch house—something we can do *together!*"

I rolled my eyes and laughed. Now I knew that Nolan Ryan really had retired. *His and her mops.* An hour or so later, the florist delivered a dozen gorgeous red roses.

Other gifts have been just as much fun—if a bit less practical. Nolan has never forgotten my birthday or our anniversary. His wedding gift to me was a pair of tiny pearl earrings; strangely enough, I don't remember what I gave him.

On one anniversary he gave me a book of poems. On our tenth anniversary he gave me a piano, a Steinway baby grand, and had someone deliver it as a complete surprise. I hadn't played in years, but I was thrilled with such a thoughtful gift. Now I love to play, but just to entertain myself. I grew up playing church hymns and songs in the Thompson piano books; that's the sum total of my training.

I try to be equally inventive in my gifts to him, although I spend a lot less money. One Christmas I gave him a wooden Indian, the kind that used to stand outside the old stores in western towns. Another year I gave him a longhorn steer, so now he has four longhorns, including the two the Rangers gave him. Another year I bought him an old gasoline pump with a light. We try to think of unusual things to surprise each other with. We also enjoy going out with six to eight other couples to celebrate our birthdays.

And remember, I have a mother, a sister, and a daughter in addition to this thoughtful husband, so my birthdays are never forgotten! My mother always made our birthdays an extraspecial day, and she could be counted on to have a special gift waiting for each of us. It might not be anything big, but it was something specifically chosen (or made) for us. It let us know she'd put some time and thought into it. It was *special,* and it made us feel special to know she cared enough to do that for us.

With that kind of inherited attitude, it's easy to understand why we make a big deal out of the kids' birthdays whenever we can. That was something my mother always did for us kids when we were young, and I know how special she always made us feel. So I try to do the same for my kids now. When they were adolescents, our kids would say, "Oh, Mom, that's so dumb." But those are the things they talk about now as some of their favorite memories.

One year when they were teenagers I planned a scavenger hunt for one of their parties. We had some Swedish relatives in town visiting us, so they came to the party, too, and their teenage daughter was on one of the teams with some kids—even though she didn't quite understand what was going on. She seemed to have a great time participating, though. We gave them the lists and let them go in groups in their cars. And as they went roaring off, I thought, *What have I done?* But they all survived, and it really was great fun.

Reid's twenty-first birthday came while his TCU baseball team was playing at Texas A&M in College Station. He couldn't come home for that weekend, so Nolan, Reese, Wendy, and I went up there. We had a party at a restaurant with some friends and relatives who lived there, and it was really wild and crazy as we reminisced about Reid's antics as he was growing up.

I missed having Reid around every day—I know we all did, including the grandparents. It was equally hard when Reese left last year to head to Fort Worth to attend TCU. Now they're both sharing a house there. Sometimes my dad goes up to Arlington to spend time with the boys on a special day—or even when it's not a birthday or holiday. He takes along a special pan he bought just to make his famous Norwegian pancakes, or he makes his delicious spaghetti or gumbo or other favorite recipes. It's a lucky day for any of us when Dad shows up with his trusty pots and pans and groceries.

Wendy, born in March, was our spring-training baby, so we celebrated all her birthdays in Florida. Usually that meant we just had a little cake and some gifts and a happy time together. But when she was ten, we went all out and rented a bus and invited some Astros families to go to a Florida attraction called Boardwalk and Baseball. Circus World was there, too, and we had the whole place to ourselves. Last year, when we celebrated Wendy's first birthday in Texas (her sixteenth), we had a big barbecue and a tennis and volleyball tournament.

The kids are very good at thinking of creative surprises for us, too, like the stadium seats Reese and Wendy had waiting for us when we returned home from Seattle. I still have a little heart-shaped box that Reese surprised me with when he was only ten. He's getting good at bigger surprises now. Last summer he surprised a friend with a puppy— he even drove to San Antonio to deliver it to her.

Sometimes I marvel at how lucky we are to have been blessed with such delightful kids. They aren't perfect by any means—they spent their share of time in detention or being grounded. I've been called to the principal's office a time or two, and my kids have gotten into their share of mischief. They've been known to sneak out at night, and they've done things they weren't supposed to do. But every day I'm thankful that they are normal, happy kids who work hard to please us and who are independent when they are away from us.

But we've done our best to be consistent in our discipline. I don't *not* believe in spanking, but it just didn't work for our kids. Spanking Reid was like hitting my own head against the wall; it had no effect on him, didn't work at all. But one swat to Wendy and she was crushed . . . cried as if her heart was irrevocably broken.

So I changed after I learned a little about parenting with Reid. I stopped spanking the kids. Instead, I got better results by saying, "If you don't do this, you can't have that," or "If you do this, you can't do that."

Nolan was good at giving advice, but he wasn't always there, and he didn't always agree with what I had already done by the time he found out about it. When he would call and I told him something they had done, he would ask me, "What did you do?" Then sometimes he'd say, "You should have done this . . . "

When the kids became teenagers, we faced those other issues all parents come up against sooner or later. First, there were the dating problems. There have been times when we haven't liked the ones our kids wanted to date. Once we told one of the boys flat-out that he could not go out with a particular girl. I dreaded it because I thought there might be a battle. But he didn't argue with us; it turned out that he had actually been looking for a way out.

Another time one of the kids was going with someone we felt uncomfortable with. I bit my tongue for several weeks, then we said the dating had to stop. When the announcement was made, the other kid called me and asked, "Mrs. Ryan, why don't you like me? Why won't you let us go out?"

Talk about being put on the spot!

I said, "It's not that I don't like you. I don't know you that well. I can only observe where you go and who you go with. As a mother, I have to worry about my kids. If anything happened to one of them and I felt I was at fault or that I could have prevented it, I would never forgive myself. I'm sorry if I have hurt your feelings, but that's just the way it is."

We've also tried to be equally direct with our kids when it comes to the issue of drinking. We've let them know we don't approve of underage drinking, and we've reminded them of the disastrous consequences of drinking and driving. They've already seen that firsthand. Last spring my friend's sixteen-year-old daughter was killed in a crash involving a driver who had been drinking, and one of Wendy's friends died when the car she was riding in crashed at what police estimate was one hundred miles per hour.

To the Ryan kids, an even bigger threat was probably the reminder that drinking could get them kicked off their sports teams. We've also pointed out that if they are even in a car with a minor who's in possession of alcohol, they could get the same citation, even if they're not drinking themselves.

We've told them they needed to behave because they know right from wrong—not because their problems would be an embarrassment to us, living in the spotlight, but because *they* have to live with the consequences of their decisions. We tried to make it clear that we loved them and wanted them to be safe. I've told them they can call me, no matter what, and I'll be there for them, no questions asked. I'm a realist. I realize if they thought they would be grounded for the situation they'd gotten themselves in, they probably wouldn't call. So I tell them we'd be much more upset if they were drinking and tried to drive home— or got in a car with a driver who had been drinking.

Sometimes I guess we go to the extreme to make that point, but it's one thing I'm glad we can afford to do. In a small town like Alvin, sometimes the kids seem to think drinking is all there is to do. We've worked hard to show our kids they can have a good time without drinking. For instance, after one of the proms, our kids invited their friends over for an all-nighter—we had a house full of them. We rented movies and played tennis and volleyball all night, and I think everyone had a good time. The kids slept all over the floor, then they all got up and went to the beach the next day.

Another time, another couple rented a house on the beach for the after-prom party, and I rented a bus to take twenty kids down there when the prom ended.

We've managed to avoid any major problems, so I feel pretty good about the alcohol issue so far; on the other hand, I don't think we've done such a great job talking to our kids about sex. Nolan isn't comfortable discussing that topic with them, and I've tried but failed. The fact is, they just don't want to talk about it.

It's like one of my friends was saying when she described her own pitiful attempt to talk to her son about sex. She bought some books that told her how to do it, and she sat him down to discuss it one day and spoke very matter-of-factly about the whole thing. When she was finished, her son looked her in the eye and said icily, "Mom, I don't ever want to hear that again. That's the grossest thing I have ever heard!"

Compared with the issues of sex and drinking, I know the issue of teenagers' appearance seems minor, but I also know how many arguments it causes. Like any mother, I've sometimes worried that the kids weren't dressed appropriately when we were going out in public. But I've tried to accept as much as I can without being critical of their hair or clothes. I honestly try to be a person who's full of optimism and praise whenever I can be.

Nolan has drawn a little tighter line. For example, he jokingly told the boys, "If you come home with your ears pierced, I'll cut your ears off!"

I asked him why it would bother him so much; I think I could handle it, although it wouldn't be what I would choose for them—and so far I'm glad it isn't what they've chosen for themselves. If I can just get them to look halfway clean and neat, I consider it a victory.

One day, though, my perspective was changed when I saw a television talk show about kids who pierced various body parts. I know I would still love my kids if they had pierced noses or navels, but I'm *so* thankful I don't have to face that problem!

Another issue we've worried about is whether our kids have learned the value of work the way Nolan did when he was growing up. I feel pretty confident in saying our kids haven't been spoiled. They mowed the yard and did chores to earn pocket money, and they had summer jobs or after-school work when possible, but our lifestyle of moving around and constantly being gone has put them in a different position from most kids. We're never sure we've prepared them for the responsibilities that will soon be coming their way, but we've done our best.

This came home to us when Reese agreed to go to the ranch for a few days to help the ranch manager work the cattle—pinning calves for branding and other hard, rugged work. He happily headed off for the ranch—a four-hour drive to a remote area outside of George West, Texas, and when he got there he realized he had forgotten his suitcase.

Out to Pasture

When I called him later that night, he admitted what he had done. I said, "Well, Reese, why don't you just go to Wal-Mart and buy yourself a couple of pairs of jeans and some shirts to get by?"

He said, "Mom, have you forgotten where I am? There are no stores close by, and we start work in the morning at daylight."

Reese paid for his forgetfulness. Every night when he came in from working cattle, he would take off his one and only T-shirt and jeans, wrap himself in a towel, and sit in the laundry room until they were washed and dried. His arms were scratched up from the thick brush and not wearing the long-sleeved shirts he'd packed in his suitcase. I don't expect he'll forget his luggage again any time soon!

All in all, I think most kids today have learned a lot of little lessons like this, the hard way, and I believe they deserve a lot more respect than adults usually give them. We should be a little more careful, I think, to look beneath an appearance that might not meet our adult expectations. Behind those baggy clothes and strange haircuts, we just might find some pretty interesting people.

One of my pet peeves is people who treat kids disrespectfully, especially when they think another adult isn't listening. One of the most memorable times that happened for our family was at a ball game in San Francisco when Reese and Wendy were five and six years old. When the kids and I got to our seats, we found a woman sitting in the middle of them. But instead of asking her to move, I motioned to the kids to sit in the row behind her.

She was wearing headphones, and the kids were sitting there, laughing and playing with their toys before the game began. Suddenly, she turned around and yelled in a viciously loud voice, "Would you kids be quiet!"

I'm not proud of admitting it, but I lost my temper. Something just flashed in me, and I said, "First of all, these kids are not bothering you. Just because they're kids, you shouldn't talk to them like that. Second, this is a ballpark. Most of these crazy people are loud and drunk. And anyway, you're sitting in our seats."

I was so mad I was shaking, but the woman just turned around. She stayed in our seats. The funny part of it was that word must have gotten around to the team that I had bawled out someone in the wives section. Ray Knight was on the team then, and he was a terrible prankster. Later that day we were all on the team bus, and he yelled to me, "Hey, Ruth! I hear you don't like my mother-in-law."

I nearly died. He really made me believe that horrible woman was his wife's mother. But of course I found out later she wasn't.

The kids thought the whole thing was pretty funny; they love jokes and pranks, and they accuse me of being "too serious" about some things. I guess I am a little too sensitive now and then, but it's hard not to be; after all, I've devoted my entire adult life to being a wife to Nolan and a mother to our three kids. So please forgive me if I have this little dream that one day our kids will look back in their own adult years and recognize that they were raised on love and faith and straight talk. And I can't help hoping that they'll understand someday that those qualities aren't always the easiest things to teach, so maybe they'll see that their mother was justified in being a little too overprotective now and then!

24

Still (Fitness) Crazy after All These Years

I wasn't ready for menopause.

First of all, I was too young. When the hot flashes and crazy mood swings and menstrual-cycle problems set in, at first I couldn't imagine what was happening to me. All sorts of dire possibilities ran through my mind as, day after day, I tried to determine where these personal lightning bolts were coming from.

I was flabbergasted when I figured it out. *Me? Going through menopause? There must be some mistake!* I always envisioned menopause as something that happened to gray-haired grandmothers. Why, I was barely in my mid-forties! How could this happen?

Second, I was too busy to deal with such a life-changing ordeal. I already had enough things in my life to cope with—an oldest child getting ready to leave for college, two other teenagers going through their own perplexing hormonal changes, and a husband whose fame seemed to be exploding just as his career was nearing an end . . .

A husband whose career hinged on a pitching arm that had a tear in the ligament . . .

My life already seemed to be saturated with things that made my emotions swing from high to low like a rowboat riding a stormy sea.

At night when I should have been falling asleep, I lay stiff and wide-eyed, staring into the darkness, wondering, *How can I cope with all of this and menopause too?*

I gained ten pounds.

I lost my positive attitude.

I was depressed.

And I was miserable.

The timing couldn't have been worse. As I was fighting this losing battle against my raging hormones, Nolan was struggling through his last season, fighting his own battle to get off the disabled list and fulfill his commitment to finish the year with his team. We needed each other, and we tried to understand what the other was going through, but I must admit that during that long, torturous summer, there were times when I was hanging on so tightly to my own emotional roller coaster that I had no energy left to worry about anyone else.

In the height of the craziness I realized I needed counseling, but I just couldn't bring myself to submit to it. For one thing, I didn't think I had any time to go to therapy. My days were filled with endless running—from home to school, from home to one of the kids' activities, from home to the ranch, from Alvin to Arlington; the days flew by, and as each one ended I had either traveled—or felt as if I'd traveled—hundreds of miles. There was no time to stop, no *way* to stop. I had to keep moving.

Another reason I didn't seek counseling was that I just didn't feel I could talk to anyone about the things that were happening to me. Even though I knew there were many trustworthy professional counselors out there, I couldn't bring myself to confide in any of them. I guess it was vain of me to assume that baseball fans—or anyone else, for that matter—would be interested in my own personal torment, but I'd seen the way headlines could take a grain of truth and turn it into a hint of scandal. I didn't want to do anything that might help that happen. In other words, I didn't want to tell anyone about my problems.

There are many times now when I look back at my life and see what I've come through—good times and bad—and I really believe there were times when exercise saved my sanity. One day I made this discovery, which should have been obvious all along. Since that time in California when I'd begun my running program by trotting, heaving and gasping, to the neighbor's driveway and back, I had rarely let a week go by without at least two or three exercise or running sessions, sometimes more. I had continued that routine devotedly all these years, and one morning in Alvin when I got out of bed feeling that I couldn't get through one more day, I automatically pulled on a leotard and headed out to the weight room. It had become such a habit, I really didn't think about it.

First, stretching. Then the weights. Next, the stairstepper, and on to the bike. By the end of an hour, I was sweating and red-faced and breathing hard.

And then I noticed it: Standing there, taking a break, I felt healthy and good.

This is my therapy, I realized. *When I'm working out, the bad things— the dark moods and turbulent emotions—disappear.*

When I go out for a run I try not to think about my problems. I don't mean to trivialize things here, because I know most problems don't just go away. But sometimes time does heal wounds, and exercise is certainly better "therapy" than drinking or overindulgence.

I really mean it when I say that exercising helped me keep my sanity during a very stressful period of my life, but I'm not necessarily saying this approach will work for everyone; it's not the cure-all for all problems. I probably should have gone to counseling when I was depressed because it took me a very long time to overcome some of my problems. I'm sure that there are many good, professional people out there who could be of great benefit to those who suffer from emotional distress, and I probably should have done that myself.

Actually, I feel a little foolish admitting that I "discovered" how much exercise helped my emotional state. After all, fitness had been a crucial part of Nolan's whole life, and I'd always worked hard to stay in shape. Those years when I had lost my fitness because I was overwhelmed by mothering responsibilities taught me an important lesson:

Out to Pasture

Taking time for exercising was essential to my well-being. It wasn't optional for me. If I intended to stay healthy and be an active participant in our busy family's lifestyle, I had to *make* time to stay fit.

After that rocky beginning when my first attempt at running lasted less than five minutes, I took Nolan's advice and set a goal of lasting a little longer, working a little harder every time I worked out. When I'd gained a little stamina, I enrolled in a ballet course in California, and later I took some advanced tennis lessons. Since then, exercising and working out have continued to be high priorities for me.

I even became a certified aerobics instructor, and I loved teaching and sharing what I'd learned. It was such a thrill to see people improving, getting healthier and gaining strength and pep. I tried to be a good motivator, the kind of teacher I had enjoyed having myself. I would modify the workout for the different levels I was teaching. The important thing for me was that the students enjoyed it. I told them, "Don't think of this as thirty minutes of aerobics. Consider this part of your lifestyle; make it a natural part of your life."

Now I try to work out one and a half to two hours almost every day if possible. I know not everyone can spend that much time—and for a lot of people it's not necessary. But for me, it's become something I enjoy, and I indulge myself whenever I can. I try to work out at least five days a week, and I also run two to three miles four days a week.

I'm a big fan of running; as I said earlier, I hate to see coaches use it as punishment for poor performance or disruptive behavior. I feel so sad for kids who are brainwashed by this kind of attitude; it stays with them all their lives. Instead, running should be used as a part of conditioning, as a training tool to develop strength and endurance.

In recent years I've exercised on my own—by myself or with Nolan or maybe Wendy—instead of attending classes. Recently I began working with one of Reese's friends who is earning a master's degree in exercise physiology. He has a program all made out for me; it's like having a personal trainer, and it's made the workouts even more beneficial. They're more fun, too, because he varies the routine so nothing gets monotonous.

My routine varies, but I usually stretch and then work out with weights. Next I use the treadmill, a stationary bicycle, and/or the stair-stepper. Usually, I wake up looking forward to my workout. I like feeling good, and when I'm in there stretching and lifting and getting my heart rate up, I *do* feel good—and I know the feeling will last. I've told people that exercise has kept me from going nuts, and I'm not exaggerating.

It's also helped me keep my weight under control. When those ten extra pounds suddenly appeared in the midst of menopause, I exercised harder to take them off. I know I would have had to starve myself to lose the weight if I hadn't been exercising.

Another thing that helped me was estrogen therapy. And finally, late last year, I gave in to a hysterectomy. All the while I was recovering from the surgery, I was thinking about my exercise workouts, missing them the way a kid who has to stay home might miss going to an amusement park with a bunch of friends. As soon as my doctor gave the okay, I eased myself back into my routine, and I'm sure it made my long-term recovery progress faster.

Even when we travel, Nolan and I try to find time to work out at least thirty minutes a day. Most hotels these days have some workout rooms with weights and machines. I think the real key to sticking with an exercise program is to find things you enjoy and make them a part of your routine. Do something to music or pop a movie in the VCR while you're on the treadmill or stairstepper. If I need a little extra boost, I watch a ball game while I'm working out. Someone told me once if there was a program on television I really wanted to see to tape it—and then watch it as I exercise. I've tried that, and my friend is right: The time flies by, and before I know it, the program is over, my workout is finished, and I feel better.

While staying in shape has become an essential part of my life, it's been by choice. That hasn't been the case for Nolan. Staying physically fit isn't something professional athletes have a choice about. They either stay in shape, or they find a different career.

In the early years, Nolan's fitness routine consisted of four steps that occurred in an annual cycle. Around the first of January (just after the holiday feasting period ended), we concentrated on low-fat meals and counting calories as Nolan began to think about spring training (step one). A couple of weeks later, I would see him doing push-ups and sit-ups on the floor at night before going to bed (step two). After that came the serious work on his stationary bicycle and endless laps in the pool (step three). Then he moved outdoors to the pitcher's mound he'd built behind our house, and he began tossing a ball around (step four). This would last until it was time to leave for Florida and the Grapefruit League games that would begin in early March.

Now, even though Nolan has retired from professional baseball, he continues to work out several days a week, year-round. Over the years, he made the same discovery I did: that he feels better, is more energetic, and stays healthier when he stays in shape. And we both believe working out is becoming more important for us as we grow older. Nolan and I are both spokespersons for "Fit over Forty: Your Doctor's Prescription," a program co-sponsored by the American College of Sports Medicine and developed by the Advil Forum on Health Education. It provides the medical community with tools to help educate older patients about the benefits of regular and moderate exercise and the health risks associated with inactivity.

Just as I did, Nolan made a life-changing discovery about exercise, but his came early in his career. When he was playing for the Angels, he discovered the weight room at Anaheim Stadium. As hard as it may be to believe this now, when working out with weights is acknowledged as being beneficial for nearly everyone—athletes and nonathletes, young and old—back then sports experts believed weight training made people musclebound. The universal gym in Anaheim Stadium wasn't there for the baseball players; it had been installed for some other group.

Out of curiosity, Nolan started slipping in and using the weights little by little, being careful not to overdo. He learned on his own how to work different areas of his body, and he carefully noted how the results affected his pitching strength and his overall fitness. He liked what was happening to his body as a result of using the weights. Now, twenty years later, he says there's no doubt in his mind that he would have been out of the game many years ago if he hadn't discovered that weight room.

When he was playing baseball, Nolan worked out from two to five hours almost every day. He had a positive attitude about his workouts;

he knew it would be easy to skip one—he had plenty of other things he could be doing—but he knew the results were worth the effort.

I always thought it was interesting to consider the mental game he played to psych himself up for working out: Nolan's exercise routine began *immediately after a game.* While his pitching arm was being iced to reduce inflammation from throwing more than a hundred pitches, he was usually riding an exercise bike—not because he needed the exercise to loosen up after a game, but because he considered it preparation for the next game he would start in. *As soon as one game was over, he started preparing for his next one.*

The next morning he would be in the weight room by nine o'clock and begin a two- to three-hour workout with ninety minutes of upper- and lower-body weightlifting. Next came the stairstepper and stationary bike, and then running and stretching to cool down. The following two days, he would reduce the workout by an hour or two, but on the third day, he would start over again with a two- or three-hour session. Only on the day before he was to start did he back off the workout routine to give his body a day to recover.

My intention in sharing our passion for fitness here is not to impress you with our strenuous routines or overwhelm you with the idea that your life must revolve around exercise equipment if you want to stay fit. The point I'm trying to make is that exercising can make a difference in your life; Nolan and I are living proof of that.

You don't have to spend hours every day to stay fit. But you do have to make an effort to stay with it on a fairly consistent basis. A thirty-minute workout once a week probably won't help much. Instead, find something you enjoy, and then make it a part of your life, as important to you as eating and bathing and sleeping. It's like Nolan told me so long ago in California—allow yourself a few days of feeling sore and tired, but keep pushing yourself every time to work just a little bit harder, last a little bit longer. Then one day I hope you'll find yourself exercising and you'll make that discovery I made when menopause had me firmly in its grasp: *Hey! This is great!*

25

The Next Season

*L*ast year when the Rangers' new stadium was about to open in Arlington, a story was making the rounds that two workmen were up in one of the skybox suites, hurriedly trying to repair a leak in the ceiling before the opening festivities began.

"We'd better hurry," one of them said. "The president of the club is due any minute."

"Yeah," his partner replied. "I hear Nolan Ryan's coming too."

The first guy smiled ruefully. "I hope Nolan gets here first," he said.

"Why?" his partner asked.

"Well, if the club president gets here first, he'll chew us out for not having everything ready. But if Nolan gets here first, he'll help us fix it."

I wasn't mentioned in the story, but I like to imagine myself there, too, holding the flashlight and joking with the guys as we all hurried to get things fixed before the "important" people got there.

I'm not mentioned in a lot of the stories about Nolan, but that's okay. I know my place, and it's usually there in the background, holding the flashlight, watching from the stands, waiting outside the clubhouse, or back in Alvin, covering home.

Out to Pasture

At first, when Nolan got to be well known and we would go out in public, I sometimes felt like the invisible woman. I could be standing there beside him, and some people actually seemed unable to see me. It still happens occasionally, but I know now that when I start feeling invisible it's only because I let other people make me feel that way. Nolan never does, and whenever he sees it happening he steps in to help.

For instance, last year at the elaborate opening-game luncheon at The Ballpark in Arlington, Nolan and I were sitting side by side at a table in the banquet room, and I got up to get something to drink. When I came back, a man was sitting in my seat next to Nolan. He had piled a bunch of stuff around him, and he was even shelling peanuts in my plate.

I just stood there, waiting, and he finally looked up and said, "Oh, is this your plate?" He just moved over one place and kept right on talking, leaning around me so he could see Nolan. The game was being delayed because of rain, and suddenly the wait seemed to stretch before me in one long, endless nightmare. My stomach was in a knot, and I felt myself starting to sweat as I sat there, looking at my plate full of peanut shells. Nolan muttered out of the side of his mouth, "I'm sorry. He sat down and started in before I knew what was happening." Then he looked at my face and said, "Let's get out of here."

He and I left the party and moved up to his office in the stadium. We sat there alone, watching the rain for an hour, and I was happy again.

The kids are good at ignoring such incidents. Sometimes when someone behaves rudely toward the kids and me so he or she can get to Nolan, Reese says something silly under his breath that makes us all laugh. He never says it loud enough for the offender to hear, but we all know it's probably what Nolan would like to say if his tolerance and his sense of responsibility to the fans weren't so strong. Reese can be sarcastically funny; he makes us all laugh, and that relieves the tension.

It also helps to know that when we get alone, away from the crowds, we'll make up for the irritations and the annoyances we have to cope with every time we go out together in public. Now that he's retired, Nolan and I try to eat lunch together every day we can; we'll either eat at home or we'll head for one of the familiar restaurants in Alvin where there usually aren't many out-of-towners and where the local folks ignore us. When we get home, we spend a lot of time together, working around the house and yard or sitting at the kitchen table, sharing a cup of coffee and talking. Nolan's always been accessible to me; he's always been willing to spend quiet time, listening and sharing with me. No television. No newspapers. Sometimes we even manage to ignore the telephone. There have been times during these talks when he hasn't liked what I had to say, but he's listened anyway, and we've worked through our problems together.

We've done the same thing with the kids. We try to take time to discuss things with them and to tell them as much as we know about what's going to happen next in our lives. But there are times when we have breakdowns in communication, when these kinds of statements are heard: "I didn't know you were going out of town," or "I have a date tonight. I can't go with you and Dad," or "Didn't I tell you I'm bringing three friends home this weekend?" I'm sure similar things can be heard in every busy family.

We also try to make a point of listening to their opinions and letting them know how much they matter to us. We've tried by our example to show them how to live a Christian lifestyle; we do our best to follow the Golden Rule, and we've taught the kids that they're no better—and no worse—than anyone else, no matter how much money their family has and no matter how much frustration and embarrassment and annoyance they must endure because their father is in the public eye.

That's not to say there are never any sharp words or arguments. One of the hardest things I think Nolan has had to do in his retirement is sit in the stands with me—that thing I'd dreamed of for so many years—and keep from spouting off. Being a spectator is a lot harder than he thought! He'll be quiet for a long time, but if something keeps happening that he doesn't like, he'll eventually yell out some "advice." At one of Reese's baseball games last year, quite a few heads turned late in the game when Nolan complained, "Come on, ump! You've got the widest strike zone in the league!"

He got his first taste of how hard "spectatoring" was going to be when he went with me a few years ago to one of Reid's high school basketball games.

Nolan loves basketball; he could probably coach it as well as he could baseball. He loves the technique of the game, the mechanics—everything about it. On this night, Reid was out there on the floor with the team, playing all out in a wild game, and he did something stupid. I can't even remember now what it was, but Reid had obviously made a mistake.

Nolan shouted loudly from the stands, "Come *on,* Reid!"

Reid looked up, stomped over to the stands, put his hands on his hips, and shouted back, "I'm *trying,* Dad!"

I think the embarrassment they caused each other that night gave them both a lot of insight into the other's situation. It's hard to do your best when you think someone—just one person or a stadium full of fans—is watching your every move. And it's equally hard to sit in the stands and appreciate just how hard an athlete is trying to do his or her best.

Over the years our kids have learned a lot about both sides of that issue. They've participated in a wide variety of sports themselves, and they've put up with a lot as kids of a sports celebrity. All in all, they've turned out very well, in my highly biased opinion.

Reid, our comic, is playing minor-league baseball now, but he's prepared himself for a career outside of baseball if that's the way his life goes. He's been careful to keep realistic goals, and despite outsiders' pressure on him to follow in his dad's footsteps, he knows that his natural abilities may lie in other directions. He says he'll seek a career in broadcasting if he doesn't progress to the majors. Already he's showing signs of real talent as an announcer; the message on his answering machine isn't "Hi, this is Reid. Leave a message." It's the major-league baseball disclaimer ("No portion of this program may be rebroadcast without the express permission of Major League Baseball"). He also has creative talents. I always thought he would make a good advertising person, making up commercials or even being a game-show host.

He has a unique and charming way with people. Recently he announced a practice game at TCU in which his brother was playing. Although there were only about six people watching from the stands, he entertained everyone with his humor and performed a "special" song for each player on both teams whenever each one came up to bat.

Reese is our sensitive middle child. He talks to me a lot, and I treasure our closeness. When he was seven years old, he and I took a trip to Sweden, just the two of us plus my mother and sister, to meet our Swedish family members—relatives of my mother's mother. We visited Mother's cousin and stayed with family members, and it was a wonderful experience. Best of all, Reese seemed as delighted with everything as I was.

Reese is a very independent young man; he doesn't always go along with the crowd, and he stands up for what he believes is right. One year at the prom he wore jeans, boots, a cowboy hat—and a tuxedo jacket. I did a double take when he walked out dressed that way, but then I had to stop and admit that he did look pretty good.

When Reese was in junior high, he would get into fights in school, and he was not a big kid. We'd get a call from the teacher: "Reese was fighting again today." It was pretty hard on all of us, but before we started lecturing him, we would talk about what had happened. We'd ask him why he was fighting. Usually it was because he was defending a friend or a principle he believed in—and whenever it was something about Reese's idea of right and wrong, he usually had some pretty darn good reasons for doing what he did.

A few years ago, Reese was at home and in charge of taking care of the animals while I was on a road trip. He went out to check on something at the barn, and one of our dogs accidentally got shut up in the house and went crazy trying to get outside with Reese. In her frenzy, she chewed up blinds and tore up some doors and curtains. When Reese got back to the house and saw what happened he knew he was responsible. He called a decorator friend of mine to come over, assess the damage, and help get it fixed. He told her that he would pay for it with his own money. The incident made me very proud that he would be conscientious enough to try to fix the problem without my help.

And then there's Wendy, our third child. We were so delighted that we finally had a daughter when she was born—and she's turned out to be everything I ever dreamed a daughter would be. We hang out together and spend time talking; sometimes she works out with me in the weight room or plays tennis with me.

Whenever I'm down or I'm having a bad week, Wendy notices. She's very perceptive about other people's feelings. She'll go to the store and buy a card and write something sweet on it, then leave it for me to find. The boys might not notice if I'm a little depressed about something; I joke that I could probably be curled up on the floor, dying of depression, and the boys would just step over me on their way out the door without even noticing. But Wendy picks up on things; we're good friends, and I feel blessed by her companionship.

Also, it should be noted, Wendy's probably the best all-round athlete in the family; while the boys focused on two primary sports (baseball and football for Reese; baseball and basketball for Reid), Wendy played softball, basketball, and volleyball and competed in swimming, diving, and gymnastics throughout grade school and junior high. She goes from one sport to the next and is good at whatever she tries. Last year she decided to drop basketball. The coach hated to see her leave the team—and said so. It made the decision hard for her, but I told her, "Wendy, we love basketball, and we love watching you play. But it has to be your decision. You're the one who has to put in the time and effort."

She worried what Nolan would think, but he told her the same thing I did: "We'll support you no matter what you do."

We don't want her to be pressured by what other people think she should do with her time. She's mature enough to make her own decisions, and I respect her judgment because she always puts a lot of thought into everything and she's very realistic about her own abilities. She makes good grades, is in the National Honor Society at school, and is a very thoughtful and beautiful young woman.

I feel close to all three of our kids; Nolan and I try to talk straight with them about situations we're facing, and we try to ease some of the pressure they feel because of comparisons with their dad.

When Reese signed a baseball scholarship with TCU, the college Reid had attended, an article in the *Fort Worth Star-Telegram* said that he was "trying to follow in the Ryan family footsteps. He may not be an all-star pitcher, but he may be the entrepreneur in the family. He may be the one who winds up owning the team."

I couldn't quite decide how to take that at first, but Reese didn't seem bothered by the comparison, and he liked the team-owner prediction, so I didn't complain.

Even Wendy finds herself compared to Nolan occasionally. When she was at a tournament, a coach from another school told her, "You walk just like your dad. Even your right arm and shoulder hang down, just like his."

She just sighed and said, "I know. I know."

Sometimes the kids feel they can't even take a step without someone trying to analyze them and see how they match up against their superathlete father.

I think we're fortunate that the kids talk to us and tell us what's going on in their lives. When they do, I try not to be critical. I grew up with a lot of praise and support, so I'm quick to look for ways to pass that gift along to my kids. When they're worried about something their friends are doing, I'll tell them, "You know right from wrong. Follow your conscience."

I try to practice positive reinforcement every chance I get, and I make it a point to find things to praise them for. I'll say, "Just look at your driving records. I'm proud of them, and I hope you are too."

But because I'm so quick to praise, sometimes I'm not sure my glowing accounts have much effect on them. I told Nolan once, "If you praise them, it means so much more to them. Why is that?" It's the same if he corrects them. I can say the very same thing and they just answer, "Aw, Mom," and walk away.

Nolan considers that attitude a natural consequence of his having spent so much time away from his children over the years. But he knows there's one situation when the kids head my way. He always tells people, "If the kids have a problem, the person they go to is their mother, not me."

Nolan is reserved, reticent, and never effusive. He has a way of taking a long moment (or two) before answering a question or offering an opinion. He is a commanding presence in his household, just as his own father was. When he speaks, his kids listen. But he has fun with them, too, and on a day-to-day basis he wants to know everything they are doing.

I see his influence when a stubborn streak shows up in each child from time to time, and now that I'm the mother of teenagers, I appreciate that stubbornness as a good trait to have when peers are pressuring them to do something they know is wrong. Our kids have also inherited Nolan's ability to block out negative things and shrug off encounters with rudeness or thoughtlessness. I'm glad to see them develop that attitude, because being vulnerable to the invisible-woman mentality has caused me a lot of grief. In this respect, I try to follow my kids' lead and not let it bother me, but it's never easy. And also, I don't want to become so hardened to the feelings churning inside me that I become cynical.

The problem is that when you're married to a celebrity, all that attention focused on your husband can magnify your own insecurity. To survive, I'm convinced, you have to be a woman who is almost overly confident, not just in your ability and looks but in your personality and in everything you do. You have to believe in yourself, and you have to understand things from your husband's perspective.

The fact is, there are women out there who make it so easy for the athletes that the men find it hard to resist the temptation these women present. When a team stays in a hotel, it's not unusual for women to try to call the players, even those who aren't yet well known. Most wives know it doesn't mean anything; some of these women just pick up the house phone and ask for a player's room. That's easy enough. Still, when I've been with Nolan and he's had some of these calls, even when I was sure he didn't know the woman who was calling—and even if I knew she was just going down a list, looking for a good time—I still felt a sick feeling deep inside me as I saw him talking to her on the phone.

Other women can threaten any wife, but I think this is especially true of those married to professional athletes. Even now, when I see how some women touch Nolan's arm when they ask for his autograph, I inwardly cringe. This troubled me at nineteen, and it still bugs me in my forties. I want to snarl at them, "Get your hands off my husband, you turkey!" but so far I've managed to just smile my frozen smile while I tug on Nolan's sleeve. It's not just the autograph seekers. When we're out in casual restaurants, women gawk at Nolan and send him notes, and it's hard to be so self-confident that these things don't bother me.

After a game last year, we went out to eat at a country-western place, and women were all over him from the minute we walked in. They wanted to dance with Nolan, talk to him, hang on him. The more attention he drew, the more invisible I became. I got irritated with myself for overreacting to it, but I let Nolan know I wasn't enjoying it.

"How would you feel if men were winking at me, coming up to me, putting their arms around my shoulder, and leaning close so they could whisper to me?"

He looked at me and smiled. "Well, if that happened, we wouldn't go in there anymore," he said.

We left after that, and we haven't been back to that place since.

I wonder sometimes when all the attention will end and we can just go back to being Nolan and Ruth, ordinary people living in an ordinary small town. Sometimes I'm convinced that may never happen, even though I try hard to steer us in that direction. But there are a few things that stand in the way—they're the same things that stand as monuments to this man I've been married to for twenty-eight years.

For example, there are the two baseball fields in Alvin that are named for Nolan. And there's that stretch of Highway 288 between Houston and Lake Jackson, the one the state legislature voted to rename the Nolan Ryan Expressway. And then there are those fifty-three entries in the baseball record books . . . And finally, there's that life-size sculpture of Nolan in front of Alvin City Hall. Wearing his Rangers uniform, caught in mid-windup . . . in statue form, Nolan is frozen in that familiar stance, and every time I go by there, it stops me. When I see it, I can't help but think of all the times I've seen him there, on the mound, poised just like that for the next pitch.

That image is such a vivid one for me, but it's not my favorite ballpark memory. That moment happened repeatedly at different times during hundreds of games in many different cities for nearly three decades. It probably happened the first time on the high school baseball diamond in Alvin in the mid-1960s. The last time I saw it was September 22, 1993, in Seattle.

The moment came when inevitably, sometime during the game, Nolan would pop up out of the dugout and quickly scan the grandstands behind home plate, looking for someone.

Looking for me.

I'd raise my hand in a quick wave and flash him a smile.

I'm here for you. Good luck!

He would find my face and grin back at me, maybe snapping his head up in a quick nod. *There you are. I'm glad.*

Then he'd duck under the roof and turn back to the game.

It was a simple moment, never noted in the baseball record books or the career summaries. But of all the moments in all the games, it was the one that was most important to me.